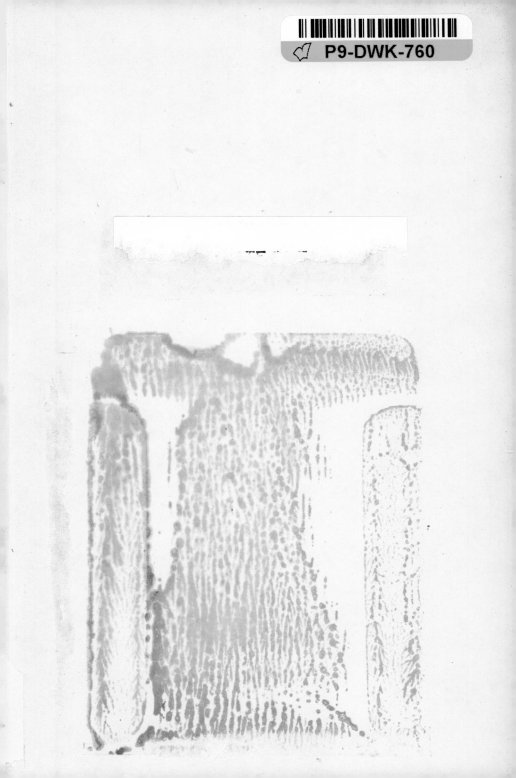

BAUDELAIRE
A Study of his Poetry

BAUDELAIRE AS A YOUNG MAN

Portrait painted by Emile Deroy in 1844 (Musée de Versailles)

BAUDELAIRE

A Study of his Poetry

BY

MARTIN TURNELL

'De la vaporisation et de la centralisation du *Moi*. Tout est là.'   *Journaux intimes.*

A NEW DIRECTIONS BOOK

*New Direction Books are published by
James Laughlin at Norfolk, Connecticut.
New York Offices: 333 Sixth Avenue.*

PRINTED IN ENGLAND

TO
LIZA

CONTENTS

7

ILLUSTRATIONS

FOREWORD

'BAUDELAIRE is at the height of his fame', said Valéry at the beginning of a famous lecture. Nearly thirty years have passed since these words were first used. We can see now that they were an understatement, that Baudelaire's fame has steadily grown and that he is a greater poet that Valéry himself perhaps realized. Copyright in his writings expired in 1917. This gave a considerable impetus to the study of the man and his work. The first volume of the great Conard Edition was published in 1922, and except for the break caused by the war volumes have continued to appear at irregular intervals until the present year. At the same time there was a steady stream of biographies, commentaries, and interpretations. I do not think that anyone who examines the literature which has grown up round Baudelaire impartially will feel disposed to contest the view that literary criticism is decidedly the Cinderella. There have been good lives, interesting interpretations of his 'thought', learned theses on his influence, fascinating speculations about his religious beliefs and his sexual peculiarities, his relations with his mother and his mistresses—we have a whole book on his mother, two on Mme Sabatier, and one on Marie Daubrun—and his patronage has been hotly disputed by contending factions. But out of this vast literature I can think of only a comparatively small number of books and articles which tell us anything useful about his art.

Baudelaire was an extremely versatile writer. He was the greatest poet of his age and its greatest critic, an admirable translator, one of the originators of the modern prose poem, the author of a remarkable treatise on the effects of drugs and of some highly provocative aphorisms on life, love, and politics. And he was of course the most intriguing 'case' of the century. But the time has come to say plainly that his immense reputation rests firmly on his one slim volume of verse. If all his other writings had perished and the *Fleurs du mal* had survived, his position in world literature would be virtually unaffected. The loss of the criticism would have been grievous not only on account of its intrinsic merits, but because we should be deprived of a standard for measuring the contribution of lesser men like Sainte-Beuve and Taine and because to a greater extent than all the other documents it helps to illuminate Baudelaire's own practice. It would not, however, have been a matter of sheer loss. There might well have been two decided gains. The French might have been saved from Edgar Allan Poe and there would have been far less danger of the 'case' coming between us and the poetry.

These are the reasons that have prompted me to confine my study to Baudelaire's poetry or, more precisely, to his verse. I have given as much of his life as seems necessary to understand his poetry. I have drawn on the criticism only in so far as it explains his practice. I have omitted the *Petits poèmes en prose* which though historically important appear to have been over-rated. No critic can escape theorizing to some extent, but I have kept as close to the text of the *Fleurs du mal* as possible and tried to avoid abstract discussion in order to concentrate on essentials. These essentials seem to me to be the meaning and artistic value of the *Fleurs du mal*, the impact of Baudelaire on French poetry, and some reflections on what is rather grandiloquently called his relevance for our own time. It also seemed desirable to include a few simple observations on two important but unpopular topics—prosody and syntax.

The essay naturally makes no claim to completeness—whole books far longer than mine have been written on the subjects of some of my six chapters—but in literary criticism completeness and finality are not virtues and are happily unattainable. One of the main qualifications of the critic is the ability to read and enjoy his authors because his primary task is to teach reading. It is not, however, sufficient to be a teacher of reading. The critic must do his utmost to send people back to the texts of the authors whom he discusses. Every work of criticism ought to be a miniature anthology of its subject's finest lines because this is the surest way of communicating enthusiasm, and one of the easiest ways of finding out whether a book of criticism is worth reading is to look at the proportion of quotations it contains. On the other hand, nothing is more mistaken than to try, as some specialists have tried, to give every possible illustration of the different manners and technical devices used by an author. It defeats the critic's aim by making the reader feel that the last word has been said, that there is nothing left for him to discover for himself, with the result that he reads the critic when he should be reading the poet.

I began to read Baudelaire exactly twenty-five years ago, and in spite of excursions into French classical drama and the French novel, I have never stopped reading him. Except for a brief period when Rimbaud took its place, I can hardly remember a time during the last fifteen of these twenty-five years when I did not have a copy of the *Fleurs du mal* by my bed or went away for any length of time without slipping a copy into my suitcase. You cannot live with a great poet with impunity. The day came when I suddenly discovered that what was intended to be a chapter in a different book had turned into a book on Baudelaire. I realized then that in spite of all the other things which had come between I was bound to write a book on him one day. Not even twenty-five years will provide all the answers or ensure that the answers are always right, and I offer the essay simply as a reading of Baudelaire.

I have to thank the following authorities who were kind enough to help me with advice and encouragement though they are naturally not responsible for the views I have expressed: the late Jacques Crépet; M. Charles Bruneau, Professor at the Sorbonne; M. André Ferran, Professor at the University of Toulouse, and M. Henri Clouard.

I wish to express my particular thanks to the Leverhulme Trustees who made me a grant to assist me in carrying out research in France.

April 1953   M. T.

BAUDELAIRE

I

THE ORIGINALITY OF BAUDELAIRE

'Un artiste, un homme vraiment digne de ce grand nom, doit
posséder quelque chose d'essentiellement *sui generis*, par la
grâce de quoi il est *lui* et non un autre.'

L'Art romantique

I

THE SURPRISING thing about the nineteenth century is not that
it was one of the greatest ages of French literature, but that such
an age should have produced any literature at all. It was like the
seventeenth century an age of transition, an age in which civilization was undergoing revolutionary changes, but there the
resemblance ends. 'For the creation of a masterwork of literature',
wrote Matthew Arnold in his great essay on *The Function of
Criticism at the Present Time*, 'two powers must concur, the
power of the man and the power of the moment.' He goes on to
speak of the poet in the age of Shakespeare as living in 'a current
of ideas in the highest degree animating and nourishing to the
creative power'. No one doubts 'the power of the man' in the
nineteenth century or that he lived in 'a current of ideas'; but so
far from being 'animating and nourishing to the creative power',
those ideas were, at any rate in appearance, fundamentally hostile
to all art. This is how a contemporary observer describes them:

'The crisis', wrote Saint-Simon, 'lies essentially in the transition
from a feudal and theological system to an industrial and scientific
system. France has become a vast factory and the nation a great work-
shop. The true temporal power is to be found today in industry and
the true spiritual power in the men of learning.'

There is truth in this diagnosis, but the pathetic faith in
industrial and scientific progress does small credit to the descen-

dant of the great Duc de Saint-Simon. Later critics have perceived the same symptoms, but have drawn different conclusions from them.

'The old aristocratic order had fallen', writes Mr. Middleton Murry; 'there was no new democratic order to supply its place: in the interval arose, like a growth of weeds on the site of a demolished building, as the sole principle of spiritual and social order, that reverence for wealth for its own sake which distinguished nineteenth-century France. Guizot's *Enrichissez-vous* marked a social nadir.'[1]

'[It was]', adds Mr. T. S. Eliot, 'an age of bustle, programmes, platforms, scientific progress, humanitarianism and revolutions which improved nothing, an age of progressive degradation.'[2]

It was, indeed, an age of extreme economic individualism, rampant industrialism, the spread of urban civilization—'the hideous eruption of great cities'—and the emergence of a new and aggressive middle class. Its large gestures produced meagre results. The annexation of Tahiti and the abortive revolutions seem trivial compared with the dangers of our own time; but the materialism and the facile optimism did their work only too thoroughly. They undermined the system which to Saint-Simon seemed so firmly founded and prepared the way for collapse before the hordes of twentieth-century barbarism.

These changes naturally left their mark on literature. There is one striking difference between the position of the nineteenth-century poet and that of the great writers of the past. He did not find his materials already present. He had first to create the conditions in which it was possible to write poetry at all. This involved not merely the creation of 'a current of ideas' which would nourish and animate his art, but the destruction of ideas which were hostile to it. It thus happens that a good deal of Baudelaire's work—the poetry as well as the prose—is an indictment of a corrupt society. It is one of the signs of his genius that his poetry sprang from a clash between the individual and society, that the difficulties of writing in such a period became one of the sources of his strength. It is partly because the evils that he

---

[1] *Countries of the Mind*, I, new ed., London, 1937, p. 117.
[2] *Selected Essays*, London, 1932, p. 375.

attacked have lost none of their virulence with the passing of time that he still speaks to us more urgently, more intimately than any other modern poet.

At the same time we must not make the mistake of thinking that his poetry is important because it can be regarded as in some sense the work of a reformer. The conflict was sharpened because social and political change had produced a change in the artist's vision, but the outer conflict was the symptom of a much deeper malaise. In the old unitary society the artist had been far more a 'craftsman' than a 'visionary'. He might criticize abuses as Dante, Chaucer, and Langland had criticized them, but there was no conflict between the writer and society. He not only expressed a communal as opposed to an individual experience; his work glorified an order in which at bottom he believed. Cracks had begun to appear in the social structure in the seventeenth and eighteenth centuries, but even in those centuries the writer was to a large extent the spokesman of an aristocratic *élite*. In the nineteenth century he was an outsider in an alien world. The old order had gone and there was no external system to which his experience could be related. He therefore proclaimed that he was a 'seer' whose work was to discover a new order which was metaphysical rather than social. He was engaged in his own way in a revision of values and, inevitably, he went into dangerous places and made discoveries which were highly disturbing to his simpler-minded contemporaries.

It follows that though social, political, and economic changes have considerable bearing on the position of the writer and the sort of work that he produces, they cannot explain it. The history of literature is an unending process of change and development. We can only appreciate Baudelaire's originality to the full when we see him in relation to the writers of the past and to his own contemporaries. I therefore propose to glance very briefly at the development of French literature from 1630 to 1830. I shall discuss some of Baudelaire's observations on his contemporaries and on his own practice. Finally, I shall interrogate one of the closest of his followers in order to try to find out what Baudelaire's example meant to the poets who succeeded him.

B

2

The great imaginative writers of the seventeenth century made a searching examination of human nature, but their world was necessarily circumscribed. Their vision was confined to the natural sphere, to man in society. Religious experience, in the sense in which we understand the term, metaphysical speculation, and Nature were virtually excluded from their work. There is not a trace of what is loosely described as 'mysticism' in *Polyeucte* or *Athalie*. M. François Mauriac has written of the working of divine Grace in the first of these plays and Sainte-Beuve claimed to detect the presence of God in the second, but the rest of us may discover something different. Corneille's own beliefs probably account for a deepening of his experience in *Polyeucte*, but the main importance of the religious motif is to provide another study of Cornelian heroism. We find in it the familiar conflict between duty and inclination, but in Polyeucte's mind duty is identified with religion. This does not apply to the other characters. In Pauline's mind Polyeucte stands for duty, Sévère for inclination, and the most moving part of the play is her love affair with Sévère. *Athalie* is a study of the disintegration of the personality of the dictator, but it differs from the other plays in that religion instead of sexual passion is the agent of destruction.

The distinction is also true of a specifically religious writer like Pascal. For Pascal was something new in literature. He was neither a professional theologian nor a professional philosopher. He was the artist-thinker whose sensibility is far more important than the mystical revelation that he is believed to have had or his thought. He was a student of Montaigne and he marks the change from one form of apologetic to another. It was not merely a change from metaphysics to psychology, from the Thomist proofs of the existence of God to the study of the mental processes of the believer. Religious practice and religious art are necessarily coloured by the temper of the age, but there is one striking difference between the Middle Ages and the seventeenth century. In the Middle Ages belief imposed the pattern on experience;

from Pascal onwards it is the man and the age which impose their pattern on belief. Religious literature conveys a complex emotional experience in which religion is only one element and which may contain other alien elements such as the erotic element in the art of the Counter-Reformation. Pascal is therefore primarily interesting on account of his inner experience and as the virtual inventor of that religious unrest which has become progressively more popular, more widespread, and more contagious with the passing of time.

It is hardly surprising that by the end of the seventeenth century the artist's experience was becoming used up. There are unmistakable signs that Marivaux—the real successor of Racine—was working an exhausted seam. The dismissal of Hortensius, the pedant who in the *Seconde surprise de l'amour* tries to convince the unruly lovers that 'la raison doit être notre règle dans tous les états', is a symbolical act. Reason is taken to the door and unceremoniously thrown out. It is one of the first protests against the Reason which had dominated the previous century, but once again there is a difference. The literature of the seventeenth century rested on what I have called in another place a regulated tug-of-war.[1] The conflict between reason and emotion took place in the mind of the individual. In the eighteenth century there was a parting of the ways. Literature divided into two branches—the literature of Reason and the literature of Sensibility—one dominated by the Rational Man, the other by the Man of Feeling. In the best work of Rousseau and Prévost we are aware of a continual attempt to break out of a closed circle and to reach a reality which transcends the world of everyday life, while the prevalence of 'illuminism' and madness is an eloquent testimony to the frustration of the more sensitive minds.

Gérard de Nerval argued in *Les Illuminés* that the 'illuminists' played a part of capital importance in preparing the French Revolution.[2] Although they appeared to belong to different camps, the exponents of sensibility and the rationalists were in

[1] *The Classical Moment*, London, 1947, p. 15.
[2] See Jeanine Moulin, *Les Chimères* (Textes Littéraires Français), Paris, 1949, p. xxvii.

fact allies in the same cause. The first group appealed to those hidden feelings which found no proper outlet in the narrow society of the *ancien régime* and the second undermined traditional checks and sanctions, with the result that the day came when society simply exploded in a deluge of violent emotionalism.

'If,' said Jacques Rivière, 'if, in the seventeenth century, anyone had taken it into his head to ask Molière or Racine why they wrote, they would probably only have been able to answer: "To amuse decent people." It was only with Romanticism that the act of writing began to be thought of as a raid on the absolute and its result as a revelation.'[1] The poets did not escape the deluge. The Romantic Movement was the triumph of the Man of Feeling. It was an article of faith that feeling was intrinsically good and what really mattered. God, Nature, Love, and Death became an excuse for turning loose emotion. Whatever their own shortcomings, however, it is only right to add that the Romantics revolutionized the existing conception of poetry. It ceased to be something 'to amuse decent people' or a superior pastime and became a *vocation*. It is almost impossible to exaggerate the importance of this change for Baudelaire and the poets who followed him.

I must turn now to Baudelaire's comments on his predecessors and contemporaries:

'Most of the errors relating to the beautiful', he said, 'are the result of the false conception of morality which prevailed during the eighteenth century. During that period nature was regarded as the basis, source, and type of every possible form of the good and the beautiful. The denial of the dogma of original sin played no small part in the general blindness of the age. In any case, if we are content simply to refer to the fact, which is apparent to the experience of every age and to the *Gazette des Tribunaux*, we shall see that nature teaches nothing or practically nothing, that is to say, she *forces* man to sleep, to drink, and to protect himself as well as he can against the elements.'[2]

We need not interpret Baudelaire's religious terminology too

[1] *Nouvelles études*, Paris, 1947, p. 313.
[2] *L'Art romantique*, ed. Crépet, pp. 95–6.

strictly. He was engaged in a literary and not in a theological controversy. What he disliked about the eighteenth century was its belief in the perfectibility of man because it seemed to him to reduce the individual to a state of uniformity, to exclude the sense of mystery and those tensions of which he was acutely aware in himself. He also disliked the cult of nature because to him nature seemed mindless, mechanical, and uncivilized. In short, the eighteenth-century conception of life was a simplification which restricted the field of human experience and did more than any other single factor to enclose man in a finite world.

The French Revolution was in some respects a salutary shock, and it provided the Romantic Movement with its initial impetus. The Romantics rebelled against the closed world and against a degenerate classicism, and they tried to bring life, colour, and imagery back into poetry. It was something, but it was not enough because 'the power of the man' was lacking. Baudelaire's summing-up is admirable in its justice and in its unerring perception of the weaknesses of the Movement:

'It would certainly be an injustice to deny the services rendered by the school known as Romantic. It recalled us to the truth of the image; it destroyed the academic commonplaces and even from the superior point of view of linguistics, it does not deserve the contempt which has been heaped on it by certain impotent pedants. But by its very nature the Romantic insurrection was condemned to a short life. The puerile utopia of *art for art's sake* by excluding morality and often even passion was a flagrant contradiction of the genius of humanity. In the name of the higher principles which constitute the universal life, we have the right to declare it guilty of heterodoxy.'[1]

When he uses the word 'insurrection', Baudelaire means that the real value of the Romantic Movement was negative and destructive. It rid poetry of the academic commonplaces; it made a breach in the walls of the finite world and it drew attention to the insufficiency of eighteenth-century language as a vehicle for poetry; but there its usefulness ended. The belief in 'art for art's sake' turned art into a cult which was divorced from life; and

[1] *L'Art romantique*, pp. 183–4.

'excluding morality' implied that the Romantics' view of life
was neither a mature nor an adult one.

I have said that 'the power of the man' was lacking, and this is
borne out by Baudelaire's specific criticisms of individual writers:

'Victor Hugo, Sainte-Beuve, Alfred de Vigny had rejuvenated or
rather resurrected French poetry which had been dead since Corneille.
For André Chénier, with his soft antiquity *à la Louis XVI*, was not a
sufficiently vigorous symptom of renovation, and Alfred de Musset,
feminine and without a doctrine, might have existed at any time and
would never have been anything but an idler turning out graceful
effusions.'[1]

Chénier and Musset are properly criticized because they were
lacking in genuine vitality and because they were not writers of
sufficient calibre to give poetry a fresh start. The tributes are more
difficult to explain because none of the three recipients exercised
a deep or lasting influence on Baudelaire. They were to some
extent dictated by personal feelings or tactics. It is understandable
that Baudelaire should have thought more highly of Vigny than
we do, and Vigny was almost the only writer to befriend him at
the time of his unfortunate candidature for the Academy. He had
admired Sainte-Beuve's verse as a schoolboy and always spoke of
him with affection in spite of the shameful treatment that he
received from him. His attitude to Hugo varied and was never
free from a certain ambiguity. The essay on Gautier, from which
this passage is taken, was first published in 1859 and belongs to
the period when Baudelaire treated Hugo with indulgence. His
earlier criticisms of him are more searching and for the present
purpose more instructive because they show what Baudelaire
thought of Hugo at the time when he was starting work on the
Fleurs du mal. This is what he has to say in the *Salon de 1846*:

'M. Victor Hugo, whose nobility and majesty I certainly do not
wish to underestimate, is a workman who is much more adroit than
inventive, a craftsman who is far more correct than creative. Delacroix
is sometimes clumsy, but essentially creative. M. Victor Hugo reveals
in all his pictures, whether they are lyrical or dramatic, a system of

---

[1] *L'Art romantique*, p. 153.

alignment and of uniform contrasts. Excentricity itself assumes in his work symmetrical forms. He is complete master of and uses coldly all the tones of rhyme, all the resources of antithesis, all the tricks of apposition. He is a composer who belongs to a period of decadence or transition, who employs all his tools with a dexterity which is truly admirable and curious. M. Hugo was naturally an academician before he was born.'[1]

It is impossible to read this passage without pausing to admire the sureness of touch and the extraordinary penetration of the twenty-five-year-old critic. It possesses the finality which only belongs to great criticism. Hugo is reduced to the status of a craftsman who skilfully but 'coldly' exploits all the latest tricks. A certain 'nobility', a certain 'majesty', are conceded to him, but he remains a rhetorician who does not possess the most fundamental gift of all—creativeness. The criticism is completed by a single damaging sentence from the *Exposition de 1855*:

'Mais M. Victor Hugo est un grand poëte sculptural qui a l'œil fermé à la spiritualité.'[2]

There is only one reference—a faintly derogatory reference— to Lamartine in Baudelaire's criticism, but Lamartine illustrates better than any other contemporary poet the situation against which Baudelaire was reacting. He is in a sense *the* Romantic Poet, the author of carefully contrived set pieces on the great abstractions:

> Éternité, néant, passé, sombres abîmes,
> Que faites-vous des jours que vous engloutissez?
> (*Le Lac*)

> Et les ombres, les vents, et les flots de l'abîme,
> Vers cette arche de feu tout paraissait courir . . .

> Flux et reflux divin de vie universelle,
> Vaste océan de l'Être où tout va s'engloutir! . . .
> (*L'Occident*)

---

[1] *Curiosités esthétiques*, ed. Crépet, pp. 105–6.
[2] *Curiosités esthétiques*, p. 247.

There is a world of difference between Lamartine's use of words in these lines and Baudelaire's in *Le Gouffre*:

> Pascal avait son gouffre, avec lui se mouvant.
> —Hélas! tout est abîme,—action, désir, rêve,
> Parole! . . .
> En haut, en bas, partout, la profondeur, la grève,
> Le silence, l'espace affreux et captivant . . .

Lamartine creates a vague impression of 'uplift' by the accumulation of highly 'poetical' words. It is the purely emotive use of language. It cannot be said that the words have any positive content or that they really mean anything. They are not doing any work. They are strung together in a way which provides a release for the reader's private emotions and gives him the sensation that he is enjoying poetry. They have none of the intense psychological reality of Baudelaire's 'gouffre' which produces the sense of inner collapse in lines 2 and 3. The difference between Lamartine's 'Flux et reflux divin' and Baudelaire's 'espace affreux et captivant' is no less striking. Lamartine's words are mere statement; they *do* nothing to us; but Baudelaire's enable us to *participate* in the vertiginous, seesaw movement of attraction and repulsion.

We must conclude that the Romantics had given the signal for rebellion, had carried out a useful preliminary work and that technically some of their verse was extremely accomplished, but that they did not possess the intelligence, the vision, or the maturity which were essential to French poetry at that time.

The development of literature is not a series of sharp changes of direction, the death of an old movement and the birth of a new one. It is a process of continual slight alteration or, to put it in another way, literature implies an internal critical activity, a constant revision of what seems dead in the immediate past and the exploitation of qualities which are latent in it because certain qualities are perennial and native to all good writing. That is what occurred during the change from Romanticism to the form of poetry invented by Baudelaire. His positive values are formulated in the *Salon de 1846* with the same sureness with which he criticized Hugo:

'Romanticism does not consist precisely in the choice of subject or in exact truth, but in the manner of feeling.

'They sought [Romanticism] outside themselves, but it is inside us alone that it is to be found.

'For me Romanticism is the most recent, the most actual expression of the beautiful.

'There are as many kinds of beauty as there are habitual ways of seeking happiness. . . . Romanticism does not lie in perfect execution, but in a certain correspondence with the morality of the century.'

Then comes the crucial definition:

'Whoever speaks of Romanticism speaks of modern art,—that is to say, spirituality, colour, aspiration towards the infinite, expressed by every means practised by the arts.

'It follows from this that there is an obvious contradiction between Romanticism and the works of its principal exponents.'[1]

Although Baudelaire's criticisms of the movement of 1830 are radical, it is clear that he did not object to being labelled a Romantic himself. The last quotation, however, shows that his Romanticism—he would presumably have called it true Romanticism—was very different from that of 1830, and he has been happily described by Mr. Eliot as a 'counter-romantic'.[2] For in these passages we can follow the workings of the complex process of acceptance-rejection-exploitation. Baudelaire accepts the individualism and the sense of exile of the Romantics, but he emphasizes that the deciding factor is 'the manner of feeling' or, as we say today, the poet's sensibility. Eighteenth-century poetry had been too external and too formal, but the Romantic 'insurrection' had simply drawn attention to the division between poetry and life without overcoming it. The poet must therefore seek his material inside himself. He must abandon the classic conception of a fixed unchanging beauty and realize that beauty is manifold, which is a long step towards the modern theory that beauty is an attribute of the perceiving subject and not an objective quality in the thing perceived.

The most important words in Baudelaire's definition are 'cer-

---

[1] *Curiosités esthétiques*, pp. 90–1.
[2] *Op. cit.*, p. 372.

tain correspondence with the morality of the century', to which I shall return later, 'spirituality', and 'aspiration towards the infinite'. Baudelaire's poetry reveals a constant effort to extricate himself from the finite circumscribed world. He is haunted by the image of the 'prison'; in *Élévation* he looks longingly in the direction of 'les champs lumineux et sereins', while there are other images which describe an endeavour to stretch, expand, or penetrate material reality in order to reach something beyond or outside it. In *Correspondances* he speaks of perfumes as

> Ayant *l'expansion* des choses infinies . . .

In *Le Poison* it is the effect of intoxicants:

> L'opium *agrandit* ce qui n'a pas de bornes,
> *Allonge* l'illimité,
> *Approfondit* le temps, *creuse* la volupté . . .

In *Le Voyage* he evokes

> De vastes voluptés, changeantes, inconnues,
> Et dont l'esprit humain n'a jamais su le nom!

This brings me to what may be described collectively as the esoteric cults which bulk so largely in nineteenth-century French literature. These cults naturally flourish in periods when orthodoxy is weak. Their vogue in the eighteenth and nineteenth centuries corresponds at a somewhat higher level to the popularity of spiritualism and Christian Science in our own time. Whenever men feel that orthodox Christianity has failed to satisfy their legitimate aspirations, they seek satisfaction in other ways and are attracted to the esoteric cults by a deep-seated conviction that there must be a reality beyond the material world. This explains the interest of some of the greatest French writers of the last century in Swedenborg, the Cabbala, 'illuminism' and magic, and their addiction to *excitants*. It also explains the tendency for literature to become a substitute for religion and the subsequent transformation of the poet into the 'Voyant' which is implicit in Baudelaire's theory of 'correspondences', but which was to receive its most explicit and its most impressive formulation in

Rimbaud's famous letter. They were all short cuts, were all attempts to force what Nerval called 'the ivory gates'.

I have a particular dislike of the word 'mysticism' when used in literary criticism because it is only too often a sign of slovenly and confused thinking; but I think that we have to admit that there is in Nerval, Baudelaire, and Rimbaud a form of non-religious mysticism which is part of the attempt to discover a way out of the world of nineteenth-century positivism and to enjoy an experience—it is a Romantic trait—which is different from and transcends all other experiences. It was the outcome of the decline of religious belief to which I have drawn attention, but it does not seem to have been a substitute for religion. It exists in Baudelaire side by side with the substratum of Christianity which we find in the *Fleurs du mal*, and it is interesting to observe that while his hell is the Christian hell, his paradise or his sense of beatitude is a sort of mystical-aesthetic paradise. A passage in one of his letters to Alphonse Toussenel throws some light on his theories:

'I have long maintained that the poet is *supremely* intelligent, that he is intelligence *par excellence*,—and that the *imagination* is the most *scientific* of faculties, because it alone understands the *universal analogy*, or what mystical religion calls *the correspondence*.'[1]

The emphasis on intelligence is another sign of Baudelaire's reaction against the Romantics, and his description of imagination as 'the most scientific of faculties' points to the theory that poetry is a form of knowledge—supra-rational knowledge—which was carried to extremes by some of his successors.

M. Georges Blin distinguishes between the 'vertical' and the 'horizontal' use of the term 'correspondence'.[2] Swedenborg, who was not the inventor of the concept, uses it in the 'vertical' sense to suggest that objects in the natural world have their reflections or counterparts in a supernatural world. Baudelaire also uses it in the same sense in a passage from one of his essays on Poe which is reproduced in the study of Gautier:

[1] *Correspondance générale*, ed. Crépet, 1, p. 368 (letter of 21 January 1856).
[2] *Baudelaire*, Paris, 1939, p. 107.

'It is this admirable, this immortal sense of the beautiful which makes us regard the earth and its sights as a glimpse, as a correspondence of Heaven.'[1]

This interpretation, however, is hardly characteristic. In the letter to Toussenel and in other places, Baudelaire confines himself to the 'horizontal' use. He was convinced of the unity of experience and was bent on discovering the hidden relations—the relation between perfumes, sounds, and colours in *Correspondances* is the classic example—which exist between things on the terrestrial plane. Imagination—'the most scientific of faculties'—is the instrument of investigation and the term 'correspondence' indicates the nature of the discovery or the poetic revelation.

Baudelaire uses the words 'correspondence', 'symbol', 'analogy', and 'allegory' in broadly the same sense. In a famous passage in the diaries he remarked:

'Dans certains états de l'âme presque surnaturels, la profondeur de la vie se révèle dans le spectacle, si ordinaire qu'il soit, qu'on a sous les yeux. Il en devient le symbole.'[2]

He is careful to say 'presque surnaturels' and the words are of some importance. They suggest that while the *content* of mystical and aesthetic experience is different, there may be a resemblance in their *appearance*. It seems to me to show, too, that his main preoccupation was to discover the inner pattern of experience and that it was to this that he was referring when he called the poet 'un traducteur, un déchiffreur'.[3] In short, what he was aiming at was an *approfondissement* of experience on the natural plane. Nothing could be more mistaken than to describe him, as he is sometimes described, as a realist. His lack of visual imagination may account to some extent for the poverty of his descriptive poems, but this was not the sole or the main reason. He was not interested in the delineation of material reality. His work marks

[1] *L'Art romantique*, p. 159. (See Professor P. Mansell Jones's admirable discussion of the subject in *The Background to Modern French Poetry*, Cambridge, 1951, pp. 1–37.)

[2] *Journaux intimes*, Édition critique établie par Jacques Crépet et Georges Blin, Paris, 1949, p. 24.

[3] *L'Art romantique*, p. 305.

the substitution of the image for direct description and for statements about the poet's feelings which was one of the most important innovations in modern literature. The women of the love
poems and the figures in the Parisian poems, for example, are all
'symbols' in the sense in which Baudelaire uses the word in the
passage from the diaries. Their function is to reveal the significance of the experience as a whole. For this reason they are
deliberately stylized and presented in non-realistic terms. When
he addresses Jeanne Duval as

> Statue aux yeux de jais, grand ange au front d'airain!

the images drawn from stones and metal are designed to bring
out her moral qualities, or rather her lack of certain moral qualities, and to indicate her place in the drama of 'Spleen et Idéal'.

'What do I care', Baudelaire once said, 'what the reality outside me is made of provided that it helps me to feel that I am and
what I am.' His theory of poetic experience was scarcely com-
patible with the dualism of subject and object that we find in the
writers of the past and in the 'grand poëte sculptural'. For the
subtlety and subjectivity of modern poetry reflects a change from
the classical metaphysic to one of the idealist systems. Experience
becomes a synthesis of the perceiving subject and the thing
perceived:

'What is the modern conception of pure art?' Baudelaire asked. 'It
is to create a suggestive magic containing at one and the same time
object and subject, the world which is external to the artist and the
artist himself.'[1]

Baudelaire's theory of poetic experience is intimately connected
with his theory of language, and terms like 'suggestive magic',
'sorcery', and 'alchemy' are key-words:

'Il y a dans le mot, dans le *verbe*, quelque chose de *sacré* qui nous
défend d'en faire un jeu de hasard. Manier savamment une langue,
c'est pratiquer une espèce de sorcellerie évocatoire. C'est alors que la
couleur parle, comme une voix profonde et vibrante; que les monu-
ments se dressent et font saillie sur l'espace profond; que les animaux
et les plantes, représentants du laid et du mal, articulent leur grimace

[1] *L'Art romantique*, p. 119.

non équivoque; que le parfum provoque la pensée et le souvenir correspondants; que la passion murmure ou rugit son langage éternellement
semblable.'[1]

The function of the language of poetry is not to describe, but
to suggest. It is essentially creative, a 'magic' operation in which
words cease to be mere signs and participate in the things that
they present or evoke. It establishes 'correspondences', uncovers
'the universal analogy', and reveals the inner significance of
experience.

Gérard de Nerval was one of the earliest exponents of *sorcellerie évocatoire*. It is commonly assumed that he had a considerable influence on Baudelaire, but it is not easy to determine
the precise nature or the extent of his influence. It is possible that
Baudelaire took the theory of 'correspondences' partly from him
and not directly from Swedenborg. We know that *Un Voyage à
Cythère* was suggested by a passage from Nerval's *Voyage en
Orient* which Baudelaire had read when it first appeared in
L'Artiste, and there is certainly no reason to assume that the
influence was limited to Nerval's verse. The bulk of the poems
known as *Les Chimères* were not published until 1854—the year
in which they were collected and included in an appendix to *Les
Filles du feu*—but three of them had appeared in *L'Artiste* in
1844–5. *Le Christ aux Oliviers* may have suggested *Le Reniement
de Saint Pierre* and *Vers dorés* may possibly have suggested
L'Homme et la mer; but the real affinities between the poets go
deeper. It is worth examining *Delfica* which was first published
in *L'Artiste* on 28 December 1845 when Baudelaire was probably
working on the early poems which belong to the Cycle of Art in
'Spleen et Idéal':

> La connais-tu, Dafné, cette ancienne romance,
> Au pied du sycomore, ou sous les lauriers blancs,
> Sous l'olivier, le myrte, ou les saules tremblants,
> Cette chanson d'amour qui toujours recommence? . . .

---

[1] *L'Art romantique*, p. 165. (The words, 'le parfum provoque la pensée
et le souvenir correspondants', are a particularly illuminating comment on
Baudelaire's own practice.)

Reconnais-tu le TEMPLE au péristyle immense,
Et les citrons amers où s'imprimaient tes dents,
Et la grotte, fatale aux hôtes imprudents,
Où du dragon vaincu dort l'antique semence? . . .

Ils reviendront, ces Dieux que tu pleures toujours!
Le temps va ramener l'ordre des anciens jours;
La terre a tressailli d'un souffle prophétique . . .

Cependant la sibylle au visage latin
Est endormie encor sous l'arc de Constantin
—Et rien n'a dérangé le sévère portique.

I do not want to suggest that there is any striking similarity
between the content of this poem and the content of any of
Baudelaire's, nor do I wish to place undue emphasis on the images
of 'le TEMPLE au péristyle immense', the 'grotte' and 'le sévère
portique' which were greatly favoured by other writers besides
Baudelaire. What I do wish to stress is the immense power of
incantation of the poem and its strange enchantment. The images
are suggestive, but not vague; they have something of the precision and the heightened reality of a dream. We do not feel that
we are being smothered by a cloud of words; we are conscious
rather of a sense of liberation and release. Our reactions are very
much the same when we turn to *Correspondances*:

La Nature est un temple où de vivants piliers
Laissent parfois sortir de confuses paroles . . .

There is the marvellous reverberation produced by the play of
vowels and nasals in

Comme de longs échos qui de loin se confondent
Dans une ténébreuse et profonde unité . . .

In other places we have:

J'ai longtemps habité sous de vastes portiques
Que les soleils marins teignaient de mille feux . . .

Ma jeunesse ne fut qu'un ténébreux orage,
Traversé çà et là par de brillants soleils . . .

Mais le vert paradis des amours enfantines,
Les courses, les chansons, les baisers, les bouquets . . .

Je suis comme le roi d'un pays pluvieux . . .

This form of enchantment, which is very evident in the refrains of some of the earlier poems, became more controlled as Baudelaire's genius ripened but it did not disappear. It is found in those two 'Symbolist' poems, *Harmonie du soir* and *La Mort des amants*; and it comes to the surface again in the work of the writers who belonged to the movement of 1886.

It is necessary to stress the extreme importance both of this element and of Nerval's contribution to the development of nineteenth-century literature. He has never had his due in this country, but though he was not a poet of the first order he was an innovator who had a decisive influence on modern poetry. The introduction of dreams, myths, magic, and the fantasies of the unconscious, which was only possible through the exploration of the resources of language, opened up a vast new seam and added a fresh dimension to poetry. It is Baudelaire's exploitation of these discoveries which has given him his dominating position in the European literature of the last hundred years. He stands at once for tradition and experiment, for discipline and revolt. His versification and syntax are in the main traditional. They provide a discipline, but they are at the same time the vehicle of a new vision. In this way he becomes, as M. Albert Béguin has pointed out, the founder of the double line of Artists and Seers. An artist like Mallarmé may make drastic modifications in syntax, but he is still the careful craftsman using traditional forms as a means of expression. Rimbaud, on the other hand, is the prototype of the revolutionary and the Seer who makes a clean sweep of traditional forms in the attempt—the impossible attempt—to present the naked vision without the intermediary of an image.

I have suggested that Baudelaire's aesthetic theories anticipate those of certain modern writers and I want to glance at some of his other pronouncements:

'But just as there is no perfect circumference, the absolute ideal is a *bêtise*. An exclusive taste for the simple leads the foolish artist to imitate the same type. Poets, artists, and the whole human species would be very unhappy if the ideal, that absurdity, that impossibility,

were found. What would each of us do after that with his poor *ego*,—
his broken line.'[1]

'All forms of beauty like all other phenomena contain something
eternal and something transitory—something absolute and something
particular. Absolute, eternal beauty does not exist, or rather it is only
an abstraction skimmed from the general surface of different forms of
beauty. The particular element in each form of beauty comes from the
emotions and as we have our particular emotions, we have our own
form of beauty.'[2]

These passages are taken from the *Salon de 1846*, but Baudelaire returns to the problem in the essay on Constantin Guys
which was first published in 1863:

'This is a splendid opportunity of establishing a rational and his-
torical theory of beauty in opposition to the theory of a unique and
absolute beauty; an opportunity of demonstrating that notwithstand-
ing the fact that the impression it produces is one of unity, the composition of beauty is always and inevitably double. For the difficulty of
distinguishing the variable elements of the beautiful in the unity of the
impression that it produces on us in no way weakens the necessity of
variety in its composition. The beautiful is composed of an eternal,
invariable element of which the quantity is excessively difficult to
determine, and of a relative, circumstantial element which is, if one
chooses to put it like that, in turn or altogether, period, fashion,
morality, passion. Without this second element, which is the amusing,
titillating, appetizing envelope of the divine cake, the first element
would be indigestible, impossible to appreciate, not adapted, and not
appropriate to human nature. I defy anyone to discover the least gleam
of beauty which does not contain the two elements.'[3]

These observations throw considerable light on Baudelaire's
own practice. In his poetry he is constantly in search of something
that he describes as the 'Ideal' or the 'Absolute', but it is evident
that he does not believe in its existence. His scepticism coupled
with the ardour of his pursuit of the chimera gives his poetry its
unending tension. Now Baudelaire was far from being a poet
who devoted himself to the cultivation of unrelated sensation or

[1] *Curiosités esthétiques*, pp. 141–2.
[2] *Curiosités esthétiques*, p. 197.
[3] *L'Art romantique*, p. 69.

C

even unrelated moments of vision, and this lies behind the theory of the double composition of the beautiful. Absolute beauty may be a myth, but there is a permanent element in experience which gives it its unity. The permanent element is the reflection of something in our basic human nature which guarantees the existence and continuity of literature as well as its intelligibility. It cannot be experienced in isolation, and there is no contradiction in the view that absolute beauty does not exist and the view that there is a permanent factor in all experience. For Baudelaire the permanent unchanging element is the substratum and the ground of life.

The theory explains some of the vagaries of literary taste. The permanent element in experience is associated with those qualities that are native to all good writing and are obviously indispensable to any literature which proves lasting. The second element is the superficial 'modernity' which Baudelaire himself calls, in the same essay, 'the transitory, the fugitive, the contingent'.[1] The ephemeral work, the best-seller, possesses only the second element and is therefore perishable or survives as a 'period piece'. It is the second element which accounts for the immediate popularity of a literary work and for subsequent fluctuations in taste. The permanent element remains; the impermanent is alternately in harmony and out of harmony with the taste or surface sensibility of the age. In this way it becomes either a help or a hindrance to the appreciation of a work which contains both elements.

One of the difficulties of Baudelaire's criticism is that though he expresses himself in the idiom of the day, he is continually using a common terminology to advance revolutionary ideas. When we look more closely at his definition of the impermanent element in beauty, we experience a shock of surprise. 'Period' and 'fashion' are clearly impermanent, but it is strange to find them classed with 'passion' and 'morality' which are generally regarded as permanent factors in art. The truth is that Baudelaire is launching an unobtrusive but far-reaching attack on conventional ideas of 'passion' and 'morality' and throwing them overboard with the 'absolute ideal' and 'absolute, eternal beauty'.

---

[1] *L'Art romantique*, p. 66.

The position becomes clearer when, later in the same essay, he writes:

'Woe to the man who studies anything in the work of the ancients except pure art, logic, and general method! By plunging too deeply into it, he loses the sense of the present; he abandons the value and the privileges conferred by circumstance. For almost the whole of our originality comes from the stamp which *time* imprints on our sensations.'[1]

The permanent element in Baudelaire's own work is clearly the classic style with its harmony and its orderliness, or what he called 'pure art, logic, and general method'. The impermanent element is the macabre imagery and some of the nineteenth-century gestures and décors which are increasingly felt to be a hindrance to the enjoyment of his greatest work. I think that we must go on to say that there is a third element which he himself might have considered impermanent and which may some day come to be regarded as such. I have said that it is a mistake to use the term 'realistic' of his descriptions of the external world, but it cannot be too strongly emphasized that he was a great *psychological* realist, that he explored not merely the mind and the emotions, but the nerves of contemporary urban man with an insight which was undreamed of in French poetry before him. His poetry is the anatomy of a highly complex mood which only crystallized in the last century and which must be identified with what he called 'the morality of the century' or 'the stamp which *time* imprints on our sensations'. The mood colours the whole of his poetry, turning 'passion' and 'morality' into something very different from the traditional concepts that he had jettisoned and giving a fresh and startling meaning to the words *ennui, spleen, extase,* and *volupté* which are its component parts and which we shall meet again and again in the *Fleurs du mal*. This is not the place to analyse the mood which belongs properly to the study of his poetry. All that need be said is that it accounts very largely for his immense stature among modern poets and for the place which he occupies in the spiritual history of our time.

[1] *L'Art romantique*, p. 69.

3

I have given an outline of Baudelaire's aesthetic theory, but it would be idle to pretend that he was a consistent thinker or to try to extract a 'system' from his criticism. His views varied during the twenty years of his literary career. They are not free from ambiguity or even from contradictions though his very inconsistencies help us to understand certain aspects of his poetry. We can see that his theories were largely the result of the situation in which he found himself, and that they are at once a criticism and an exploitation of the Romantic conception of poetry. We can also see what he considered to be the particular problems of the poet in his time and how he thought they should be solved; but that is as far as they take us. No amount of theory can explain a poet's achievement or tell us to what extent he succeeded in his aims and what his example meant to his successors. We can only find this out by studying the poetry and seeing what his successors had to say about it.

Nearly every critic who has written well about Baudelaire has dwelt on his originality, his impact on French poetry, and his influence on later generations of poets. Jules Laforgue, writing less than twenty years after Baudelaire's death, gives a list of things that he was 'the first' to do. It provides a valuable introduction to his work.

'He was *the first* to relate his experiences in the subdued tones of the confessional and did not assume an inspired air.

'He was the first to speak of Paris like any ordinary lost soul of the capital [*en damné quotidien de la capitale*], the street lamps tormented by the wind, "the prostitution which lights up in the streets", the restaurants and their ventilators, the hospitals, gambling, the wood that is sawn into logs which echo on the paving-stones of courtyards, the chimney corner, cats, beds, women's stockings, modern makes of perfume, but all of it in a noble, distant, superior manner. . . .

'He is the first who is not triumphant, but accuses himself, reveals his wounds, his laziness, his bored uselessness in the midst of this hardworking, devoted century.

'The first who brought into literature the feeling of apathy in pleasure [*l'ennui dans la volupté*] and its bizarre décor . . . *spleen* and sickness (not poetical Consumption but neurasthenia) without once using the word.

'He was the first to discover after the daring of the Romantics the crude comparison which casually introduces a note of flatness into the middle of a harmonious period. . . .

'He was the first to break with the public.—The poets addressed themselves to the public—human repertoire—but he was the first to say to himself:

' "Poetry will be something for the initiated.

' "I am damned on account of the public.—Good.—The public is not admitted." '[1]

Laforgue's tantalizingly fragmentary notes are the most perceptive criticism of Baudelaire made in the nineteenth century, not merely for what they say, but because they convey the atmosphere of his poetry. In the passages that I have detached from them he draws attention to nearly all the essentials of his originality and leaves later critics to elaborate them.

With Baudelaire the poet ceases to be a 'bard' and abandons the oratorical style because poetry has become a record of inner experience—the intimate tensions and stresses of contemporary urban man which Laforgue labels 'neurasthenia'—and the style must be adapted to the matter. It must be sufficiently flexible to reflect the whispered tone of the confessional and on occasion to rise to the heights of the grand manner. It is a varied style which switches deliberately from the solemn to the ridiculous to express the peculiar sense of bathos which for Baudelaire seemed to be characteristic of urban life. This may have prompted Laforgue to describe his work, as he does more than once, as 'Yankee' and to remark, in a brilliant phrase, of his language: 'C'est l'américanisme appliqué aux comparaisons du *Cantique des Cantiques*', anticipating Claudel's 'extraordinary mixture of the style of Racine and the journalistic style of his time'.[2]

---

[1] *Mélanges posthumes*, Paris, 1903, pp. 111–12, 113, 115. *Entretiens Politiques et Littéraires*, Vol. II, No. 13, April, 1891, pp. 99, 100, 103, 112.

[2] Quoted by Jacques Rivière in *Études*, 8th ed., Paris, 1924, p. 15.

Laforgue insists on Baudelaire's closeness to us. He is not a distant figure communing with nature, but a fellow-citizen who is out of sympathy with a utilitarian age, a divided and tormented soul walking the streets of the capital at our side. The whole life of the great modern industrial city—its sights, its sounds, its smells—is added to the subject-matter of poetry. It is not seen from without; it becomes part of our inner landscape.

There is only one serious omission in Laforgue's notes. He mentions Baudelaire's irony, his love of startling and disconcerting the reader and his 'Americanism', but he does not bring out the sardonic humour which informs his poetry and gives it its toughness and resilience as well as its immense power of deflation. It is pre-eminently a moral quality which is the product of Baudelaire's own heart-searching and which is entirely free from self-pity. In *Au Lecteur* and *Bénédiction* the alexandrines sound like the crack of a whip. In the first of these poems irony is used to puncture the reader's complacency, to force him to take sides with the poet, and in the second it is directed against the hostile society into which the poet is born. It is also one of Baudelaire's most influential qualities. Rimbaud used it in his first poems with greater ferocity and less discrimination. The tone of certain of Corbière's poems like *La Rapsode foraine* and *La Fin*, which recall some of the 'Tableaux Parisiens', is much closer to Baudelaire, but in *Femme* the irony is self-regarding. Laforgue himself was undoubtedly influenced by it, but he did not possess the 'punch' of the other two poets and his irony is to a large extent defensive.

The attitude implicit in Baudelaire's irony shows why 'he was the first to break with the public' and why the words 'déclassé et déraciné' are no more than a factual description of his vocation. He thought of himself like the 'dandy' as a member of an exclusive 'caste' which is characterized by its attitude of 'opposition and revolt'; of a 'new kind of aristocracy all the more difficult to break because it will be founded on the most precious, the most indestructible faculties, and the celestial gifts which work and money cannot confer'.[1] The art produced by the

[1] *L'Art romantique*, p. 91.

élite is not merely an art for the 'initiated'; it is necessarily individualist, sensitive, subtle, analytical, precarious, and abstruse. It reflects an attitude of 'opposition and revolt' towards the complacent, hard-working middle classes and it is in the nature of things subversive, a threat to stability and complacency and to a civilization based on the bank and the stock exchange.

'Je me suis mis à traduire tous mes rêves, toutes mes émotions', said Gérard de Nerval. Baudelaire would certainly have endorsed his aim. For we can say of him, as Mr. Eliot said of the English Metaphysicals, that he 'possessed a mechanism of sensibility which could devour any kind of experience'.[1] In his work poetry was extended to all sorts of strange and unfamiliar places, and the sensibility of people capable of reading him was immensely enlarged. It is not in the last analysis what a poet *says*, but what he *does* to us, that matters. It is a sign of the greatest writers that they not only enlarge our sensibility, but produce a radical modification in our experience and our capacity for experience.

'I know of nothing more compromising than imitators, and there is nothing I like so much as to be alone', said Baudelaire in a letter written to his mother a few weeks before his stroke. 'But it is not possible and it appears that *l'école Baudelaire* exists.'[2] This brings me to a last point. Baudelaire was not the leader of a literary movement; he was the founder of a school of poetry. There is a clear distinction between a movement like the Romantic Movement and the School of Baudelaire. A literary movement means that a number of poets use a similar style to express feelings which are to some extent common to them all. The founder of a school is the creator of a new manner of feeling and a new style. He succeeds in handing on his outlook and certain elements of his style to his successors who, within the limits of this framework, express their individual reactions to the new situation. Without Baudelaire there might have been no Corbière and no Laforgue while Rimbaud would have been a very different poet. It is a tribute to Baudelaire's vitality that after some early imita-

---

[1] *Op. cit.*, p. 273.
[2] *Corr. gén.*, 5, p. 303 (letter of 5 March 1866).

tions of his work the development of later writers was always *away* from the master. It shows that his poetry instead of inviting the imitation that he feared, was a genuine source of inspiration, a stimulus which encouraged further experiments and led to the discovery of Laforgue's free verse, Corbière's familiar style, and the prose poetry of Rimbaud. But that will have to be the subject of another book.

II

A NINETEENTH-CENTURY VOCATION

1. The Poet and his Mother

'Mais persuade-toi donc bien une chose, que tu sembles
toujours ignorer; c'est que vraiment pour mon malheur, je
ne suis pas fait comme les autres hommes.'
Letter to Mme Aupick

IT IS impossible to separate Baudelaire from his mother, and it is
not easy to be fair to her. It is commonly said that his biographers
have been too hard on her, that she was not lacking in taste or
wit, that the story of the Œdipus complex has been exaggerated,
and that if mother and son were on bad terms for many years it
was because they were too much alike.

There may be some truth in this view, but when we read the
pathetic begging letters that he wrote to her with their sad little
sums showing that financial stability was almost in sight, or his
careful refutation of the charges contained in one of her 'cruel'
letters, we can scarcely avoid the feeling that she played too large
a part in his life or that she comes between the poet and ourselves
as she may have come between the poet and his work. We find
ourselves wondering what the effect on European literature would
have been if the young wife instead of the elderly husband had
died in 1827. General Aupick was probably less formidable and
less grim than he appeared to his stepson, but the mother's second
marriage was undoubtedly a disaster for the poet. It is difficult to
believe that Mme Aupick's constant lecturing did her son anything but harm; and while we must agree with Feuillerat that there
is no need to 'invoke Freudian theories', we must also agree that
there was 'something equivocal', something which was 'not completely innocent' in the relationship between mother and son.[1] I

[1] A. Feuillerat, *Baudelaire et sa mère*, Montreal, 1944, pp. 14, 17.

41

think that we must add that the peculiar love-hate which they seem to have felt at times for one another was highly unfortunate for the poet, and that its harmful effects were accentuated by the mother's narrow middle-class outlook.

There is, however, a more serious charge to be brought against Mme Aupick. There is no doubt that her intentions in setting up the *conseil judiciaire* were admirable as there is no doubt that she and Ancelle were firmly convinced that they were acting in Baudelaire's interests during the twenty-three years they administered it. It must be said plainly that in spite of the excellence of their intentions the arrangement was cruel and stupid, and that the material as well as the psychological effects on the poet were deplorable. He himself never ceased to complain in the bitterest terms of the humiliation that they had inflicted on him or of the difficulties that it created for him. His complaints and his reproaches were fully justified. For the *conseil judiciaire* ensured two things. It ensured that he would never have sufficient income from his investments to enable him to live tolerably—it came to about seventy-five pounds a year—and it also ensured that he would never be able to pay off the debts incurred in his early twenties or be free from the persecutions of his creditors.

It cannot be denied that he was extravagant or that Mme Aupick assisted him to the limit of her slender means, but not even M. Sartre's psychological ingenuity can convince us that he deserved what he got, still less that he had secretly desired the *conseil judiciaire*.[1] It turned his life into a burden, created conditions which were so inimical to writing that we must feel a certain surprise that his finest work was written at all. That it should have driven the greatest French poet of the century into practices which M. Sartre elegantly describes as 'verging on fraud' was among the least of its evils.[2]

Caroline Archimbaut-Dufays was born in London on 27 December 1793 and died at Honfleur on 16 August 1871.[3] She

[1] *Baudelaire*, Paris, 1947, p. 18.

[2] *Ibid.*, p. 51.

[3] According to Crépet, her correct name was Archenbaut-Defayis (*Corr. gén.*, I, p. 4 n.).

was left an orphan at an early age and was brought up by friends. Although delicate, she is said to have been good-looking, smart, ambitious, and to have had an equable temper; but she had one great disadvantage which outweighed all these gifts. She had no *dot*. Her guardians probably felt that she was lucky when on 9 September 1819 she married Joseph François Baudelaire, a widower who was over thirty years her senior. She may have shared their views, at any rate for a time; but when we look back on this marriage and its consequences, we can hardly deny that Feuillerat's account of it as 'cette union, par trop raisonnable' is decidedly mild.[1]

'M. Baudelaire', we are told, 'malgré son âge, était fort séduisant.'[2] He was born on 8 June 1759 and had begun his career as a teacher of drawing at the Collège Sainte-Barbe, but had later been appointed tutor to the family of the Duc de Choiseul-Praslin. He lived very comfortably and was able to indulge his taste for luxury, which was inherited by his son, until he was deprived of his livelihood during the Revolution. He took no active part in events, earned his living by giving drawing lessons, and remained loyal to his old master and old pupils. They did not forget him when they regained their position, and he was given a sinecure in the Senate. In 1803 he married Rosalie Janin, a woman of means who was eight years older than himself and had studied art in the same studio. A son, Claude Alphonse, was born in 1805. Nine years later his wife died leaving him what in those days was a substantial fortune. His career at the Senate came to an end in 1814 owing to the undecided political views of the Choiseul-Praslins, but he received a generous pension which with his wife's estate freed him from material cares.

In an interview that he is supposed to have given in Belgium, Baudelaire spoke with extreme bitterness of the marriage of his parents. He called it 'a disproportionate, pathological, senile union', attributed his own ill-health to the fact that he was 'the chancy fruit of such a coupling', and in order to make it sound

---

[1] *Op. cit.*, p. 13. Porché is less indulgent and calls it a 'union . . . quasi monstrueuse' (*Baudelaire: Histoire d'une âme*, Paris, 1945, p. 8).

[2] Feuillerat, *op. cit., loc. cit.*

more convincing added ten years to his father's age at the time of his second marriage.[1] 'My father', he said in one of his letters, 'was a detestable artist.'[2] Although he asked his interviewer, who was studying physiology, to obtain Claude Bernard's opinion of the effects of the marriage, we may doubt whether physiologists would endorse his view. It is by no means certain that the age of his father had anything to do with his poor health. His half-brother was a sickly ailing man who died comparatively young, and his mother was decidedly neurasthenic. Nor must we overlook the credit side of the account. François Baudelaire was an intelligent and cultivated man who had been the friend of Helvétius and Condorcet. He may have been a 'detestable artist', but we can scarcely doubt that his intelligence as well as his sensibility played a part in his son's formation. Genius is incalculable, but it seems probable that François Baudelaire's sensibility determined the form which his son's genius assumed.

Charles Pierre Baudelaire was born in Paris on 9 April 1821. His father died on 10 February 1827 and on 8 November of the following year his mother married Major Aupick, a handsome and brilliant young officer who was destined for a great career. The influence of those first six years on Baudelaire was decisive. The mother, who had made a first marriage which was 'par trop raisonnable', naturally lavished all her tenderness on her son and it was during those years that the 'equivocal' relationship was formed. When she married a man who possessed the qualities which were lacking in her first husband, the son took second place. He naturally felt cheated, an outcast, and developed a sullen resentment towards the stepfather whom he could only regard as an intruder who had wrecked his happiness.

We know little of Baudelaire's early life. He went to school at the Collège Royal at Lyons where his stepfather had been sent to put down a riot. His only academic success there was a drawing prize. When the parents returned to Paris, he transferred to the Lycée Louis-le-Grand. His stepfather proudly presented him to

[1] Quoted in E. and J. Crépet, *Charles Baudelaire*, Paris, 1907, pp. 155–6, n. 2.

[2] *Corr. gén.*, 2, p. 111 (letter to Mme Aupick of 30 December 1857).

the authorities as a pupil who would do honour to the school, but he was wrong. Baudelaire's school career was undistinguished academically and ended in disgrace. His reports were bad; he was already something of a rebel, and seems to have displayed little aptitude for anything except Latin verse for which he won a prize at the Concours Général—a competition open to all the schools in France—in 1837. He had to leave the Lycée the following year. There has been some controversy about the reasons for his expulsion, and one of his school-fellows alleged that it was on account of an 'histoire de dortoir'. It seems, however, that the reason was nothing more serious than his refusal to give up a note which had been passed to him in class.[1]

He was then sent to live at the home of a man named Lasègue, who coached him for the *baccalauréat* which he passed in August 1839. This was followed by the traditional quarrel over his future. His parents wanted him to read for the diplomatic service. Aupick, who was now a brigadier-general and knew the Duc d'Orléans, could have helped; but Charles would not hear of it and shocked the family by announcing that he intended to become a writer. He was sent to lodge at the Pension Bailly and was inscribed at the École des Chartes, where he is said to have attended lectures intermittently for the next ten years.

At this period the Latin Quarter was virtually a student city. Baudelaire plunged with relish into student life, or at any rate the gayer side of it. He made friends with Gustave Le Vavasseur, the founder of *l'école normande*, Louis Ménard, and Ernest Prarond, and seems to have met Balzac, Gérard de Nerval, and Gautier. He soon became one of the most prominent figures among the students, ran into debt, and probably contracted the disease from which he is said to have died twenty-five years later. He was allowed to enjoy student life for nearly two years when his family became alarmed over his friends and his extravagance. General Aupick paid his debts, which amounted to three thousand francs, out of his own pocket, but the *conseil de famille* was hastily summoned and decided that something drastic must be done. They

---

[1] *Corr. gén.*, 1, p. 6 n.

made up their minds to send him on a voyage and five thousand francs were taken from his father's estate to cover the costs. He was placed in charge of the captain of a ship called the *Paquebot des Mers du Sud*, which was bound for India, and sailed from Bordeaux on 9 June 1841 on a voyage which was meant to keep him out of harm's way for two years.

He disliked his fellow-passengers while they were incensed by his youthful intellectual arrogance and his outrageous *boutades*. The ship ran into a storm, lost its mainmast, and was nearly wrecked. Captain Saliz, the skipper, was obliged to put into Mauritius for repairs which took nineteen days. Baudelaire went to live at an hotel, sought out such intellectual company as was to be found on the island, and met M. and Mme Autard de Bragard. It was to Mme Autard that the poem in the *Fleurs du mal* called *A une Dame créole* was addressed and sent in a letter to her husband of 20 October 1841. The ship called next at the Ile Bourbon. Baudelaire decided that the voyage had lasted long enough, refused to go on, and persuaded Saliz to allow him to return to France. He sailed from Bourbon on 4 November and was back in Paris in February of the following year.

'Posterity', writes M. André Ferran, 'owes General Aupick a debt of gratitude which he never sought to incur.'[1] His one aim had been to keep his stepson out of mischief, but it is scarcely an exaggeration to say that the punitive voyage changed the course of French poetry. The sights, sounds, scents, and colours of the East had a decisive effect on the development of Baudelaire's genius. They enriched his sensibility and provided him with a vast store of brilliant exotic images which he could not have acquired in any other way and which are one of the most fascinating characteristics of his poetry.

Baudelaire reached his majority on 9 April 1842 and came into possession of the seventy-five thousand francs which he inherited from his father. In June he left his parents' house, where he had been living since his return, and took a flat on the Quai de Béthune in the Ile Saint-Louis, moving a little later to the famous Hôtel

[1] *L'Esthétique de Baudelaire*, Paris, 1933, p. 32.

de Lauzun. The next two years were among the most fateful of his life. It was probably during this period that he developed the habit of taking hashish and other drugs. He met Jeanne Duval and wrote a number of poems which were to take their place in the *Fleurs du mal*. He also set up as a leader of fashion, trying to emulate the exploits of the wealthy Roger de Beauvoir; and partly through extravagance but partly through the cunning of trades-people contracted the bulk of the debts which were to be a growing burden until his dying day.

In 1844 his horrified family discovered that he had spent half his capital and a *conseil judiciaire* was proposed. Baudelaire implored his mother not to allow it, but she was adamant and in September it was appointed. It was the beginning of a nightmare which was to have no end. 'I shall die without having done anything with my life', we find him writing to his mother in 1860. 'I once owed 20,000 francs; I now owe 40,000. If I have the misfortune to live long enough, the debt may be doubled again.'[1] The same year he describes the *conseil judiciaire* as 'that appalling mistake which has ruined my life, blasted my days, and tinged all my thoughts with hate and despair'.[2] A few months later it is 'that accursed invention, the maternal invention of a mind too anxious about money' which has dishonoured him and interfered with his education as an artist and a man of letters.[3]

The year 1845 was marked by Baudelaire's mysterious attempt to commit suicide by stabbing himself in the chest while sitting in a café with Jeanne Duval. His biographers have never been able to decide whether the attempt was serious or whether he was merely trying to play on the sympathies of his family. There is no doubt, however, that the four years which followed the appointment of the *conseil judiciaire* were years of tribulation. He was deeply humiliated; his financial position was impossible, and he was already leading a cat-and-dog life with Jeanne. In spite of this he managed to write some poetry, and the first of his famous *Salons* was published. He was also extending his connections in

[1] *Corr. gén.*, 3, p. 174 (letter of 21 August 1860).
[2] *Corr. gén.*, 3, pp. 191–2 (letter of 11 October 1860).
[3] *Corr. gén.*, 3, p. 267 (letter of 1 April 1861).

the world of art and letters. He met Murger, Courbet, the poet Pierre Dupont, and Champfleury, who was one of the earlier realistic novelists, and probably Delacroix. These were professional acquaintances, but he also laid the foundations of his friendship with two men who were to play an important part in his later life. The first was the faithful Asselineau, a man of letters and a book-collector whom he is thought to have met through the painter Deroy, whose portrait of Baudelaire as a young man now hangs in the gallery at Versailles. The second was Poulet-Malassis who was to become his publisher.

The events of 1848 are among the most curious episodes in Baudelaire's career. For we find him taking part in the revolution on the side of the insurgents. With Champfleury and Toubin he founded a revolutionary newspaper called *Le Salut Public*, of which only two numbers were published. Buisson has described him during the February uprising brandishing a gun which had obviously never been used, claiming to have fired a shot and shouting, excitedly, 'We must go and shoot General Aupick.'[1] He also seems to have been back on the barricades in June, but after abortive efforts to edit a conservative paper, which he changed into an opposition paper, at Dijon in 1849, and a local paper at Châteauroux in 1850, he ceased to take any further interest in politics and had severed his connection with all the parties by 1851. When he looked back on the events of 1848, he found it difficult to explain his actions. 'What was the nature of my intoxication in 1848?' he asked in his diaries. He replied: 'Thirst for revenge. Natural delight in destruction. A literary intoxication; the memories of books I had read.'[2]

It may at first seem difficult to reconcile his association with the insurgents and the theory of dandyism set out in the famous essay on Constantin Guys, but in reality it is not so. The exclusive 'caste' described in the essay was the first attempt to form a writers' party in order to resist the encroachments of the new middle class which had issued from the Revolution. The spectacle

---

[1] E. and J. Crépet, *op. cit.*, pp. 78–9. On Baudelaire's political activities, see J. Mouquet and W. T. Bandy, *Baudelaire en 1848*, Paris, 1946.

[2] *Journaux intimes*, p. 56.

of the poet with his gun urging the mob to go and shoot General Aupick is the symbol of the artist at odds with society. Baudelaire was to insist on the dandy's attitude of 'opposition and revolt', and like many writers he made the mistake of entering into an alliance with the extreme left in the hope of defeating his particular enemies—the bourgeois—failing to see that if the revolutionaries had come to power their first action would have been to 'liquidate' the artist. For in a classless society there is no room for an exclusive caste of artists which would be an obvious challenge to the 'Party'. What in fact happened in 1848 was that the Revolution was suppressed, a new constitution was introduced which under cover of vesting full executive powers in the people, ensured that it remained in the hands of the professional politicians and that the party-political game continued. The writers saw that they had lost and wisely retired from the scene.

During the next seven years Baudelaire devoted himself largely to his critical writings and to the translation of the works of Edgar Allan Poe. He had first come across some tales of Poe's in a French translation in 1846 or 1847 and had experienced 'a strange commotion', seeing in the American author a sort of spiritual brother who had expressed perfectly feelings and ideas which he himself had only perceived dimly.[1] English and French readers are unlikely ever to agree about Poe. In England we can only lament that Baudelaire should have spent so many years translating the American, and sympathize with his lack of experience in allowing Michel Lévy to buy the copyright of the translations from him for a paltry sum in 1861. Poe's influence really amounted to very little and what there was of it was largely bad, but in discovering him Baudelaire provided research students and dons with a heaven-sent subject for theses and dissertations.

On 28 April 1857 General Aupick died suddenly. On 25 June the *Fleurs du mal*, first announced under the title of *Les Lesbiennes* as long ago as 1846, was published.[2] The two attacks on the mora-

[1] *Corr. gén.*, 2, pp. 249–50 (letter to Armand Fraisse thought to have been written in 1858).

[2] The final title was suggested by a man of letters named Hippolyte Babou about 1854–5.

lity of the book, which appeared in the *Figaro* on 5 and 7 July, were the beginning of one of the most famous of all literary *causes célèbres*. Four days later the authorities confiscated the sheets held at Poulet-Malassis's and de Broise's printing works at Alençon, and on 20 August Baudelaire was prosecuted for an offence against public morality in the Sixième Cour Correctionnelle—a court which normally tried cases of petty larceny, burglary, and vagrancy. The prosecution seems to have been somewhat half-hearted, but the court ordered the suppression of six poems, fined Baudelaire three hundred francs and the publishers a hundred francs each. Baudelaire's fine was later reduced to fifty francs—possibly owing to the intervention of the Empress Eugénie to whom he had appealed—and in 1949 by a peculiarity of French law the conviction was annulled.

We must once again challenge M. Sartre's view that Baudelaire desired the condemnation of his work and discount the terms in which his appeal to the Empress was couched. In spite of his professed contempt for authority, he was shattered by his conviction and was not consoled by Hugo's letter telling him that he had achieved the only real distinction that the State could confer. His conviction was the origin of the unfortunate attempt to rehabilitate himself by standing for the French Academy in 1861–2. He met with real kindness and genuine understanding from Alfred de Vigny who was dying of cancer and whose good influence was probably responsible for inducing him to avoid another rebuff by withdrawing his name. Sainte-Beuve had already disgraced himself by his silence at the time of the trial, and his notorious article discussing the chances of the different candidates was characteristically perfidious. Baudelaire's accounts of his official 'visits' to the fifth-rate men of letters whose support he was soliciting are highly entertaining, but he loathed the whole business and spoke from the heart when he remarked in a letter to Arsène Houssaye: 'Vous savez quelle odysée horrible c'est, odysée sans sirènes et sans lotus.'[1]

The years that followed the publication of the *Fleurs du mal* were among the most difficult of Baudelaire's life, and his letters

[1] *Corr. gén.*, 3, p. 29 (letter written at Christmas 1861).

to his mother are filled with complaints about his lot. He was depressed at the thought of having to revise the book and write fresh poems in place of the condemned pieces. His debts and the *conseil judiciaire* preyed on his mind. 'These cursed *Fleurs du mal* that I have got to start over again', he said bitterly in a letter written in February 1858. 'I need rest for that. To think that I have got to become a poet again, artificially through an effort of the will, return to a trail that I thought I had blazed once for all, deal over again with a subject that I thought I had exhausted— and all that out of obedience to the will of three magistrates, one of whom is *Nacquart*.'[1] 'If ever a man suffered from spleen and hypochondria in his youth, I am that man', he said in another letter. 'And yet I want to live and I should like to enjoy a little security, a little fame and feel a little satisfaction with myself. Something terrible inside me says: *never*, but something else says: *try*.'[2] 'I am alone,' we find him writing in the middle of the year 1861, 'without friends, without a mistress, without a dog, and without a cat to whom I can complain. I have only my father's portrait and it is dumb.'[3] 'You see, what I suffer through being alive is inexpressible.'[4] His lamentations never cease. Two years later he is still dwelling on his loneliness and his *ennui*. 'I experience such *ennui* in my unlighted room, I suffer so much from the lack of *friendship* and *luxury*; I am so crushed by my loneliness and my laziness that I keep putting off my obligations until to-morrow, even those that I am most anxious to fulfil.'[5] 'What I feel is a complete disgust with everything and above all else with every form of pleasure . . . the only feeling that convinces me that I am still alive is a *vague* desire for celebrity, vengeance, and money.'[6]

The deepening depression of these years seems to be reflected not only in the letters, but in the new poems he was writing for

[1] *Corr. gén.*, 2, p. 128.
[2] *Corr. gén.*, 3, p. 263 (letter of February or March 1861).
[3] *Corr. gén.*, 3, p. 282.
[4] *Corr. gén.*, 4, p. 18 (Christmas Day 1861).
[5] *Corr. gén.*, 4, p. 206 (letter of 25 November 1863).
[6] *Corr. gén.*, 4, p. 219 (letter of 31 December 1863).

the Cycle of Spleen and in the portraits that we have of him. The bearded Adonis with long curly chestnut hair, whom Deroy painted in 1844, appears to change suddenly in Nadar's photographs into the prematurely aged man of letters. In each of them the lips appear more pinched, the furrows round the mouth deeper and the expression of horror in the eyes—it is always the eyes that haunt us in Baudelaire's portraits—more intense. There is a frightening photograph of Carjat's, taken when he had had to have his long hair cropped on account of illness, in which he looks like an old man of sixty though he was only forty-two at the time.[1] When we gaze at the anguished expression and the thin straggling hair, we may feel that the letter-writer and the poet are one and the same person and that M. Sartre is right in describing his life as 'the story of a very slow, very painful decomposition'.[2] But when we recall that the second edition of the *Fleurs du mal* contains far more than six new poems, that *Le Voyage*—described by Crépet as 'un des plus magnifiques joyaux des lettres françaises'—was written in 1859, *La Chevelure* almost certainly about the same time, and that his vigorous championship of Wagner and the famous essay on *Tannhäuser* belong to the years 1860–1, doubts arise.[3] The situation described in the letters provided the raw material for the Cycle of Spleen, but it is a mistake to assume that the experience of the man and the experience of the poet are identical and to fail to take into account the transforming power of poetry. The man who wrote the letters, who took drugs, who could not bring himself to work, who was untrustworthy over money, and who savagely denounced contemporary civilization and women in the diaries can only be regarded as a radical case of maladjustment. He was out of sympathy with his age, incapable of dealing with the problems of everyday life, and his experiences as a lover suggest that he suffered from some form of sexual maladjustment. The poems

[1] He was apparently referring to this photograph, with which he was delighted, in the letter written to Carjat on 6 October 1863 (*Corr. gén.*, 4, p. 193).
[2] *Op. cit.*, p. 223.
[3] *Corr. gén.*, 2, p. 278 n.

BAUDELAIRE IN 1863

From a photograph by Carjat

unquestionably sprang from this maladjustment; but while the letters are a display of human frailty, the poems exhibit the strength of a great artist. In them the self-pity of the letters is replaced by the toughness, the resilience, and the sardonic humour of which I spoke in the last chapter.

Although Baudelaire painted everything as black as possible in his letters to his mother and was inclined to practise a subtle form of emotional blackmail in these last years, he was certainly further than ever from having the sort of life he deserved. The second edition of the *Fleurs du mal*, on which he had expended great labour and which he modestly described as '*presque bien*', was published in January 1861 and was not a success.[1] The following year Poulet-Malassis went bankrupt. Baudelaire had parted with the copyright in his translations, which had brought him in a modest income for some years, and now that his creditors were becoming more pressing he had nothing with which to pay them. His troubles were aggravated in 1862 by another attack of the syphilis of which he had believed himself cured.

In the course of a somewhat chequered career, which had included traffic in obscene books, Poulet-Malassis had had occasion to visit Belgium where there was no censorship. It was with his encouragement that Baudelaire conceived the idea of going to that country in the hope of arranging a new edition of his work, earning some money by lecturing and gaining a respite from his creditors. After many delays and postponements, he left for Brussels in April 1864. His stay in Belgium was a calamity. He detested the people. His publishing plans came to nothing. His lectures were a failure, and the Belgians cheated him over his fees. There was a moderate attendance at his first lecture on Delacroix which he gave in May though it was already too late in the season for public lectures. He began his second lecture on Gautier by thanking the audience for their attendance at the first, but imprudently added that it was among them that he had lost his virginity as an orator, 'virginité qui n'est d'ailleurs pas plus regrettable que l'autre'. The more prudish among them left the hall, and as the lecture went on for some two hours he found himself at the

[1] *Corr. gén.*, 3, p. 221 (letter to Mme Aupick of 1 January 1861).

end addressing rows of empty seats. He lost his nerve and gabbled through his third lecture on the *Paradis artificiels*, which was a fiasco.

The failure of his publishing plans and his lectures meant that he was soon in fresh financial difficulties and unable to leave his hotel because he could not pay his landlady. In April 1866, while visiting the Jesuit church of Saint-Loup at Namur with some friends, he had a slight stroke and fell. This was followed by aphasia. He was partially paralysed and unable to speak coherently. He was brought back to Paris by his mother and friends on 2 July and entered a nursing home in the Rue du Dôme where he died on 31 August 1867. The funeral was a fitting end to the grim story. There were inexcusable 'abstentions' on the part of well-known writers. A thunderstorm broke over the cemetery, making the speeches inaudible and scattering the handful of mourners.

2. The Poet and his Mistresses

The controversy over Baudelaire's sexual life begins with Nadar and is perpetuated in his ramshackle volume of memoirs and its provocative sub-title: 'Le Poète Vierge.' The memoirs were written many years after the events when Nadar was an old man, and it is impossible to verify his assertions. Baudelaire was extremely reticent in such matters, but he was an intimate friend of Nadar's and might possibly have confided in him. Nadar's championship of his virginity, however, does not rest on alleged disclosures; it is based on the gossip of cheap prostitutes, on the story of Jeanne Duval's giggles when anyone suggested that Baudelaire was her lover, and her description of him as a 'doux rêveur inoffensif, un maniaque dont toute la flamme s'épuisait en rimailleries'.

It is impossible to prove that Baudelaire actually had sexual intercourse with any of his official mistresses or with the women whose names and addresses appear in his *carnet*. It is not disputed that he suffered from syphilis. It is conceivable, but unlikely, that the syphilis was hereditary or was contracted by some indirect means. There remains the hypothesis that he was impotent. It has been interestingly discussed by Dr. Enid Starkie, who points out that even if impotent, he might have been capable of some sort of partial relations with women which would dispose of the difficulty of explaining the syphilis.[1]

Whether we accept or reject Nadar's view is not a matter of great moment. It is evident that Baudelaire's sexual life and his attitude towards the sexual connection were not altogether normal, and fortunately we have ample material in his own writings to enable us to reach some conclusions about this intriguing subject.

In the early autobiographical story called *La Fanfarlo*, Baudelaire remarks of his hero that 'l'amour était chez lui moins une affaire des sens que du raisonnement'.[2] There are indications in his work that he himself suffered from excessive cerebration. It is not uncommon among intellectuals and is not necessarily a sign of impotence. It produces on occasion the temporary sexual incapacity which Stendhal labelled 'le fiasco'. We know that he himself suffered from it, but we have the testimony of Alberthe de Rubempré that he was fully equal to the not inconsiderable demands that she made on him, and the manuscript of *La Vie de Henri Brulard* apparently contains some startling and highly entertaining statistics about his exploits with a certain Mme Galice.

Temporary incapacity, however, is by no means the most important or the most interesting symptom of excessive cerebration. The most striking characteristic of the cerebral type is his tendency to lose his simplicity and his single-mindedness, to treat love as something to be studied instead of lived, to become a *voyeur* instead of a performer. This undoubtedly applies to Baudelaire. The poems addressed to Jeanne Duval are not love poems in the accepted sense, but erotic poems. The poet is not so much the lover as the connoisseur of erotic effects; he is more concerned with the diverse ways of arousing desire than with its satisfaction, and it may be this that he had in mind when he spoke

---

[1] *Baudelaire*, London, 1933, pp. 74–8.
[2] *Les Paradis artificiels*, ed. Crépet, p. 274.

of 'le savant amour', meaning the love experienced by a man on the threshold of middle age.[1]

Baudelaire throws some further light on his own peculiarities when he goes on to tell us that Samuel Cramer's conception of love was 'surtout l'admiration et l'appétit du beau' and that 'la jouissance avait engendré chez lui ce contentement savoureux, cette rêverie sensuelle, qui vaut peut-être mieux que l'amour comme l'entend le vulgaire'.[2] This illustrates very well what I meant when I spoke of the loss of simplicity and single-mindedness. For Baudelaire's work is a reversal of the normal process of artistic creation. It is not a straightforward expression of sexual or erotic experience. He either uses poetry as a substitute for love or he uses love as a means to induce a state of mind which at bottom has very little to do with it. When we come to *La Chevelure*, for example, we shall find that the woman is used as a means for satisfying a different need which may provisionally be called 'l'admiration et l'appétit du beau'. The tendency to make art a substitute for sexual experience is confirmed by the remark attributed to Jeanne Duval which assumes a new importance in the light of these observations. He was, she said, 'un doux rêveur inoffensif, un maniaque *dont toute la flamme s'épuisait en rimailleries*'. It receives even more striking confirmation in a curious entry in the diaries. 'Plus l'homme cultive les arts', said Baudelaire, 'moins il bande. Il se fait un divorce de plus en plus sensible entre l'esprit et la brute. La brute seule bande bien, et la fouterie est le lyrisme du peuple.'[3] There is no reason to doubt the

---

[1] 'L'amour (sens et esprit) est niais à 20 ans, et il est *savant* à 40 (*Corr. gén.*, 3, p. 71. Letter to Alphonse de Calonne, March 1860.).

'For the child the caress comes without the knowledge of the woman from all the graces of woman. He therefore loves his mother, his sister, his nurse on account of the agreeable titillation of satin and furs, the smell of breasts and hair, the chink of jewels, the play of ribbons, etc. . . . on account of that *mundus muliebris* beginning with underclothes and expressing itself even through the furnishings on which the woman places the imprint of her sex' (*Corr. gén.*, 3, pp. 96–7. Letter to Poulet-Malassis of 23 April 1860. Compare *Les Vocations* in *Petits poèmes en prose*, No. XXXI).

[2] *Les Paradis artificiels*, pp. 274, 275–6.

[3] *Journaux intimes*, p. 95.

correctness of M. Sartre's assertion that it is a personal admission, or to refrain from adding that the last sentence reveals the *voyeur* and the connoisseur.

The substitution of aesthetic for sexual experience is probably not uncommon and is certainly not abnormal, but it must be recognized that there was undoubtedly a perverse element in Baudelaire's attitude to women. There is something monstrous about his association with the appalling Louchette, and the early poem that he wrote to her beginning, 'Je n'ai pas pour maîtresse une lionne illustre', seems to me to be pathological in the strict medical sense. Nor can we dismiss as a mere *boutade* the passage in *Fusées* in which he compares the act of love to 'torture or a surgical operation' with one of the partners playing the part of 'executioner' and the other that of 'victim' in 'a tragedy of dishonour'. He goes on to speak with horrified fascination of 'ces gémissements, ces cris, ces râles . . . ces yeux de somnambule révulsés, ces membres dont les muscles jaillissent et se roidissent comme sous l'action d'une pile galvanique . . .' 'Certes,' he concludes, 'je croirais faire un sacrilège en appliquant le mot "extase" à cette sorte de décomposition.'[1] We must remember that the diaries are a late work which should be used with circumspection, that Baudelaire's hostility to women and his emphasis on prostitution may have been accentuated by the recurrence of the syphilis which he is reputed to have caught from a prostitute.[2] It is apparent from his work, however, that the attitude was by no means new. Even in his most sensual poems—the poems written to Jeanne Duval—there is an unmistakable sexual antagonism beneath the raptures. There is merely a difference of degree between poems like 'Tu mettrais l'univers entier dans ta ruelle, Femme impure!' or *Duellum* and the attacks on women in the diaries, while in *A Celle qui est trop gaie* even the difference of degree vanishes.

The last text to which I want to draw attention occurs in a curious letter written to Asselineau on 20 February 1859, and describes a local scandal at Honfleur:

[1] *Journaux intimes*, p. 10.
[2] The editors of the critical edition suggest that *Fusées* belongs to the period 1855–62, and *Mon Coeur mis à nu* to the period 1859–66 (See p. 182).

'On avait surpris, il y a déjà longtemps, la femme du maire se faisant
f . . . dans un confessionnal. . . . C'est une femme insupportable . . .
mais qui doit avoir un cul superbe (elle). Cette histoire de fouterie
provinciale, dans un lieu sacré, n'a-t-elle pas tout le sel classique des
vieilles saletés françaises?'[1]

Writers on Baudelaire sometimes describe his attitude to love
as 'manichæan' without realizing the full implications of the
term. The diaries and the poems undoubtedly reveal a morbid
revulsion from the sexual connection mingled with a strong sense
of guilt which was probably associated with his 'equivocal' relationship to his mother; but puritanism is not a purely negative
attitude and is seldom the outcome of sexual deficiency. On the
contrary, it is often a form of overcompensation which is found
in very highly sexed people who either have strong religious
convictions or like Baudelaire some personal feeling of guilt.
There is no mistaking the relish behind the words, 'C'est une
femme insupportable . . . mais qui doit avoir un cul superbe
(elle)', but it is still the relish of the *voyeur* and the reference to
the 'vieilles saletés françaises' is significant. It removes a 'true
story' to the realm of literature.

I think we can conclude that in Baudelaire we find excessive
cerebration, a tendency to subordinate sexual to aesthetic experience, to use women as a means instead of an end, and a curiously
ambivalent attitude to the act of love. This is of considerable
importance for an understanding of his life and poetry, but it
cannot be said to solve the problem of his virginity or his
impotence.

La Vénus Noire

Crépet has declared categorically that Baudelaire's liaison with
Jeanne Duval began 'without any doubt' in 1842.[2] We know
nothing of her origins. There are highly circumstantial accounts
of her first meeting with Baudelaire, but like the descriptions of
her personal appearance they depend on recollections written
down many years after the events and cannot be accepted without

[1] *Corr. gén.*, 2, p. 274.
[2] *Charles Baudelaire*, p. 54 n.

reservation. She was probably a prostitute who managed to earn a little extra money by playing very minor parts at the theatres on the Left Bank. It is said that at the time of the meeting she was appearing in a vaudeville at the old Théâtre du Panthéon, which has long since been pulled down, and that her part was confined to announcing: 'Dinner is served, madame.' Baudelaire's biographers have suggested that she must have been chosen for her personal appearance and not for her ability as an actress, but the views of contemporary observers on her beauty are not unanimous and tell us less than the poetry. She was a half-caste and is said by Nadar to have been a tall dark girl with perfect nose and mouth and a large mass of dark curly hair which fell in a cascade over her shoulders. Banville spoke of 'une chevelure violemment crespelée', and added that there was something 'at once divine and bestial' about her movements.[1]

The meeting was probably a chance one. Baudelaire is thought to have dropped casually into the theatre where she was employed one evening after dinner for want of anything better to do. He at once picked her out and began to court her as though she were a prima donna, sending her bouquets of hot-house flowers, asking permission to drive her home, and finally establishing her in a flat decorated in oriental style in the Rue de la Femme-sans-Tête near his own residence in the Ile Saint-Louis.

That a young man should choose an actress for his first mistress has nothing surprising about it. It is or was the traditional start of a young man about town, particularly a young man with literary or artistic leanings. Nor is it surprising that a shy young man should have found his actress at a small theatre in the Latin Quarter instead of at one of the fashionable theatres on the Right Bank. What seems at first surprising is that he should have chosen a woman who was playing not merely an insignificant part, but an insignificant part in a curtain-raiser. The poet, however, had good reasons for his choice. The management may have given Jeanne her job on account of her looks; Baudelaire selected her for the part that she was to play in his life, not merely for her

---

[1] *Mes souvenirs*, Paris, 1882, pp. 74–5.

looks but for her origin and the colour of her skin. He had come back from the East with his mind stored with memories of an exotic scene, but except for the spectacle of the heaving buttocks of a black woman servant who was being publicly thrashed—a spectacle which had made a powerful impression on him—the scene was empty, and he needed an inhabited scene. Jeanne offered him exactly what he was seeking. We have to admit that she was chosen partly to enable him to project the morbid element in his attitude towards sexual love—she was the exotic creature whom he could worship and with whom he could indulge in strange practices—but it is no exaggeration to say that she acted on his imagination as a catalytic agent, that the combination of the woman and the country he had seen was essential to set the machinery of poetic creation in motion. Life with Jeanne was a nightmare, but the finest poems inspired by her are among his main achievements.

Baudelaire was soon to discover that Jeanne's looks were her only real asset. She was indolent, rapacious, and unfaithful to him with his friends and possibly even with the tradesmen who came to the house. She was incapable of understanding or taking the slightest interest in his work and, as he was to remark bitterly, would gladly have burnt his poems if that would have brought in more money than publishing them. When he had first singled her out she had perceived at once that he came of good family, but she had believed mistakenly that he possessed a large fortune. As soon as the *conseil judiciaire* was appointed and she discovered her error, the trouble began.

Dr. Starkie suggests that passionate love between them, always supposing that it had existed, was over by 1845; but Baudelaire was to cling to her for years to come, partly out of a sense of duty, partly from habit, and partly, we may suspect, from an obscure sense that she was still necessary to his work. 'Jeanne', he said in a letter to his mother, 'has become an obstacle not merely to my happiness . . . but to the perfecting of my mind. . . . *In the past, she had certain qualities* but she has lost them, while I have gained in clear-sightedness.' He goes on to denounce her stupidity and rapacity, recalls a violent scene in which he had cut her head open, and announces that he is going to leave her 'for ever', that he 'will never see her again'.[1]

The letter was written on 27 April 1852. They certainly parted about this time, but when he said that he would never see her again Baudelaire exaggerated his own determination. In 1854 he was already thinking of going back to her and the following year he did so. He had decided, he said, to 'rentrer dans le concubinage', adding that if he were not living with Jeanne by the beginning of the next year, it would be with 'the other'. 'Il me faut à tout prix *une famille*.'[2] The reconciliation is thought to have produced at least one notable poem—*Le Balcon*—but it did not last long. On 11 September 1856 we find him writing to his mother: 'My liaison with Jeanne, a liaison which lasted fourteen years, is at an end. I did everything that was humanly possible to prevent the breach. The wrench and the struggle went on for a fortnight. Jeanne always replied, imperturbably, that I had an impossible character and that in any case I myself would one day be grateful to her for the decision. . . . I shall always regret this woman . . . she was my only distraction, my only pleasure, my only companion and in spite of all the shocks of our stormy liaison, the idea of a final separation had never seriously entered my head.'[3]

They parted for the second time in the autumn of 1856, but it was not definitive. In 1858 they were living together once more, but this time Baudelaire seems to have been moved by pity and speaks of Jeanne as a 'pauvre infirme'.[4] The following year she entered Dr. Dubois's nursing home, where she was treated for paralysis and dipsomania, and tried characteristically to swindle Baudelaire over the medical fees. When she left the nursing home in 1860 Baudelaire gave a dinner in her honour and rented a flat for her at Neuilly. While she was there a man claiming to be her brother came to live with her which increased the inevitable friction between Baudelaire and herself. When she had to go into hospital—the workhouse hospital this time—for further treatment, the brother sold her furniture and absconded with the proceeds. This was too much. Baudelaire left the house at Neuilly

---

[1] *Corr. gén.*, 1, p. 163.
[2] *Corr. gén.*, 1, p. 315.
[3] *Corr. gén.*, 1, pp. 397–8.
[4] *Corr. gén.*, 2, p. 184.

and never lived with Jeanne again, but he did not cease to worry and fret about her—we know from his letters that in 1864 she was threatened with blindness—to send her money when he had any, or to ask his mother to see that she did not want after his death. Mme Aupick behaved as we should expect. She took good care to destroy the correspondence between the poet and the most famous of his mistresses and she ignored the request to help the wretched, ailing woman. Nadar claims to have seen her on crutches in 1870. Then she disappears from history.

La Vénus Blanche

In spite of her great though involuntary services to French literature, Jeanne Duval has never been popular with Baudelaire's biographers. They have felt, understandably enough, that on the human plane she was unworthy of him and that she treated him abominably. Madame Apollonie Sabatier, the second of his mistresses in order of fame but not of time, has been much more fortunate. The poems that he wrote to her are inferior to those inspired by Jeanne Duval and Marie Daubrun, but most of his biographers have thought well of her, have given her 'a good press', and two of them have devoted charming monographs to her.

Her real names were Aglaé Joséphine Savatier and she never married. She was born at Mézières on 7 April 1822 and was the natural daughter of the Vicomte d'Abancourt, a former Prefect of the Ardennes, and a sewing-maid named Léa Marguerite Martin who used to work at the Prefecture. The Vicomte persuaded André Savatier, a forty-three-year-old sergeant in the 47th Infantry Division, which was stationed at Mézières at the time, to marry the mother before the birth of the child and give it a name. The family moved to Strasbourg, but when André Savatier retired from the army, 'covered with wounds and decorations' as one of Baudelaire's biographers puts it, they went to Paris and settled at Batignolles.[1] The father died there on 27 September 1833, and the following year Mme Savatier gave birth to another

---

[1] Porché, *op. cit.*, p. 269.

daughter who was named Adèle Irma and familiarly known as Bébé.

Apollonie showed a disposition for the arts, studied at the studio of Ernest Meissonier who became one of her closest friends, and had some miniatures accepted by the Salon des Amis des Arts in 1847. She also had a promising voice, and the headmistress of a girls' school at Batignolles paid for her to have singing lessons. It was at a charity concert in which she was taking part that she met Count Alfred Mosselman, a wealthy Jewish banker belonging to an ancient Belgian family, who installed her in the best nineteenth-century manner in a flat at 4 Rue Frochot.[1] We do not know the date of the meeting or whether Mosselman was her first lover. She herself was always modest about her successes, but she never had the reputation of being 'difficult'. M. André Billy puts it very happily. 'Let us place her, if you wish,' he writes, 'above *la haute bicherie* among the absolute *élite* of the profession; but we cannot alter the fact that she was *une biche du quartier Bréda.*'[2]

Apollonie was a woman of considerable beauty and Mosselman employed the sculptor, Jean Baptiste Clésinger, to model her. The method used was somewhat unorthodox and decidedly uncomfortable. She was wrapped in modelling clay; a plaster statue was cast from the mould and exhibited at the Salon of 1844 under the title of *Rêve d'amour*. It attracted little attention. The banker and the sculptor were annoyed, and the model is said to have been hurt. They decided on bolder tactics which proved highly effective. A marble sculpture of the naked Apollonie called *Femme piquée par un serpent* was sent to the Salon of 1847. It was severely handled by the more serious-minded critics. One of them was nearly involved in a duel for hinting that the sculptor had used the same method as for *Rêve d'amour*; others remarked on the weaknesses of the artist's lines and curves, but no one failed to observe that the model's convulsions were not of the kind that were usually produced by a snake-bite. It was precisely this that

[1] Not, as most biographers have supposed, Hippolyte Mosselman, who was his brother.

[2] *La Présidente et ses amis*, Paris, 1945, p. 27.

turned the work into a *succès de scandale* and sent enthusiastic crowds scurrying to gaze at it in open-mouthed admiration. Clésinger's bust of her, which was exhibited the same year, is today in the Louvre; and three years later Gustave Ricard's portrait, *La Femme au chien*, attracted a good deal of favourable comment.

La Présidente, as Gautier called her, was by this time something of a celebrity. The Sunday dinners at the Rue Frochot had begun in 1850. The regular guests included Baudelaire, Gautier, Flaubert, Clésinger, Feydeau, the elder Dumas, Barbey d'Aurevilly, Louis Bouilhet, and Maxime Du Camp. She had a kind heart and was no prude. The atmosphere at her Sunday evenings is said to have been extremely free and easy and highly agreeable.[1]

Judith Gautier was taken to see Apollonie by her father, and has left a vivid picture of her in her prime. She describes her as being on the tall side, well proportioned, graceful with charming hands, while her silky chestnut hair fell in long waves. Her complexion was clear, her features regular, her mouth small and smiling. She was always good-humoured and gay. 'Son air triomphant', adds Judith Gautier, 'mettait autour d'elle comme de la lumière et du bonheur.'[2] The Goncourts, who became regular visitors towards the end of her career as a fashionable hostess, were less kind. They repaid her hospitality by calling her 'une grosse nature, avec un entrain trivial, bas, populacier', 'une belle femme un peu canaille', and finally, 'une vivandière de faunes'. The Goncourts were notoriously spiteful, but it is possible that Judith Gautier's sketch errs on the side of generosity. Our ideas of beauty are no longer those of the mid-nineteenth century, which strike us today as somewhat coarse and vulgar. The Ricard portrait shows a large, fleshly woman whose face is not remarkable for its intelligence and has a hint of the barmaid about it; but

[1] The tone can be divined from the letters written to Mme Sabatier by her friends or rather from those which are considered printable. I have not seen Gautier's notorious *Lettres à la Présidente*, which were published clandestinely, but M. Billy gives a sample of his occasional verse in *La Présidente et ses amis* (p. 95), and some curious letters from Maxime Du Camp (pp. 188–9) and Flaubert (pp. 195, 198–9, 201).

[2] *Le Second rang du collier*, Paris, n.d., pp. 182–3.

Flaubert, who is said to have drawn on Mme Sabatier for the character of La Maréchale in *L'Éducation sentimentale*, may well have been describing the general impression made by her on his contemporaries when he remarked in a letter to Feydeau: 'C'est une excellente et surtout saine créature.'[1]

Baudelaire is believed to have had his first glimpse of the Présidente in 1842 when she was a fine-looking girl of twenty returning from the swimming-baths with some friends. He was introduced to her in 1845 and brought to her Sundays by Gautier in 1851. It was not merely her beauty, but her particular style of beauty which had a decisive effect on him. He deliberately ignored both her reputation and her fleshly appearance and concentrated on her colouring when he chose her as a foil to the 'Vénus noire', and tried to set her up as the emblem of Sacred Love.

The year after his introduction at the Rue Frochot, he began writing her anonymous love letters in a disguised handwriting and enclosed with them six of the nine poems which originally formed the Cycle of Mme Sabatier in the *Fleurs du mal*, and a seventh which was omitted from the first two editions.[2] The tone of the letters is curiously equivocal and has been described as *roué*:

'As for myself, it seems to me that *les âmes bien faites* cannot help feeling proud and happy at their beneficent action. I do not know whether I shall ever be granted the supreme joy of speaking to you myself about the hold that you have gained over me and of the perpetual radiance that your image creates in my mind. For the present, I am happy simply to swear over again to you that no love was ever more disinterested, more ideal than the love that I secretly cherish for you, and that I shall always hide it with the care which this tender respect commands.'[3]

'Lastly, in order to explain my silence and my ardours—ardours which are almost religious—I must tell you that when my whole being is plunged in the darkness of its natural wickedness and folly, I dream

---

[1] M. Billy rejects the idea that she was the original of La Maréchale.

[2] The poems are *A Celle qui est trop gaie* (9 December 1852); *Réversibilité* (3 May 1853); *Confession* (9 May 1853); *Le Flambeau vivant* (7 February 1854); *L'Aube spirituelle* (? February 1854); *Que diras-tu ce soir* (16 February 1854); *Hymne* (8 May 1854; not included in the *Fleurs du mal*).

[3] *Corr. gén.*, 1, p. 263 (letter of 16 February 1854).

E

deeply of you. This exciting and purifying meditation generally produces a happy accident.—For me, you are not merely the most attractive of women;—of all women, but more still, the dearest and most precious of superstitions. . . . How happy I should be if I could be certain that this lofty conception of love stands some chance of being received in a secret corner of your adorable thoughts.'[1]

'You are more than an image that I cherish and dream about, you are my *superstition*. When I am guilty of some great piece of stupidity, I say to myself: *Good heavens! if she knew*. When I do something good, I say to myself: *That's something which brings me closer to her,—in spirit*.'[2]

The correspondence was spread over five years. When we remember Mme Sabatier's appearance, her reputation and the tone of the Sunday dinners, it is difficult to convince ourselves that Baudelaire can have been entirely serious when he said that 'no love was ever more disinterested, more ideal' or used those equivocal phrases, 'my ardours—ardours which are almost religious', and 'you are my *superstition*'. It is still more difficult to believe that Mme Sabatier was unaware of the identity of her anonymous correspondent or could have imagined that anyone but Baudelaire was capable of writing the poems which accompanied the letters. In any case, if his identity were ever a secret it cannot have remained a secret for very long. It is unthinkable that a person in Mme Sabatier's position failed to read three of the poems sent to her when they were included in the selection published over Baudelaire's signature in the *Revue des Deux Mondes* on 1 June 1855. We know, too, from the letter of 18 August 1857, that he had met Mme Sabatier's younger sister, that 'the little monster' had burst out laughing and asked him whether he was still in love with her sister and still writing her 'superb love letters'.[3] It was not, however, until this letter that he wrote to

---

[1] *Corr. gén.*, 1, p. 276 (letter of 8 May 1854).

[2] *Corr. gén.*, 2, p. 88 (letter of 18 August 1857). Italics in the text.

[3] Bébé shared her elder sister's weakness for artists. She had a natural son by Fernand Boissard, a painter whom Mosselman had used as a screen for his liaison with Apollonie. She later married Ernest Christophe, the wealthy sculptor to whom Baudelaire dedicated two of his poems, *Le Masque* and *Danse macabre*.

her in his own name and handwriting to ask her to use her influence in the case which was being brought against the *Fleurs du mal* in two days' time. This led to the curious event which produced the still more curious letter of 31 August.

'A few days ago', he wrote, 'you were a divinity which is so convenient, so beautiful, so inviolable. Now you're a woman. . . . Well, come what may. I am a bit of a fatalist, but there's one thing I am sure about. I have a horror of passion because I know it with all its ignominy;—and now the beloved image which dominated every adventure has become too seductive.'[1]

Baudelaire speaks in this letter as though a meeting had taken place between them the day before and mentions two distraught letters from her to which he was replying. This may be correct, but it must be emphasized that all we know with certainty is that there was a meeting about this time and that something went wrong. We do not know, we shall never know, precisely what happened or where the meeting took place. 'She had made up her mind to go to bed with Baudelaire', said Porché bluntly, and the letters they exchanged do suggest that she took the initiative.[2] A reference in the same letter to 'cette sale rue J.-J. Rousseau' has led most of the poet's biographers to assume that the meeting occurred at an *hôtel meublé*, that the Lady offered herself and the Poet took fright. This theory presents one obvious difficulty. When a man and woman meet in an hotel room, they usually do so for one purpose and one purpose only. If therefore Mme Sabatier and Baudelaire did meet at an hotel, it becomes extremely difficult to explain the poet's fright. Crépet has tried to resolve the difficulty by suggesting that the Rue J.-J. Rousseau was the address of the 'poste restante of the Central Post Office, the only one in existence at that time'.[3] I am not sure that Baudelaire's actual words will bear this interpretation, but it is a plausible suggestion. They may have used the post office either for the

---

[1] *Corr. gén.*, 2, pp. 93–4.   [2] *Op. cit.*, p. 290.

[3] *Corr. gén.*, 2, p. 94 n. Baudelaire's words were: 'Il me paraît impossible de vous faire aller ainsi dans cette sale rue J.-J. Rousseau. Car j'ai bien d'autres choses à vous dire. Il faut donc que vous m'écriviez pour m'indiquer un moyen.'

purpose of concealment or because Baudelaire was always changing his lodgings. It disposes of the hotel bedroom, but it implies that the meeting took place at Mme Sabatier's flat and throws us back on the theory of the brazen Lady and the frightened Poet. Mme Sabatier was undoubtedly a delightful woman and not the sort of person to trifle with anyone's affections, but she seems to have been one of those women who give themselves naturally, freely, and without any sense of disloyalty to the wealthy Jew who paid the bills. It is unlikely that she was capable of understanding what Baudelaire called 'ces hautes conceptions de l'amour' or of taking them altogether seriously. The view that Baudelaire administered a rebuff—it must have been a rebuff because she was too experienced to be put off by a mere Stendhalian 'fiasco'—and rubbed it in by the unhappy reference to passion 'with all its ignominy' and to the fear of 'hurting an *honnête homme*' (meaning Mosselman), would certainly account for the shattering effect that the meeting had on her. I still find it difficult to believe, however, that Baudelaire was really taken by surprise when Mme Sabatier offered herself or that he really wanted her to remain the chaste Idol. It seems to me to have been a case of sexual maladjustment. I think that Baudelaire wanted something more than what he called, in the first of the poems sent to her, 'les trésors de ta personne' which was all she had to offer, that he wanted a deeper passion than 'une biche du quartier Bréda' was capable of giving. It is also possible that he was genuinely anxious to break the tyrannical hold that Jeanne Duval exercised over his senses, but that when the moment came it could not be done. That seems to have been Mme Sabatier's view. 'What am I to think when I find you avoiding my embraces', she said in one of her letters, 'except that you are thinking of the other whose spirit and whose black face come between us?'[1] And her copy of the *Fleurs du mal* contained a photograph of Jeanne on which she had written: 'Son idéal!'

We come finally to the difference between what may be called the *poetic* and the *human* reasons for Baudelaire's conduct. It is the eternal drama of the Poet and the Lady that in the last resort

[1] Quoted, Billy, *op. cit.*, p. 134.

the Poet will always prefer the book to the Lady whatever the consequences for her. Jeanne Duval was poetically and sexually the most successful of his mistresses, but the time came when he wanted something more and something different. He therefore tried to impose on Mme Sabatier a poetic role. The role of Platonic mistress was not new, but it had been given fresh currency by the Romantics. Mme Sabatier was the untouchable Idol of the Romantic myth and was designed to play the same part in Baudelaire's life as Jenny Colon in Gérard de Nerval's or Élisa Schlésinger in Flaubert's. Unfortunately, Baudelaire never believed in her with the conviction of Nerval or Flaubert. That explains the anonymous letters. The anonymity may have been transparent, but it was sufficient to keep the Idol on her precarious pedestal until the book was published. When the woman, who had been unexpectedly chosen as the model for Sacred Love in the book, turned out in life to be another incarnation not merely of Profane Love, but of the wrong kind of Profane Love, she was severely punished.

We are told by some of Baudelaire's biographers that there is a danger of taking the letter of 31 August too seriously and that its tone—particularly in the closing paragraphs—is not tragic:

'Adieu, chère bien aimée; je vous en veux un peu d'être trop charmante. Songez donc que, quand j'emporte le parfum de vos bras et de vos cheveux, j'emporte aussi le désir d'y revenir. Et alors quelle insupportable obsession!'

The tone is, as usual, ambiguous. It is far from being that of the traditional *lettre de rupture*, but there is none the less a finality about both the unhappy incident and the letter. The exchange of letters shows that Mme Sabatier was anxious to try again, but that Baudelaire was not. He continued for a short time to write affectionate notes to her, to send her small presents, and to find bad excuses for not appearing at her Sundays. They remained in fact what is known as 'good friends', but except that the sudden change in their relationship produced *Semper eadem* the career of Mme Sabatier had ceased to matter for French poetry.

This does not mean that it was without interest. Mosselman was financially ruined in 1859 or 1860, and seems to have withdrawn his protection of Mme Sabatier in the spring of the latter year. Her friends were convinced that he offered her a settlement of 6,000 francs a year and that she refused because she had found a successor to him. There is no proof of the truth of this story and it seems unlikely, particularly as a good many of her belongings were sold by auction in 1861 and fetched 43,000 francs. She did not give up her interest in art or her position as a fashionable hostess. The number of distinguished works refused by the Salon of 1863 was so large that another exhibition, known as the Salon des Refusés, was organized and Mme Sabatier's rejected miniatures were shown beside Manet's *Déjeuner sur l'herbe* and Whistler's *Dame blanche*. Mme Sabatier had left the Rue Frochot and gone to live in a more modest flat in the Rue de la Faisanderie where the Sunday dinners continued until 1863–4. About this time she lost a considerable sum of money in the failure of the Société de Navigation Mexicaine and met Richard Wallace, who was either the natural son or the illegitimate half-brother of the fourth Marquess of Hertford. She became his mistress and the pair travelled widely in England and Italy. The liaison came to an end, at any rate officially, on the death of the Marquess in 1870.[1] The kinsman of the English *milord* behaved more handsomely than the Jewish banker and settled 25,000 francs a year on her.[2]

[1] He inherited all the fourth Marquess's unentailed property. This vast fortune included the great art collection which he had helped Lord Hertford to assemble and which is now the Wallace Collection. It is said that he wished to marry Mme Sabatier, but that the match was prevented by her liaison with a third party. On 15 February 1871 he married the daughter of a French army officer, Julie Amélie Charlotte Castelnau, who had borne him a son many years earlier. He remained in Paris throughout the siege of 1870 and is said to have spent 2½ million francs to relieve the suffering of British subjects who were resident there. In recognition of these services he was created a baronet on 24 December 1871. He was M.P. for Lisburn from 1873 to 1885. He was born on 26 July 1818 and died in Paris on 20 July 1890. Lady Wallace bequeathed the Hertford-Wallace collection to the nation in deference to an implied wish of her husband's. (Consult *The Dictionary of National Biography*; Bernard Falk, '*Old Q's' Daughter*, London, 1937, and *The Naughty Seymours*, London, 1940.)

[2] French writers put the figure at 50,000 francs, but this is considered an exaggeration by British authorities.

When she found herself a rich unattached woman, she tried to restart the weekly dinners; but the group had been dispersed, and though she kept in touch with individuals it proved impossible to bring them all together on the same day. Her later years were spent at Neuilly where she died on 31 December 1889.

La Belle aux Cheveux d'Or

Marie Daubrun was an actress. She made her Paris début at the age of nineteen, playing the name part in a one-act vaudeville called *Mademoiselle Lange* which was produced at the Théâtre de la Gaîté on 15 July 1846. She also appeared in a costume representing a pansy in another one-act vaudeville, *Les Fleurs animées*, which was included in the same programme. She enjoyed one of her greatest successes when she took the chief part in *La Belle aux cheveux d'or* which was produced at the Théâtre de la Porte-Saint-Martin on 18 August 1847, ran with a number of breaks until 22 February 1848, and was never revived. She was a woman of considerable beauty with a striking mass of golden hair, was well spoken of as an actress and frequently praised for the clarity and correctness of her diction.

Baudelaire's relations with her have provided scholars with an interesting problem of literary detection. We do not know precisely when they met, but Marie fancied herself as the friend of men of genius and besides being an actress used to sit for painters. It is possible that the first meeting took place about the time of her Paris début in Deroy's studio. There is considerable evidence to support this theory in the poems and the correspondence. The poem now known as *L'Irréparable* was originally published in the *Revue des Deux Mondes* under the title of *La Belle aux cheveux d'or*. The first part of the poem, with its emphasis on 'remorse' and the eclipse of 'hope', seems to refer to misunderstandings between the lovers, while the 'fée' and 'l'Être aux ailes de gaze' in the second part must be a recollection of a production which is described in French as a *féerie*.

There no longer seems to be any reason to doubt that Marie Daubrun was the recipient of the letter sent to the mysterious 'Madame Marie'. The letter was once thought to have been written in the middle of October 1852, only seven weeks before the first of the letters to Mme Sabatier. Crépet and Feuillerat, however, now think that it must be assigned to the year 1847.[1] It is addressed to a woman whom Baudelaire has met at the studio of a friend. He has made some sort of advances to her, but has been rebuffed because she already loves another. Her resentment is so strong that she has decided to give up the sittings in order to avoid any further meetings with the poet. The letter contains this remarkable sentence:

'I love you, Marie. It's undeniable; but the love that I feel for you is that of the Christian for his God. Therefore never give a terrestrial name, and a name which is so often shameful, to this incorporeal and mysterious cult, this sweet and chaste attraction which unites my soul to yours. It would be a sacrilege.'

It goes on:

'Through you, Marie, I shall be strong and great. Like Petrarch, I will immortalize my Laura. Be my guardian Angel, my Muse and my Madonna, and lead me into the path of Beauty. [*Soyez mon Ange gardien, ma Muse et ma Madone, et conduisez-moi dans la route du Beau.*]'[2]

It will be observed that phrases from the last sentence were later incorporated in 'Que diras-tu ce soir' and *Le Flambeau vivant*, two of the poems sent to Mme Sabatier in 1854. Only one inference seems possible. The recipient of the letter was intended for the role subsequently played in spite of herself by Mme Sabatier. This lends colour to Feuillerat's view that *A Celle qui est trop gaie*, which was enclosed in Baudelaire's first letter to Mme Sabatier and included by him in her Cycle in the first edition of the *Fleurs du mal*, was in fact written *against* Marie Daubrun in revenge for the initial rebuff.[3] That a shy young poet who

[1] *Corr. gén.*, 1, p. 100 n. Feuillerat, *La Belle aux cheveux d'or*, London, 1941, p. 13.

[2] *Corr. gén.*, 1, pp. 101–2.

[3] *La Belle aux cheveux d'or*, pp. 27–9. He argues convincingly, with the help of a contemporary portrait, that the 'ballet de fleurs' is an allusion to the dress she wore in *Les Fleurs animées*.

writes an anonymous love letter to a woman should send such a poem as his first offering is so extraordinary that we are bound to seek a psychological explanation. Nor is it difficult to find one. Marie Daubrun had failed in the role of 'guardian Angel' that he had chosen for her. In his exasperation he wrote a poem describing the symbolical destruction of the woman who had played her part so badly. As soon as he found a *remplaçante*, his first action was to offer her the poem as a trophy or a 'scalp' which was the sign of her victory.

This view presents two difficulties. The first is that the recipient of the letter appears to have rejected advances of a very different kind. The second is that if the letter was in fact written in 1847, it was not until five years later that Baudelaire turned his attention to Mme Sabatier. We must therefore consider the view that the theory of the 'guardian Angel' and the reference to Petrarch, which was calculated to appeal to a woman who liked to think of herself as the friend and comforter of men of genius, were a ruse, and that after the initial rebuff Baudelaire simply tried a fresh form of attack in the hope of persuading Marie to become his mistress. This is a possible explanation of his conduct towards her at the time, but it must be remembered that the theory of the untouchable Idol was deeply rooted in the age and that in spite of his innate scepticism, Baudelaire badly wanted to believe in it. I suggest, therefore, that in the case of Marie Daubrun the theory of the 'guardian Angel' was not merely a ruse, but a ruse which eventually achieved a certain measure of success. My next suggestion is that the ruse gave him the idea of the letters to Mme Sabatier, and that in December 1852 he re-created the mood of 1847 and convinced himself that Marie Daubrun had really failed in the role he had chosen for her.

This view is strengthened when we turn to the poetry written to the three women. Jeanne Duval's Cycle is usually regarded as the Cycle of Profane Love, but in it the poet is continually reaching out towards the Ideal, continually oscillating between the heights and the depths. There is far less conflict in the other two Cycles. Mme Sabatier's is dominated by the idea of Sacred Love and Marie Daubrun's by the idea of Profane Love. This leads me to the conclusion that Jeanne was originally intended to play a double role and failed in one side of it, and that after her partial failure Baudelaire decided, no doubt subconsciously, to divide the role between two women. This accounts for the fact that during a good deal of the period covered by the correspondence with Mme Sabatier, Baudelaire was living either with Jeanne or Marie, who were both emblems of Profane Love and were rivals of one another but not of Mme Sabatier. It also accounts for the irregularity of the letters to Mme Sabatier which depended on whether at a given moment Baudelaire felt in need of Sacred or Profane Love.

What I have been saying is borne out by the correspondence. The letter about the 'guardian Angel' is the only letter that we have from Baudelaire to Marie Daubrun, and there is no other reference to her in the correspondence until 1854. It will be recalled that Baudelaire and Jeanne parted in April 1852—nearly eight months before the first of the letters to Mme Sabatier—and that the separation lasted until January 1855. Two more letters were written to Mme Sabatier in May 1853 and a further four in February and May 1854. Then, in a letter to his mother written on 14 August of the same year, he suddenly remarks: 'Today is Marie's *fête*.—The person of whom I spoke to you spends her nights looking after her dying parents after playing her stupid five acts. I am not rich enough to give presents; but a few flowers sent this evening would be sufficient proof of sympathy.—I don't want your forty francs. . . .'[1] It is evident from this letter and from another written on 21 July, in which he said that he sometimes went to the Gaîté (where Marie was then playing), that Baudelaire had been seeing her and that he had told his mother about her.[2] We do not know what their relations were, but they appear to have been intimate. The next direct reference occurs in the letter to his mother of 4 December 1854, in which he announces that by 9 January he will have set up house again with Jeanne or 'the

[1] *Corr. gén.*, 1, p. 294. (Baudelaire seems to have been confused about his dates. Marie's *fête* must have been on 15 August which is the Feast of the Assumption.)

[2] *Corr. gén.*, 1, p. 286.

other'. The other—Baudelaire underlines the word—was undoubtedly Marie. She had been a friend of Banville's in 1852–3 but it is thought that he made way for Baudelaire in 1854. We know that in this year Baudelaire intervened with people who were prominent in the theatrical world in an unsuccessful attempt to help her to return to the Théâtre de la Porte-Saint-Martin. In the autumn she was playing the part of the Duchesse de Guérande in *Les Oiseaux de proie* at the Gaîté. There was some sort of quarrel with the management and at the end of the year she broke her contract. This meant that for the time being she could not hope for further employment in Paris. At the beginning of the following year she set out for Italy as a member of a touring company, which explains why it was Jeanne and not 'the *other*' with whom Baudelaire eventually set up house.

The touring company went bankrupt and in August 1855 Marie was at Nice. She appealed to Baudelaire to intervene once more with the Paris managements. He tried hard to obtain a part for her in George Sand's *Maître Favilla* which was just going into production, but he was again unsuccessful. She returned to Paris and went to live not with Baudelaire, but with Banville whose health had broken down and who needed someone to take care of him. She lived with him until, in the spring of 1857, he had to go into hospital which put an end to the *ménage*. We lose sight of her until 1859 when Baudelaire made his third unsuccessful attempt to obtain employment for her in Paris. At the end of the year she accepted an engagement in a company which was going to Nice, where she lived openly with Banville. Baudelaire had accepted the earlier liaison with equanimity and in 1856 had tried to persuade Daumier to do a frontispiece for Banville's *Odes funambulesques*, but he took the final blow hardly.[1] Marie was undoubtedly capricious and it is difficult to believe that she was ever very serious about Baudelaire, but she had filled a gap at the time of his difficulties with Jeanne and Mme Sabatier. She went to Nice when Jeanne had lost her beauty and was in hospital being treated for dipsomania, and when the final parting

---

[1] I recall that the reconciliation with Jeanne, which took place in 1855, lasted until the beginning of September 1856.

from her was imminent. This means that Marie's *trahison* marked the ultimate collapse of 'family life' for Baudelaire which contributed so largely to the gloom and loneliness of his later years.

She lived with Banville in the south until 1860 when they parted, possibly by mutual consent and certainly without a *rupture*. He was the last of the men of genius whom she 'consoled' or who 'protected' her. She returned to Paris in 1860, did three seasons in Brussels from 1861 to 1863, was at Algiers in 1867, Reims in 1868, and toured with the company from the Châtelet from 1869 to 1874. She was back at the Théâtre de la Porte-Saint-Martin from 1875 to 1883, but though her diction is said to have been unimpaired we do not know what sort of parts she was playing. Her contract was not renewed in 1883 and for the next four years she was on tour at Liége and Cannes possibly, as Porché suggests, owing to the indulgence of some leading lady in the company. She retired from the stage in 1889 and died in poor circumstances in February 1901 at the age of seventy-three.

3. The Poet and his Poetry

The critic of Baudelaire is faced at the outset by one very difficult problem. It is the dearth of manuscripts. The critical edition of the *Fleurs du mal* contains a hundred and fifty-eight poems, but there are only manuscripts or copies of manuscripts of thirty-four of them. Several of the manuscripts are undated and difficult to date and they are, with a few exceptions, examples of his less important work. This means that the date of composition of most of the poems is a matter of inference. There are four ways of approaching the problem: the oral evidence of contemporaries and occasional references in the correspondence; the date of publication of those poems which first appeared in reviews; allusions in the poems to events in the poet's life, and the internal evidence of the poems themselves. With the exception of the few direct references in the correspondence, none of these approaches is conclusive and they must be treated with reserve.

Baudelaire's contemporaries maintained that many of the *Fleurs du mal* were written by 1845, and Prarond has given a list of sixteen poems which are said to have been written not later than 1843. They are *L'Albatros, Allégorie, L'Ame du vin, A une Malabaraise, Une Charogne, Le Crépuscule du matin, Don Juan aux enfers, La Géante*, 'Je n'ai pas oublié, voisine de la ville', 'Je t'adore à l'égal de la voûte nocturne', *Le Rebelle*, 'Une Nuit que j'étais près d'une affreuse Juive', 'La Servante au grand cœur', *Le Vin de l'assassin, Le Vin des chiffonniers*, and *Les Yeux de Berthe*. Other witnesses like Cousin, Banville, and Dozon assign *A une Mendiante rousse* to the year 1842, *Le Mauvais moine* to the year 1843, and *L'Ame du vin* to the year 1844. The internal evidence suggests that most of the poems in Prarond's list are in fact early work, but his statement depends on memories which were more than fifty years old when he made it and his dates can only be regarded as approximate.

The most important surviving manuscript is the one published by Van Bever under the title of *Douze poëmes*. The twelve poems are: *A une Mendiante rousse, Bohémiens en voyage, La Fontaine de sang, Le Guignon, Les Métamorphoses du vampire, La Mort des pauvres, La Rançon, Le Vin des chiffonniers, Un Voyage à Cythère*, the two *Crépuscules*, and *Le Reniement de Saint Pierre*. The manuscript is not dated, but it is known that Baudelaire lived at the address given on it—25 Rue des Marais du Temple —from 15 June 1851 to 7 April 1852. This does not mean that the twelve poems were all written in 1851–2. The internal evidence suggests again that some of them were written much earlier, and it will be observed that the list contains three poems which oral evidence assigns to the years 1842–4. All it proves is that the twelve poems were written by 1852.[1]

The Correspondence enables us to date *A une Dame créole* and some of the poems to Mme Sabatier, though there are doubts about *A Celle qui est trop gaie*, and *Hymne* is described as having been written 'a long time, a very long time ago'.[2]

It will be remembered that a collection of poems was announced under the title of *Les Lesbiennes* at the beginning of 1846. We can therefore assume that a substantial number of poems were

[1] The last three poems on the list were all published in 1852.
[2] *Corr. gén.*, I, p. 275.

written by that date, and the choice of title makes it probable that they included not only the three Lesbian poems, but others which originally belonged to the chapter of the *Fleurs du mal* to which Baudelaire gave the same title as the volume.

This is as far as oral evidence and documents will take us in the case of poems which were contained in the first edition of the *Fleurs du mal*, or which Baudelaire decided for some reason to exclude from it. The problem is complicated by the fact that he polished or rewrote many of his early poems though he did not invariably do so. *Le Vin des chiffonniers* underwent considerable revision, but only a few unimportant changes were made in *A une Dame créole* which is the earliest poem known to have been included in the *Fleurs du mal*. It takes the traditional form of a sonnet offered by the Poet to the Lady, but in spite of its traditional form it bears everywhere the unmistakable sign of Baudelaire's *griffe*:

> Au pays parfumé que le soleil caresse,
> J'ai vu dans un retrait de tamarins ambrés
> Et de palmiers d'où pleut la paresse,
> Une dame créole aux charmes ignorés.
>
> Son teint est pâle et chaud; la brune enchanteresse
> A dans le cou des airs noblement maniérés;
> Grande et svelte en marchant comme une chasseresse,
> Son sourire est tranquille et ses yeux assurés.
>
> Si vous alliez, Madame, au vrai pays de Gloire,
> Sur les bords de la Seine ou de la verte Loire,
> Belle, digne d'orner les antiques manoirs,
>
> Vous feriez, à l'abri des mousseuses retraites,
> Germer mille sonnets dans le cœur des poëtes,
> Que vos regards rendraient plus soumis que des noirs.[1]

It will be seen that phrases like 'pays parfumé', 'd'où *pleut* . . . *la paresse*', 'charmes ignorés', 'brune *enchanteresse*', and 'vrai pays de Gloire' already look forward to Baudelaire's mature style and support the view that he matured early.

[1] This is the primitive version of the sonnet given in *Corr. gén.*, 1, p. 16.

Except in cases where it is corroborated by other evidence, the date of first publication is of little assistance for the early poems because many years often elapsed between composition and publication. *A une Dame créole* was written in the autumn of 1841 and published in 1845; *Don Juan aux enfers*, *L'Albatros* and *Les yeux de Berthe*, which all appear in Prarond's list, were published in 1846, 1859 and 1864 respectively; and to add to the difficulty slightly over half the poems in the first edition of the *Fleurs du mal* were unpublished.[1] It is more useful in the case of late poems published between the first and second editions because pieces like *Un Fantôme*, *Semper eadem*, and *A une Madone* clearly refer to changes in Baudelaire's relations with his mistresses. There are also references in the Correspondence to *Le Cygne*, *Les Sept vieillards*, and *Le Voyage*.[2] *La Chevelure* is of particular interest. Nothing is heard of it until it appeared in *La Revue Française* on 20 May 1859. In feeling it seems to belong to the period of the poet's 'passionate love' for Jeanne Duval, but it is unthinkable that Baudelaire would have omitted one of his supreme masterpieces if it had been written in time for the first edition.

We are on slightly firmer ground in relying on biographical data contained in some of the poems, but it must be emphasized that with the exception of some of the late poems that I have mentioned, it remains almost impossible to date individual poems as distinct from groups of poems with any certainty. It is a fair inference that a number of the poems addressed to Jeanne Duval were written by 1845, but the suggestion that *Le Balcon* was written to mark the reconciliation of 1855 is no more than an intelligent guess; and it is difficult even to guess the date of *Duellum* which was first published in 1858—the year in which the poet once again set up house with Jeanne.[3] All that we can say of

---

[1] The unpublished poems include seven from Prarond's list and six from *Douze poëmes*.

[2] A MS. version of *Les Sept vieillards* is contained in the letter written to Jean Morel in June 1859 (*Corr. gén.*, 2, pp. 321–4).

[3] Crépet, however, suggests that it was written at the time of the rupture in 1856.

the poems to Marie Daubrun is that one of them may have been written in 1846 or 1847, that several must have been written between 1847 and 1855, and that *A une Madone* was almost certainly written in 1859 or 1860.

The study of the internal evidence gives rise to interesting speculations. 'J'aime le souvenir' and *Les Phares* are both among the unpublished poems included in the first edition. The marked influence of Chénier and the mechanical transitions suggest that the first of these poems is very early while the second appears from its maturity of expression to be a late composition, but this is no more than an inference. Similar criticisms can be and have been made of the transitions in *Le Masque*, though it undoubtedly refers to a statue which Baudelaire first saw when he was writing his *Salon de 1859*.[1] In spite of this, we are reasonably safe in assigning most of the poems written in couplets like *Paysage*, *Le Soleil*, and the two *Crépuscules* to the early period on the ground that they are much less complex in feeling than poems known to be late work, and this view is not invalidated by the decidedly impressive qualities of *Le Crépuscule du matin*. We can also assume from the Romantic elements in them that *La Vie antérieure* and *L'Homme et la mer* are both early poems, but the three poems in 'Révolte' give rise to a different problem. Most critics are inclined to regard them as early work because the attitude expressed appears characteristic of a young man and of a young man writing in the early forties of the last century. This view is strengthened by the style and is probably correct, but it is only right to point out that the attitude does not differ fundamentally from that of the two prose poems, *La Tentation* and *Le Joueur généreux*, which are known to be very late work.

The only conclusions that can be drawn are necessarily tentative. Very few of the individual poems can be dated with any certainty and it is impossible to provide a detailed account of

---

[1] *Curiosités esthétiques*, pp. 359–60. The figure seen by Baudelaire was apparently never exhibited, but the artist exhibited a much larger and more ambitious work on the same subject in 1876. It was acquired by the State and today stands in the Tuileries (*Les Fleurs du mal*, éd. crit., pp. 330–2). The poem is discussed on pp. 244–7 below.

Baudelaire's poetic development. Oral evidence, style, and content suggest strongly that a number of poems were written in his early twenties and are possibly anterior to his meeting with Jeanne Duval. A comparison between the differing merits of *A une Dame créole* and *Le Crépuscule du matin*—one was naturally written to a woman and the other was not—is instructive. It suggests that Baudelaire had reached the point where a woman had become necessary for the development of his art. The first of the poems is evidence of a precocious talent and the second shows that he was already technically, but not emotionally, mature. I believe that as soon as he met Jeanne there was a sudden rapid maturing of his genius and that she was in fact the catalytic agent for which he had been waiting. The rest is pure speculation. We may believe firmly that he had reached full maturity by 1845, but it cannot be proved. *Un Voyage à Cythère* is the only one of his supreme achievements which is known with absolute certainty to have reached what was virtually its final form by 1852.

III

THE CIRCULAR TOUR

In *Le Voyage* Baudelaire describes a little band of travellers setting out on a voyage round the world. They leave in a mood of great elation, but it changes almost at once to a mood of profound disillusionment. The poem opens with one of Baudelaire's finest and most characteristic images:

> Pour l'enfant, amoureux de cartes et d'estampes,
> L'univers est égal à son vaste appétit.
> Ah! que le monde est grand à la clarté des lampes!
> Aux yeux du souvenir que le monde est petit!

In nearly all Baudelaire's greatest work the theme is contained in embryo in the opening image and the poem seems to unfold like a tapestry in a series of images which follow one another logically. The underlying theme of *Le Voyage* is the tragic disproportion between aspiration and reality. The poet begins by evoking the 'cosy' world of childhood—the world of lamplight, maps, and prints—in which there is no gap between the two, and in which the human being feels for the first and last time secure and satisfied. In the second line we have the sensation of the world swelling to fulfil the child's desires, but this world is artificial like the prints and the lamplight which illuminates it. For Baudelaire the word 'souvenir' nearly always has poignant associations, and in the next line we are aware of the opposite sensation of sudden contraction:

> Aux yeux du souvenir que le monde est petit!

The movement of expansion and contraction is the basic movement of the poem. It is used to express the changing feelings of the travellers, and through them the poet's own attitude to civilization. The travellers are constantly buoyed up by fresh hopes which are invariably the source of fresh disillusionment:

Un matin nous partons, le cerveau plein de flamme,
Le cœur gros de rancune et de désirs amers,
Et nous allons, suivant le rhythme de la lame,
Berçant notre infini sur le fini des mers . . .

'Infini' is another word with special associations. In Baudelaire the emphasis always falls on the inadequacy of 'reality' and never on the excessive nature of the demands made on it. The world is no longer 'equal' to these demands and this produces a sense of frustration.[1]

The motives of the travellers are various, and the poet begins by dividing them into three classes. The first are anxious to flee 'une patrie infâme', the second 'l'horreur de leurs berceaux', the third the hold of a woman—it is perhaps a memory of Jeanne Duval—which has become tyrannical. The 'patrie infâme' appears to stand for contemporary civilization, the France of 'progress', 'steam', 'gas', and 'table turning' which Baudelaire loathed. The distinction between it and 'berceaux' is not altogether clear, but 'berceaux' may be a personal reference to the poet's own unhappy childhood. It may also stand for the monotony and boredom of the travellers' birthplace without the political nuance which belongs to 'patrie infâme'. The reference to women introduces the theme of prostitution and the debasing effect of love:

Astrologues noyés dans les yeux d'une femme,
La Circé tyrannique aux dangereux parfums.

The lines are a good example of the current of ironical disillusionment which permeates the poem and of its remarkable sophistication.

---

[1] The word is used in a slightly different sense in the two *Femmes damnées*:
Faites votre destin, âmes désordonnées,
Et fuyez *l'infini* que vous portez en vous!

De la réalité grands esprits contempteurs,
Chercheuses *d'infini*, dévotes et satyres . . .
In the first couplet it stands for the perverse desires which 'reality' cannot satisfy; in the second for the pursuit of pleasures which blind them to 'reality'. In both cases, however, the result is frustration and dislocation.

All three groups have one thing in common. They were bored at home and their hearts filled with 'rancune' and 'désirs amers'. It is possible to rid oneself of the external symptoms of these desires—what Baudelaire calls 'la marque des baisers'—but not of the real cause; and this is expressed in two lines which display the same virtuosity and sophistication as the 'Astrologues noyés':

> La glace qui les mord, les soleils qui les cuivrent,
> Effacent lentement la marque des baisers.

The fifth verse introduces a fresh class of traveller:

> Mais les vrais voyageurs sont ceux-là seuls qui partent
> Pour partir; cœurs légers, semblables aux ballons,
> De leur fatalité jamais ils ne s'écartent,
> Et, sans savoir pourquoi, disent toujours: Allons!

The first two lines are a triumph of versification. One critic points out that the long first line, the *enjambement* and the repeated *partent-partir* concentrate the attention on the vessel pushing off into space; and indeed we almost hear the rattle of the chains as the anchor is being raised. The 'cœurs légers, semblables aux ballons' seem to float away into the unknown, only to be brought sharply back to the real problem—the inescapable internal problem—in the next line:

> De leur fatalité jamais ils ne s'écartent.

For in the last resort it is not the horrors of contemporary civilization, but an inner spiritual malady which drives them on.

The idea of 'infinity' as an escape from an intolerably oppressive 'reality' is reintroduced, and the image of the 'balloons' reinforced in the sixth verse where we return to the insatiable demands made by man on his world:

> Ceux-là dont les désirs ont la forme des nues,
> Et qui rêvent, ainsi qu'un conscrit le canon,
> De vastes voluptés, changeantes, inconnues,
> Et dont l'esprit humain n'a jamais su le nom!

In this verse the words 'jamais' and 'toujours' alternate, echoing and answering one another mockingly. The travellers can 'never' escape from their problem; they must 'always' wrestle with it, but they cannot be satisfied because they have never been able to give a name to their 'desires'. The image of the conscript and the cannon is interesting because it suggests that at bottom they are seeking not satisfaction but self-destruction.

The voyage becomes a crazy pursuit of an unknown and unattainable goal. The 'balloons' of the first section are replaced by the 'tops' and 'bowls' of the second; the travellers are reduced to mechanical toys driven onwards by a power over which they have no control:

> Nous imitons, horreur! la toupie et la boule
> Dans leur valse et leurs bonds; même dans nos sommeils
> La Curiosité nous tourmente et nous roule,
> Comme un Ange cruel qui fouette des soleils.
>
> Singulière fortune où le but se déplace,
> Et, n'étant nulle part, peut être n'importe où!
> Où l'Homme, dont jamais l'espérance n'est lasse,
> Pour trouver le repos court toujours comme un fou!

Every time they think that they are in sight of 'Eldorado'— the promised land where even the most exorbitant desires will find satisfaction—it turns out to be no more than a reef:

> Chaque îlot signalé par l'homme de vigie
> Est un Eldorado promis par le Destin;
> L'Imagination qui dresse son orgie
> Ne trouve qu'un récif aux clartés du matin.

The 'clartés du matin', which reveal the mistake, recall ironically the 'clarté des lampes' and the artificial world of childhood illusion which 'Imagination'—'the most scientific of faculties'—tries in vain to recapture.

In the first two sections the poet uses the narrative form and describes the voyage in the historic present. In the three following sections he makes very effective use of the dramatic form to expose the illusions of the travellers. It is clear that they are back home and an anonymous speaker addresses them mockingly as

> Étonnants voyageurs! quelles nobles histoires
> Nous lisons dans vos yeux profonds comme les mers!

The voice is evidently the voice of a stay-at-home, one of those for whom the 'berceau' has become a 'prison'; but it may also be the voice of the poet, who was an inveterate stay-at-home, interrogating us, the readers. It goes on:

> Nous voulons voyager sans vapeur et sans voile!
> Faites, pour égayer l'ennui de nos prisons,
> Passer sur nos esprits, tendus comme une toile,
> Vos souvenirs avec leurs cadres d'horizons.
>
> Dites, qu'avez-vous vu?

The answer marks the opening of a new section, presumably to indicate the pause while the travellers reflect on their reply and to give the fullest weight to their damaging report:

> 'Nous avons vu des astres
> Et des flots; nous avons vu des sables aussi;
> Et, malgré bien des chocs et d'imprévus désastres,
> Nous nous sommes souvent ennuyés, comme ici.'

In these lines with the 'stars', 'waves', and 'sands'—symbols of the obvious, the monotonous—we have the impression that the travellers are scanning the horizon, moving their heads backwards and forwards, and seeing nothing. The impression is strengthened a few lines later when we read:

> Grandiras-tu toujours, grand arbre plus vivace
> Que le cyprès?

where we find ourselves gazing again into empty space. We are prepared for disappointment by the weariness of the speaker's tone and by the way in which lines peter out with an adverb or a subordinate clause:

> nous avons vu des sables aussi . . .
> Nous nous sommes souvent ennuyés, comme ici.

They have seen nothing but monotonous wastes of sea and sky and the meaningless freaks which can be seen by any ordinary tourist:

> 'Nous avons salué des idoles à trompe . . .
>
> 'Des femmes dont les dents et les ongles sont teints,
> Et des jongleurs savants que le serpent caresse.'

The voice of the questioner becomes more insistent:

> Et puis, et puis encore?

The traveller answers derisively:

'O cerveaux enfantins!

> Pour ne pas oublier la chose capitale,
> Nous avons vu partout, et sans l'avoir cherché,
> Du haut jusques en bas de l'échelle fatale,
> Le spectacle ennuyeux de l'immortel péché . . .'

This introduces a moral note, and the tone becomes savagely contemptuous. The travellers have seen a repetition of the same horrors that digusted them at home:

> 'La femme, esclave vile, orgueilleuse et stupide,
> Sans rire s'adorant et s'aimant sans dégoût;
> L'homme, tyran goulu, paillard, dur et cupide,
> Esclave de l'esclave . . .

> 'Le poison du pouvoir énervant le despote . . .

> 'Plusieurs religions semblables à la nôtre,
> Toutes escaladant le ciel . . .'

The section ends with the disillusioned:

> '—Tel est du globe entier l'éternel bulletin.'

It will be seen that these references to the vanity and cruelty of women, the corruption of men, the tyranny of politics, and to religion are really a summing-up of the principal themes of the *Fleurs du mal*, and are intended to be the poet's final comment on contemporary civilization.[1] In the last two sections, indeed, he abandons the dramatic form and strikes a note of embittered reflection:

> Amer savoir, celui qu'on tire du voyage!

The 'amer savoir' echoes the 'désirs amers' which filled the travellers' hearts at the start of the journey. He has already commented on the absurdity of the hopeful man who

> Pour trouver le repos court toujours comme un fou!

[1] Compare the description of women with the portrait of the poet's wife in *Bénédiction*:

> Je ferai le métier des idoles antiques,
> Et comme elles je veux me faire redorer;

> Et je me soûlerai de nard, d'encens, de myrrhe,
> De génuflexions, de viandes et de vins.

But now a new note of desperation, almost of hysteria, creeps in and is reflected by the breathless:

> Faut-il partir? rester? Si tu peux rester, reste;
> Pars, s'il le faut.

They finish exactly where they started with nothing left to do but to start out on another journey. This time it is the final journey. For *Le Voyage* is an allegory of man's life from the cradle to the grave. It leaves the travellers disillusioned, battered, and exhausted, waiting for Death in the hope that this last voyage may bring them '*du nouveau*':

> O Mort, vieux capitaine, il est temps! levons l'ancre!
> Ce pays nous ennuie, ô Mort! Appareillons!

Le Voyage is rightly regarded as one of Baudelaire's supreme achievements. It is remarkable for its extraordinary range and variety of tone, for its sardonic, astringent humour, and for its extreme poise and sophistication. The main theme is also the main theme of the *Fleurs du mal*. Baudelaire's poetry is filled with voyages and plans for voyages. There are voyages round the world, voyages to fabulous islands, voyages round Paris, and even the 'voyage' of a bored monk pacing ceaselessly round and round his narrow cell. Although a passionate interest in travel is characteristic of modern poetry, it is not altogether new. It had already made its appearance in medieval poetry, but there is a world of difference between the journeys described in *The Divine Comedy* or *The Canterbury Tales* and those described in *Le Voyage* or *Le Bateau ivre*. The medieval traveller was a pilgrim moving steadily towards a known goal and overcoming all obstacles in a spirit of Christian fortitude. In spite of the use of the word in *Bénédiction*, Baudelaire was no 'pilgrim'.[1] He was in a special sense a tourist whose goal remained tantalizingly unknown:

> Singulière fortune où le but se déplace . . .

The voyages that he plans are many and varied, but the traveller is always the same. When we turn the pages of the *Fleurs du mal* we are constantly coming face to face with a solitary figure

[1] Et l'Esprit qui le suit *dans son pèlerinage*
Pleure de le voir gai comme un oiseau des bois.

wearing a frock-coat and black cashmere trousers, with a high
waistcoat unbuttoned at the top to display a shirt of the finest
linen partly hidden by the flowing black silk tie, and a curious
conical-shaped hat of his own design. The deep furrows round
the mouth, the expression of suffering on the face, and the thin-
ning grey hair escaping under the hat give him the appearance of
an old man; and when you look at him closely you notice that his
clothes, too, are showing signs of wear that careful treatment is
doing its best to conceal.

He moves slowly along the banks of the Seine, pausing, perhaps, to flick over the pages of a book on one of the *bouquinistes'*
stalls—he is an authority on the erotic writings of the seventeenth
and eighteenth centuries—then he continues his walk into the
poorer parts of the city, a strange and incongruous figure in his
splendid apparel. His eyes are fixed moodily on the ground as he
broods over his debts, the trouble that he has had with his landlady, and the begging letter that he will have to write to his
mother. From time to time he glances up at the concierges
shuffling along in their carpet slippers on their way to market.
His feelings are mixed. The tall buildings remind him of the
masts of ships and the possibility of flight from these sordid surroundings to some exotic island; but he remembers that early
voyage to the East, puts the thought out of his mind, and returns
to the fascinated contemplation of the problem of civilized man
amid the squalid horrors of modern industrialism.

For the setting as well as the purpose of the journey has
changed. Dante's careful logical universe, with its heaven above
and its hell below, and Chaucer's wide tranquil English country-
side have been replaced by the shapeless indifference of the great
modern city. There are striking similarities between the 'Eldorado
banal' with its symbolic figure dangling on the end of a gibbet
and 'the Waste Land', where the ruined impotent monarch
reigns, between Baudelaire's Paris and Eliot's London.[1] Baudelaire's Paris is not a local affair, a mere emanation of his personal
sensibility as to some extent Laforgue's is. Its significance is uni-

[1] Je suis comme le roi d'un pays pluvieux,
   Riche, mais impuissant, jeune et pourtant très-vieux . . .

versal. It is the modern world and it is a sign of Baudelaire's great-ness that he manages to present it as a physical—a terrifyingly oppressive physical—reality.

His choice of theme gives his poetry its distinctive style. When we look into it, we find that it possesses a highly personal movement. This movement is reflected not merely in the general structure of the *Fleurs du mal,* but in the six 'chapters' into which the book is divided, in the different 'cycles' of certain of these chapters, and in some of the most characteristic of the individual poems like *La Chevelure, Le Beau navire, Un Voyage à Cythère,* and *Le Voyage.* It contributes largely to the internal coherence of his poetry, making us feel that the whole work is present in the separate poems. It is not a *forward,* but a *circular* movement. A monologue of Racine's moves steadily forward from one fixed point to another and carries the entire play a stage further. Baudelaire uses a different method. He takes a scene or a situation and examines it from every angle until the last drop of feeling has been extracted from it, but in the end he always returns to his starting-point. All sorts of mysterious feelings emerge, but the dominant mood remains unchanged. For this reason images suggesting circular movement recur constantly like shorthand references:

> Mais la tristesse en moi monte comme la mer . . .

> Onduleux, mon Désir qui monte et qui descend . . .

The sea is a symbol of liberation in his poetry, but it is also a symbol of ceaseless, exhausting movement which brings no rest and no relief. Desires revolve in circles, rising and falling, shift-ing and changing, until at last feelings destroy themselves by their own internal friction.

We conclude from this that the *Fleurs du mal* is a circular tour of the modern world which begins with *Bénédiction* and closes with *Le Voyage.* In the course of his circular tour Baudelaire examines all the great spiritual problems of the age. His age was a turning point in contemporary European history. It is because it is still our age and its problems our problems that his work has acquired what can only be called an extra-literary importance.

IV

THE ARCHITECTURE OF THE
FLEURS DU MAL

'THE ONLY praise that I ask for the book', said Baudelaire in a letter to Alfred de Vigny which accompanied a presentation copy of the second edition of the *Fleurs du mal*, 'is the recognition that it is not a mere collection of verse, but that it has a beginning and an end. All the new poems are designed to fit into the singular framework [*cadre singulier*] that I had chosen.'[1]

There is abundant evidence to show that Baudelaire prepared the second edition of his poems with particular care, but his insistence on the order in which they were printed was not new. He had shown the same concern when the selection of eighteen poems was published in the *Revue des Deux Mondes* in June 1855 and when he was preparing the first edition.[2] The choice of individual poems was rigorously subordinated to the design of the book and the poet did not hesitate to make sacrifices in the interests of his design. The logical necessity of the chapter called 'Révolte' is plain, but it consists of three of Baudelaire's least successful pieces. On the other hand, he did not scruple to omit fine poems which did not fit into the design or which reflected moods that had already been satisfactorily expressed.[3]

It follows that the order of the *Fleurs du mal* is highly artificial. The poems are nearly all autobiographical, but they are not printed in chronological order or in the order of composition. They are moods and experiences. The poet cannot control the

[1] *Corr. gén.*, 4, p. 9. (Letter of 12 or 13 December 1861.)

[2] *Corr. gén.*, 1, p. 330 (letter to Victor de Mars of 7 April 1855); *ibid.*, p. 408 (letter to Poulet-Malassis of 9 December 1856).

[3] It is difficult to speak with certainty on this point owing to the problem of dating the poems. We know that he omitted *Hymne*, a poem sent to Mme Sabatier in 1854, and *Le Jet d'eau*. It is possible that *Recueillement* was written before publication of the second edition, but it was not printed until it appeared in a periodical in November 1861.

order in which they occur, but he is entitled to arrange them in a particular order, to claim that *the book* corresponds to a certain fundamental pattern in his experience and that it expresses the meaning of his life as a poet. This pattern cannot be a substitute for the inner unity which belongs to the work of a great poet, but the correspondence between the inner and the outer unity may add considerably to the power of the work; and in view of the importance that Baudelaire attached to the matter I do not think that we have the right to dismiss it, as Porché does, by contrasting what he calls 'l'ordre factice et l'ordre vrai des *Fleurs du mal*'.[1]

This determines the approach of the critic. In order to appreciate Baudelaire's work to the full, it is clearly necessary to grasp what he meant by the *cadre singulier*. It has been exhaustively discussed by his critics who have been at pains to emphasize what is known as the 'architecture' of the *Fleurs du mal*. The first of them to show a real understanding of the poet's aim was Barbey d'Aurevilly in a review of the first edition. 'Elles sont moins des poésies', he said, 'qu'une œuvre poétique de la plus forte unité. Au point de vue de l'art et de la sensation esthétique, elles perdraient donc beaucoup à n'être pas lues dans l'ordre où le poète, qui sait bien ce qu'il fait, les a rangées.'[2] Barbey's immediate successors did not show the same perspicacity. The order was sadly mangled in the third or posthumous edition published by Asselineau and Poulet-Malassis in 1868. This edition was regarded for many years as definitive, and it was not until the appearance in 1896 of Prince Ourousof's essay that writers on Baudelaire began to pay proper attention to the architecture of the *Fleurs du mal*.[3] Prince Ourousof was followed by L. F.

---

[1] *Op. cit.*, pp. 292–8.

[2] It was intended for publication in *Le Pays* in 1857, but owing to the prosecution did not appear until 1860. Reprinted in *Poésie et poètes*. See p. 109. In view of Porché's comments we should do well to note Barbey's 'le poète, qui sait bien ce qu'il fait'.

[3] See *Le Tombeau de Baudelaire*, Paris, 1896. In this brief, but highly intelligent essay, the Prince remarks with modesty and charm that 'ces notes ont été faites très loin des Bibliothèques de Paris, par un dilettante moscovite, mais fervent'. He goes on to speak of himself as working 'dans mes neigeuses et paisibles retraites villageoises, si éloignées de Paris!' (pp. 15, 37).

Benedetto, Robert Vivier, M. A. Ruff, and Albert Feuillerat.[1] In spite of the penetration of some of these studies, the last word has not yet been said. In their anxiety to do justice to the architecture, critics have either overlooked certain *défaillances*, certain gaps between intention and execution in the individual poems, or they have failed to bring out to the full the subtleties of the internal structure of the book which Barbey called 'l'architecture secrète', possibly to distinguish it from the external division into chapters.

The first problem that faces the critic is the problem of the authority of the first and second editions. The first edition contained a hundred poems—a hundred and one with *Au Lecteur*—which were divided into five chapters:

1. Spleen et Idéal.
2. Fleurs du Mal.
3. Révolte.
4. Le Vin.
5. La Mort.

The six poems condemned by the court were omitted from the second edition, but Baudelaire added thirty-two 'new' poems, making a total of a hundred and twenty-seven.[2] The Paris poems were arranged in a separate chapter of eighteen pieces, of which ten were new, and the order of the other chapters was altered:

1. Spleen et Idéal.
2. Tableaux Parisiens.
3. Le Vin.

[1] L. F. Benedetto, 'L'Architecture des "Fleurs du Mal"' in *Zeitschrift für Französische Sprache und Literatur*, Vol. 39, 1912. R. Vivier, *L'Originalité de Baudelaire*, Brussels, 1926. M. A. Ruff, *Sur l'architecture des 'Fleurs du mal'*, Paris, 1931. A. Feuillerat, 'L'Architecture des *Fleurs du mal*' in *Studies by Members of the French Department of Yale University* (Yale Romanic Studies, No. XVIII), New Haven and London, 1941.

[2] I have placed the word 'new' in inverted commas because not all the additional poems were written specially for the second edition or since the first. Part of *L'Albatros* was probably written in 1841–2, but the last tercet was added later at the suggestion of Asselineau. I have followed previous writers in counting the four poems grouped under the title of *Un Fantôme* as one poem.

4. Fleurs du mal.
5. Révolte.
6. La Mort.

'Spleen et Idéal' expresses the conflict between aspiration and despair. In the first edition the poet rebels against the invading *spleen* and plunges into the world of evil. The significance of the chapter called 'Fleurs du Mal' is twofold. It represents the world of evil certainly, but it is also the world of sexual perversion, and I shall try to show later that perversion stands for rebellion on the moral and social planes. Moral and social rebellion leads direct to the religious rebellion of 'Révolte'. When 'Le Vin' was first written, Baudelaire regarded intoxicants as a harmless indulgence. The chapter was therefore intended as an 'artificial paradise'—a temporary refuge from the violence of the first three chapters. It lowered the tension and provided a pause before the poet turned, with relief, to the prospect of death which alone could offer a final release from his torment.

It is apparent that the whole design underwent a radical modification in the second edition. The poems added to what is known as the Cycle of Spleen in 'Spleen et Idéal' were written in a much more sombre mood than the existing poems. At the end of the chapter the poet is the prisoner of his own mood, trapped in the closed circle of the self. He therefore decides to mingle with the crowds in the streets and tries in 'Tableaux Parisiens' to re-establish contact with everyday life and common humanity in the hope—the vain hope—of breaking out of his prison. He made no change in the six poems contained in 'Le Vin', but its new position between 'Tableaux Parisiens' and 'Fleurs du Mal' is not an improvement. On the contrary, it spoils what might have been the highly effective transition from the psychological and physical loneliness of the Paris poems to the sense of moral ostracism which pervades 'Fleurs du Mal', while the transition from 'Révolte' to 'La Mort' is not particularly effectual. The change in the placing of 'Le Vin' can only have been made for personal reasons. Baudelaire's whole attitude to intoxicants altered between the first and second editions. He no longer regarded them as a harmless indulgence; he regarded them with 'horror'.[1] I think we must assume that the new position was intended, possibly unconsciously, to neutralize the whole chapter which in the second edition appears irrelevant.

There were additions to all the love cycles reflecting the changes which took place in Baudelaire's relations with his mistresses between 1857 and 1861, and three poems were added to 'La Mort' including *Le Voyage*. The book originally ended with *La Mort des artistes* which seems to suggest some final resolution of the problems dealt with in the rest of the book. The three new poems were written in a different mood and the second edition closes on a note of agnosticism with the poet's gesture towards '*du nouveau*'.

There were other changes which will be considered in the appropriate places, but these are the most important ones and they have led to a division of opinion among Baudelaire's critics. Feuillerat, whose study is the most searching that has yet been made and whose argument recalls forcibly his treatment of Proust's alterations to the original plan of *A la Recherche du temps perdu*, thinks that though the second edition is richer in detail and the regrouping of the Parisian poems an improvement, the structure is much less clear and coherent.[2] He emphasizes the loss in vitality and suggests that the introduction of the new poems into the Cycle of Spleen creates a discordant note which harms its artistic unity.[3] The majority of Baudelaire's editors base their preference for the second edition on the fact that the poet himself prepared it and think that the alterations in the pattern must be accepted.

[1] 'I have developed a horror of every intoxicant because of the amplification of time and the sense of enormity which any intoxicant gives to everything. It is impossible to be not simply a business man, but even a man of letters with a continual spiritual orgy going on' (*Corr. gén.*, 3, p. 168. Letter to Armand Fraisse of 15 July 1860.). Compare, too, *Du Vin et du haschisch*, written in 1851, and *Le Poëme du haschisch*, written in 1860.

[2] *Comment Marcel Proust a composé son roman* (Yale Romanic Studies, No. VII), New Haven, 1934. For a criticism of his views, see the present writer's *The Novel in France*, London, 1950, pp. 337–8.

[3] They are *Une Gravure fantastique, Obsession, Le Goût du néant, Alchimie de la douleur, Horreur sympathique* and *L'Horloge*.

There is clearly something to be said for both views, but neither strikes me as wholly satisfactory. The poet is not necessarily the best judge of the precise order in which his work should be arranged, and a number of Feuillerat's detailed criticisms are valid. We cannot deny that the architecture of the second edition is in some ways less impressive or that there are discordant notes; but it must be remembered that a poet's experience does not stand still, that it is bound to change and develop with the years in a way which modifies our view of the artist, and that Baudelaire was contemplating still further alterations and additions in the third edition which he himself intended to be definitive.[1] 'Force' and 'coherence' cannot therefore be the final criterion. The main criticism of the second edition, however, seems to me to be the omission of the 'condemned pieces'. It is idle to argue that they were reprinted during the poet's lifetime in *Les Épaves* and should be kept as an appendix to the *Fleurs du mal*. In preparing the second edition, the poet was not a free agent; he had to do the best he could without the condemned poems and either produce unsatisfactory substitutes or, where this was impossible, leave a gap. Now at least three of the six are key poems and the remaining three are important. It is obvious that the first of the love Cycles is grievously mutilated by the omission of *Les Bijoux* and the suppression of two of the Lesbian poems does irreparable damage to 'Fleurs du Mal'. The only rational approach is to accept the loss and the gain which resulted from Baudelaire's own changes —the gain includes at least five of his greatest poems—to treat the second edition as the canon, but to restore the condemned pieces to their original places. That is what I shall do in discussing the poems in detail.[2]

---

[1] 'In the third edition, which I shall call the *Definitive Edition*, I shall add ten or fifteen poems and a long preface in which I shall explain my tricks and my method and teach everyone *the art of doing the same*' (*Corr. gén.*, 4, p. 105, letter to Michel Lévy, ?August or September 1862).

[2] A comparative table of the contents of the first and second editions is given in the Appendix on pp. 307–13 below.

V

THE INTERPRETATION OF THE
FLEURS DU MAL

Prologue

THE FIRST poem of all, called *Au Lecteur*, is not a mere formality. It is the Prologue in which the poet states his fundamental attitude to life and glances at some of the principal themes with which he will deal. The editors of the critical edition describe it with felicity as 'son admirable pièce de proue', and point out that it possesses 'l'allure carrée, la véhémence, l'âpreté tant des grands prédicateurs que des satyriques de la Renaissance' as well as the tone of the writers of the pre-classic period.[1] In spite of certain weaknesses, it is in the main a brilliant performance. It opens with immense verve:

> La sottise, l'erreur, le péché, la lésine,
> Occupent nos esprits et travaillent nos corps . . .

The reference to sin introduces the preacher, but in the next verse we hear another voice:

> Nos péchés sont têtus, nos repentirs sont lâches.

The other voice is the voice of the penitent. For the poem is, as Jean Prévost observes, a general confession—'the general confession of an age and not of an individual which is nonetheless personal '.[2] Sin and vice are the two primary facts about the human condition as Baudelaire sees it. The sins and vices mentioned here do not appear to differ greatly from those attacked by his sixteenth-century predecessors, but there is no doubt that he was thinking of the specifically nineteenth-century sins

[1] J. Crépet and G. Blin, *Les Fleurs du Mal*, Édition critique, Paris, 1942, p. 279.
[2] *Baudelaire*, Paris, 1953, p. 213.

and vices which are criticized with such vehemence in other parts
of his work.[1] I think that 'erreur' and 'péché' stand collectively
for *sins* against the spirit, and the flesh, and that 'sottise' and
'lésine' are intellectual and emotional *vices*. When we come to
the end of the poem, we shall find that they combine in something which is at once a sin and a vice.

Sin normally leads to repentance and vice to remorse, but
preacher and penitent chide the age for its supine acquiescence
in both:

> . . . nous alimentons nos *aimables remords*.
>
> . . . nos *repentirs sont lâches*.
>
> . . . nous rentrons *gaiement* dans le chemin bourbeux.

Baudelaire's references to the devil are often suspect, but the
devil mentioned in the third verse is not a melodramatic figure.
It is he who makes sin and vice seductive, and is responsible for
the supine attitude of the age.

> Sur l'oreiller du mal c'est Satan Trismégiste
> Qui berce longuement notre esprit enchanté,
> Et le riche métal de notre volonté
> Est tout vaporisé par ce savant chimiste.

It is a sign of Baudelaire's immense power of suggestion that
the pillow and the simple words 'berce' and 'enchanté' in the
first two lines are sufficient to create a dreamy, voluptuous atmosphere in which man is lulled into a false sense of security. The
effect is prolonged by 'riche', but the richest metal is also the
softest and in the next two lines he suddenly realizes that something irrevocable has happened. The hiss of the s's makes us feel
that not merely the will, but the whole man is disintegrating in a
wisp of steam.

There is a falling off in the next three stanzas where the devil
becomes the devil of Romantic horror stories, and the image of

---

[1] The parallels cited by the editors of the critical edition include:

> Le désir, l'avarice et l'erreur insensée. (*Ronsard*)

> L'ennuie, le mespris, le discord inconstant,
> La peur, la trahison, le meurtre, la vengeance. (*Régnier*)

the 'sein martyrisé de l'antique catin' is an unfortunate but not uncommon lapse. The catalogue of monsters in the eighth verse takes us back to the tone and method of the pre-classic period:

> Mais parmi les chacals, les panthères, les lices,
> Les singes, les scorpions, les vautours, les serpents,
> Les monstres glapissants, hurlants, grognants, rampants,
> Dans la ménagerie infâme de nos vices,
>
> Il en est un plus laid . . .

The seething, howling mass of monsters and reptiles belong to the medieval menagerie, and it is significant that they are all or nearly all beasts of prey. Their number can hardly be fortuitous. They either represent the Seven Deadly Sins or, as one writer suggests, seven of the meaner sins which to Baudelaire seemed no less deadly.[1] The immense effectiveness of the lines lies in the contrast between the catalogue and the solitary monster to which the poet directs his attention in the last two verses—the eighth sin or, as I have suggested, the combination of 'sin' and 'vice', which is far deadlier than the other seven:

> Il en est un plus laid, plus méchant, plus immonde!
> Quoiqu'il ne pousse ni grands gestes ni grands cris,
> Il ferait volontiers de la terre un débris
> Ets dans un bâillement avalerait le monde;
>
> C'est l'Ennui!

The carrying over of the main verb—'Il en est un plus laid . . .' —from one verse to another is the signal for a change of scene and a change of tone. The rhetoric of the earlier verses sinks to a quieter and more frightening note. The monsters disappear as though a wand had been waved over them. The howling grows fainter and dies away. It is not after all the somewhat melodramatic daggers and poisons catalogued in the seventh verse which are the real menace, but the subterranean activities of 'Ennui'— carefully isolated and emphasized—which rot away the very fibres of our mind and will and, unostentatiously, without

[1] C. A. Hackett in *An Anthology of Modern French Poetry*, Oxford, 1952, p. 189.

'grands gestes ni grands cris', reduce the world to a condition of stagnation:

> Il ferait volontiers de la terre un débris
> Et dans un bâillement avalerait le monde . . . [1]

Ennui is a malady which belongs to late civilizations, and it is characteristic of some of its victims that they have sought distraction from it in acts of violence and cruelty which will stimulate their jaded senses. This explains Baudelaire's 'Ennui':

> —l'œil chargé d'un pleur involontaire,
> Il rêve d'échafauds en fumant son houka.

It is the allegorical manner of medieval poetry. The figure smoking its hookah—a symbol of ease and luxury—is deliberately grotesque and immensely effective. Baudelaire was completely absorbed in his own inner life. His aim was to exteriorize his malady and in doing so to show us—the readers—that whether we like it or not, we too are victims. That is the intention of the last two lines where he suddenly turns on us, whispers in our ear:

> Tu le connais, lecteur, ce monstre délicat,
> —Hypocrite lecteur,—mon semblable,—mon frère!

He is trying to break down our complacency, to shock us out of our conventional habits, and make us admit that we are fellow-sufferers so that we shall be 'on his side' in the next phase of the attack. While admiring the intention, however, we may feel that the transition is too abrupt and that the very impressiveness of the allegorical figure weakens the final effect.

1. 'Spleen et Idéal'

'Who among us', asked Baudelaire in a review of Asselineau's *La Double vie*, 'who among us is not a *homo duplex*? I mean those whose minds have since infancy been *touched with pensiveness*; always double, action and intention, dream and reality; one

---

[1] The isolation distinguishes Baudelaire from his predecessors. In the examples quoted in the critical edition 'ennui' is merely one of the catalogue of sins and vices.

always harming the other, one usurping the part of the other.'[1]
The *Fleurs du mal* is not merely the autobiography of a soul; it is
the autobiography of the divided modern man, peering at his
reflection in the cracked and misted mirrors of *Bénédiction* or in
the sea and trying to decide what manner of man he is. The first
and longest chapter certainly expresses the gap between 'action
and intention, dream and reality'; but it is also the expression of
a more fundamental division which runs all through the poet's
experience and appears in the contrasts between the different
chapters and cycles as well as in the contrasted images of individual poems and the joining of 'contrary' words to which
Baudelaire refers in one of the draft prefaces.

The editors of the critical edition have provided us with a
learned gloss on the words *ennui* and *spleen*. There is no doubt
that Baudelaire often used them—particularly in this first chapter
—as practically synonymous terms, but strictly speaking *spleen*
seems to be a physical and *ennui* a moral malady. 'C'est ainsi',
write the editors, 'que du caprice des nerfs l'on passe au malaise
métaphysique.'[2]

Spleen and *ennui* are matched by two positive terms, *volupté*
and *extase*. Baudelaire's use of them is not always free from
ambiguity, but the distinction between *spleen* and *ennui* can also
be applied to them. *Volupté* usually stands for some form of
physical pleasure and is therefore a counterpart of *spleen*. *Extase*,
on the other hand, is used to denote an intellectual or spiritual
rapture, or what might be called a 'bien-être métaphysique' and
corresponds to *ennui*. I have used the words 'counterpart' and
'corresponds', but there is one important reservation to be made.
Spleen and *ennui* are moods which are rooted in man's nature, but
volupté and *extase* are essentially transitory and in the last analysis
ineffectual antidotes to the negative states to which they correspond.

The nature of the malady and the attempted remedies will be
explored in greater detail later on, but it is necessary to draw

---

[1] *L'Art romantique*, p. 409. (The words in italics are in English in the
original.)

[2] *Op. cit.*, p. 257.

attention to a further parallel. *Spleen* and *Idéal* are closely related to those other pairs: the 'deux postulations simultanées, l'une vers Dieu, l'autre vers Satan'; 'spiritualité et animalité'; the 'deux sentiments contradictoires: l'horreur de la vie et l'extase de la vie'.[1] What is described in the first chapter particularly, but also in the rest of the volume, is a state of intolerable and well nigh unbearable tension. The poet is caught between two conflicting impulses—'simultanées' is a crucial word in the celebrated formula—between a reaching-out to something beyond the present horror, which may be called 'God' or 'spirituality' or the 'Ideal', and the sensation of being continually sucked back into it by *spleen*, *ennui*, or *animalité*.

The principal theme of 'Spleen et Idéal' is a perpetual oscillation between two opposite poles, but the forms through which it is expressed are highly complex. The poems divide into three main groups: the Cycle of Art, the Cycles of Love, and the Cycle of Spleen. The first two groups record the poet's attempts to conquer *spleen* and to reach the *Idéal* through art and through love; the third describes the victory of *spleen*.

The Cycle of Art

The Cycle of Art is sub-divided into a number of smaller groups which deal with the vocation of the poet, his status in the modern world, theories of art and beauty—Romantic, Parnassian, and Symbolist—and the personal difficulties experienced by Baudelaire in producing his poems. There is a final group, consisting of poems like *La Vie antérieure*, *Bohémiens en voyage*, and *L'Homme et la mer*, which deals with the condition of man as well as with the personal qualities of a particular man. They are early work and *La Vie antérieure* verges on Romantic pastiche, but their place in the design of the *Fleurs du mal* is clear. They form a link between *Au Lecteur* and the Cycle of Spleen.

I think we should add that several of the poems in this cycle are not merely early poems, but deal specifically with the experience of a young man and with the problems of youth. The poems on the difficulty of writing describe the peculiar difficulties of a

[1] *Journaux intimes*, pp. 62, 96.

young man who is trying to make a *start*. Those on life describe the disillusionment of youth as compared with the mature disillusionment of the best poems in the Cycle of Spleen.

Bénédiction is an account of the birth and vocation of the poet. Professor Mansell Jones points out that the opening lines,

> Lorsque, par un décret des puissances suprêmes,
> Le Poëte apparaît en ce monde *ennuyé*,

repeat the main theme of *Au Lecteur* and that the word 'ennuyé' forms the 'ground-bass' of the poem.[1] It also repeats the idea that *ennui* drives men to persecution. The poet is presented as the persecuted hero of the contemporary world, a shame to his mother, a scandal to his wife and the public. It looks at first like the Romantic conception of the poet, but Baudelaire introduces a fresh note. He describes two contrasted orders—the human order where the poet is persecuted and the divine order where he hopes to be rewarded—and these in turn correspond to *spleen* and *Idéal*, the 'horror' and the 'ecstasy' of life. The monster of *Au Lecteur* was a 'monstre délicat', but there is nothing 'délicat' about the bourgeois inhabitants of 'ce monde ennuyé'. They are denounced with extreme bitterness:

> Tous ceux qu'il veut aimer . . .
> Cherchent à qui saura lui tirer une plainte,
> Et font sur lui l'essai de leur férocité.

This gives place at the close to scarcely less extravagant flights of rhetoric:

> Je sais que vous gardez une place au Poëte
> Dans les rangs bienheureux des saintes Légions,
> Et que vous l'invitez à l'éternelle fête
> Des Trônes, des Vertus, des Dominations . . .

It has been suggested that the poet's reward can only be earned through suffering or what he himself chose to call 'la fertilisante douleur'. It is true that Baudelaire regarded suffering as inseparable from the contemporary poet's vocation, but in these lines the 'bienheureux', the 'saintes', and the echo from the liturgy are

---

[1] *Baudelaire*, Cambridge, 1952, p. 31.

intended to emphasize that his vocation is a divine vocation, that he will have his place 'dans les rangs bienheureux des saintes Légions' in virtue of his calling as a poet.[1] He suffers because he is a poet trapped in a world of 'horror', but it is because he is a poet and not because he suffers that he is entitled to the 'couronne mystique'.

Bénédiction is in no sense a flawless poem, but it is important for an understanding of Baudelaire's work and contains in embryo most of the themes dealt with in the Cycle of Art. A number of these poems raise again the problem of the gap between intention and execution. The intention, however, is clear. Poetry is a vocation. It is only in the act of poetic creation that there is any possibility that the tension may be resolved, the 'horror' and the 'ecstasy' reconciled. I make no excuse for stressing the extreme importance of this view. Baudelaire held it with such conviction that it becomes one of the articles of faith of the *Fleurs du mal* and must be taken into account in any attempt to assess Baudelaire's achievement as a whole.

Whatever the shortcomings of individual poems, we cannot fail to be impressed by the care and comprehensiveness with which the first Cycle is planned. *Bénédiction* closes with a rhetorical flourish and the spectacle of the poet crowned in glory, but in the next poem he is compared to an albatross—'ces rois de l'azur'—which is brought crashing down on to the deck of a ship where it is tormented by the barbarous crew who represent the public of *Bénédiction*.[2] At the end of *L'Albatros* we leave him

> Exilé sur le sol au milieu des huées,
> Ses *ailes de géant* l'empêchent de marcher.

But in the third poem, *Élévation*, he is soaring up again 'd'une *aile vigoureuse*' into 'l'immensité profonde' and leaving far behind him

[1] The last line of the verse quoted is a translation of part of the Preface of the Mass:

'Et ideo cum Angelis et Archangelis, cum Thronis et Dominationibus, cumque omni militia cælestis exercitus, hymnum gloriæ tuæ canimus . . .'

[2] The poem is said to have been inspired by an incident which actually took place during Baudelaire's voyage to the East.

les *ennuis* et les vastes chagrins
Qui chargent de leurs poids l'existence brumeuse.

The contrasted images and contrasted movements of the two poems illustrate once again the way in which the essential movement of the book—the oscillation between contrary states and moods—is reflected in the individual poems.

The importance of *Bénédiction* for the architecture of the *Fleurs du mal* is brought home still more forcibly when we compare it to 'J'aime le souvenir'. It repeats the theme of the two orders, but this time the process is reversed. Instead of opening with a picture of the torments of the poet and ending with a vision of him among the ranks of the blessed, it opens with a vision of the 'earthly paradise' and closes with a nightmare picture of the horrors of industrial civilization and the poet transfixed

Devant ce noir tableau plein d'épouvantement.

What is still more striking is the contrast between the subject-matter of the poet in the golden age and that of the contemporary poet. For the first it is:

L'homme, élégant, robuste et fort, [qui] avait le droit
D'être fier des beautés qui le nommaient leur roi.

For the second:

des beautés inconnues:
Des visages rongés par les chancres du cœur.

This leads naturally to the sixth poem. *Les Phares* stands out among the early pieces as an example of Baudelaire's mature style, and the maturity is apparent in the peculiar felicity of the phrasing:

Rubens, fleuve d'oubli, jardin de la paresse,
Oreiller de chair fraîche où l'on ne peut aimer.

It is difficult to imagine a more impressive description of the lack that we sometimes feel in those paintings of massive Flemish beauties disguised as goddesses or disporting themselves at a Kermesse. But the poem is also interesting as a development with concrete examples of the situation described both in *Bénédiction* and in the final section of 'J'aime le souvenir'. It is an

account of *individual* artistic vocations from Leonardo to Delacroix and of the theme of their work. The movement like that
of 'J'aime le souvenir' is a *downward* movement. The poet
altered the chronological order and placed what Jean Prévost
calls 'les deux grands artistes souriants'—Rubens and Leonardo
—before the 'tourmentés'.[1] Rembrandt's 'triste hôpital'
and his 'ordures', Goya's 'cauchemar', 'fœtus', and 'sabbats',
and Delacroix's 'lac de sang hanté des mauvais anges' are all
leading to the 'visages rongés par les chancres du cœur'; and
when the poet sums up the different 'messages' of all the artists,
past and present, in the lines

> Ces malédictions, ces blasphèmes, ces plaintes,
> Ces extases, ces cris, ces pleurs, ces *Te Deum*,
> Sont un écho redit par mille labyrinthes;
> C'est pour les cœurs mortels un divin opium!

he is also describing all the different notes which combine to give
the *Fleurs du mal* its special resonance. The 'labyrinthes' suggest
very well his exploration of the hidden places of the personality,
and the contradiction implicit in 'divin opium', which conveys
the simultaneous ideas of 'transcendence' and 'illusory escape',
points to a doubt about the efficacy of the poet's message and
his experience.

The account of the poet's vocation leads to a consideration of
some of the poems dealing directly with poetic theory. I have
already said something of the importance of *Correspondances* for
the development of nineteenth-century poetry, but its placing
immediately after *Élévation* deserves comment. The idea of a
'correspondence' between sounds, colours, and perfumes was
not new and was, perhaps, the product of a confused psychology;
but Baudelaire is evidently trying to work out a form of poetic
alchemy which will not only enable him to reach something
behind the world of appearances, to understand what he calls in
the last line of *Élévation*

> Le langage des fleurs et des choses muettes!

He is trying to find a way of maintaining the *élan* described in

[1] *Op. cit.*, p. 186.

that poem until the dualism of everyday life is resolved in 'une ténébreuse et profonde unité'. *Correspondances* appears at first to be in strong contrast to *La Beauté*, which is placed among the Parnassian exercises like *Don Juan aux enfers*. For here the poets, prostrate in front of an impassible beauty,

> Consumeront leurs jours en d'austères études.

There seems to be no escape through alchemy. 'Consumeront' must be given its full sense of 'use up', 'wear out'. 'Études' is a word of limitation and seems to stand for a formal, representational art. This impression is strengthened by the following poem called *L'Idéal* which appears to be a criticism of contemporary ideas of the beautiful:

> Ce ne seront jamais ces beautés de vignettes,
> Produits avariés, nés d'un siècle vaurien,
> Ces pieds à brodequins, ces doigts à castagnettes,
> Qui sauront satisfaire un cœur comme le mien.

He goes on to denounce Gavarni as a 'poëte des chloroses' and to exalt the great tragic artists—Shakespeare, Æschylus, and Michelangelo. *Hymne à la Beauté* is still more Romantic in its conception of beauty:

> Viens-tu du ciel profond ou sors-tu de l'abîme,
> O Beauté? ton regard, infernal et divin,
> Verse confusément le bienfait et le crime,
> Et l'on peut pour cela te comparer au vin.

The poem exhibits some of the least admirable traits of the Romantic aftermath, but though the 'infernal' and 'divin' are a typical piece of nineteenth-century jargon they illustrate Baudelaire's habit of looking at the world in terms of conflict or contrast. The identification of art or beauty with wine—with an *excitant*—is something that occurs many times in his work, and we discover from the last verse that the function of art, as conceived in this poem, is to bring consolation:

> De Satan ou de Dieu, qu'importe? Ange ou Sirène,
> Qu'importe, si tu rends,—fée aux yeux de velours,
> Rhythme, parfum, lueur, ô mon unique reine!—
> L'univers moins hideux et les instants moins lourds?

It would be a mistake to attach too much importance to the apparent contradictions in these poems. It is an understatement to say that Baudelaire was not a consistent thinker. His approach was essentially experimental and even opportunist. In this group of poems he is simply exploring different approaches to the problem of æsthetic experience and extracting from each of them what seems of value for his particular purposes. His genius does not lie least in his power of assimilating the disparate elements of experience and of reconciling opposites. He succeeded, as we shall see, in maintaining the grand style and in adapting it to fresh subjects as well as in discovering new relationships between different regions of experience. For the appeal of his own poetry lies at once in its formal perfection, its depth, and in something for which 'poetic alchemy' is not altogether an unsatisfactory term.

The poems I have discussed are nearly all impersonal statements of the difficulties of the poet who is hampered by the hostility of the public, the elusiveness of his goal, and the intractability or frivolity of his subject-matter.[1] These impersonal statements are matched by three personal statements. *La Muse malade*, *Le Mauvais moine*, and *L'Ennemi*, which are among the most moving of the early poems, express the difficulties of a particular poet and his fear that he may not achieve his goal. In *La Muse malade* he is a prey to *spleen* rather than to *ennui*, and the accent falls on physical sickness. In *Le Mauvais moine* and *L'Ennemi* he is paralysed by *ennui* and unable to write. It is instructive to compare *Le Mauvais moine* and 'J'aime le souvenir'. In the second poem he speaks enviously of the artist whose subject was 'l'homme, élégant, robuste et fort' and attributes the difficulties of the contemporary artist, faced with 'des visages rongés par les chancres du cœur', to a deterioration in his *subject-matter*. In *Le Mauvais moine* failure is attributed to a deterioration in the *artist* who has lost the vigour and conviction which belonged in former ages to the artist-monk 'embellishing' the walls of his cell with representations of 'la sainte vérité' and who has become a 'moine fainéant':

[1] These are the themes of *Bénédiction*, *Correspondances*, *La Beauté*, and *L'Idéal*.

> —Mon âme est un tombeau que, mauvais cénobite,
> Depuis l'éternité je parcours et j'habite;
> Rien n'embellit les murs de ce cloître odieux.
>
> O moine fainéant! quand saurai-je donc faire
> Du spectacle vivant de ma triste misère
> Le travail de mes mains et l'amour de mes yeux?

L'Ennemi is inspired by his very personal sense of life slipping away with his work unwritten:

> Et qui sait si les fleurs nouvelles que je rêve
> Trouveront dans ce sol lavé comme une grève
> Le mystique aliment qui ferait leur vigueur?
>
> —O douleur! ô douleur! Le Temps mange la vie,
> Et l'obscur Ennemi qui nous ronge le cœur
> Du sang que nous perdons croît et se fortifie!

When we turn back to the lines that I quoted from *Les Phares*:

> Ces malédictions, ces blasphèmes, ces plaintes,
> Ces extases, ces cris, ces pleurs, ces *Te Deum*,

we see how closely the conception of the poet, poetic theory, and the personal experience of a particular poet are woven into one another.

It is sometimes assumed that art and love are two separate methods by which Baudelaire tries to overcome *spleen* and escape from 'the horror of life', but the connection between them is closer than that. We know that the tension can only be resolved if at all through poetic creation. The argument of the Cycle of Art appears to be that poetic creation can only take place if the poet has a suitable subject and is in a condition to write about it. He turns to love in the hope that it will provide him with a subject and deliver him from *spleen*, but his hopes are only partly realized. Love certainly provides him with a subject, but it offers no more than a temporary escape and becomes the source of new disasters which finally leave him more hopelessly than before the victim of *ennui*. I will anticipate by saying that the glory of Baudelaire lies, paradoxically, in the manner in which he has expressed what the French call an *échec* and in the penetration with which he recorded the final triumph of *ennui* reducing art and love to 'débris'.

The Cycle of Art leads straight to the four love cycles: the Cycles of Jeanne Duval (XXII to XXXIX), Madame Sabatier (XL to XLVIII), Marie Daubrun (XLIX to LVII), and the seven poems belonging to what Crépet calls the Cycle of the 'héroines secondaires' (LVIII to LXIV).[1] The three main cycles represent three different types of liaison which the French with their genius for this kind of distinction have somewhat misleadingly classified as 'l'amour-passion', 'l'amour spirituel', and 'l'amour-tendresse'.[2]

The Cycle of Jeanne Duval

The poems written to Jeanne Duval are the most remarkable of Baudelaire's love poems. They are not simply the expression of sensual love, they are what might be called an erotic drama. What Baudelaire does is to present most of the classic phases of a love affair—'le coup de foudre', 'la lune de miel', 'la vie commune', 'les premières désillusions', 'décristallisation', 'rupture insidieuse', 'rupture consommée'—but in doing so he contrives to give each of them a personal interpretation. In the first edition the Cycle opened with *Les Bijoux*. It is the equivalent of the 'coup de foudre' and corresponds ironically to the traditional picture of the Knight of Chivalry at the feet of the Beloved or the Poet at the feet of the Lady:

> La très-chère était nue, et, connaissant mon cœur,
> Elle n'avait gardé que ses bijoux sonores,
> Dont le riche attirail lui donnait l'air vainqueur
> Qu'ont dans leurs jours heureux les esclaves des Mores.
>
> . . . .
>
> Elle était donc couchée et se laissait aimer,
> Et du haut du divan elle souriait d'aise
> A mon amour profond et doux comme la mer,
> Qui vers elle montait comme vers sa falaise.

The actors as well as the setting have undergone a change. The

---

[1] The numbering is that of the second edition.
[2] M. A. Ruff, *op. cit.*, p. 17.

ethereal beauty of legend has become a prostitute deliberately trying new positions in order to excite the customer:

> Et la candeur unie à la lubricité
> Donnait un charme neuf à ses métamorphoses.

The operative word is 'neuf'. *Les Bijoux* is a description of a highly ingenious erotic game, our attention is concentrated on the various incidentals which titillate desire beginning with the woman's nakedness and her 'bijoux sonores'. Laforgue speaks of 'lubricités correctes', and she is not strictly speaking a *person* at all; she is a being who is constantly changing, suffering a 'metamorphosis', and only exists in so far as she arouses desire. The Knight, too, has undergone a transformation and become a fetishist, a connoisseur of the erotic effect of jewels on a naked body:

> Quand il jette en dansant son bruit vif et moqueur,
> Ce monde rayonnant de métal et de pierre
> Me ravit en extase . . .

of cosmetics on dark skin:

> Sur ce teint fauve et brun, le fard était superbe!

or of the twist of thighs and the curve of a breast:

> . . . son bras et sa jambe, et sa cuisse et ses reins,
> Polis comme de l'huile, onduleux comme un cygne,
> Passaient devant mes yeux clairvoyants et sereins;
> Et son ventre et ses seins, ces grappes de ma vigne . . .

In the hiss of the s's in the first line we hear the sound of saliva caught back as desire mounts, but in 'mes yeux clairvoyants et sereins' the connoisseur stifles the lover. He watches the woman going through the performance in a mood of cool appraisement, and the hand stretched out to finger 'ces grappes de ma vigne' shows that the performance has been an effective one. The description of the lamp dying down in the final verse is the sign that desire, too, has died down. The curtain is lowered after a splendid performance, but there has been no connection. In the last line of all:

> Il inondait de sang cette peau couleur d'ambre!

the sight of cosmetics changes, sadistically, to a vision of blood.

Parfum exotique and *La Chevelure* belong to the 'lune de miel' and are poems of rich, warm, drowsy fulfilment, but of the sort of fulfilment which was peculiar to Baudelaire. In the first of the two poems the fetish is perfume, and when he writes:

> Quand, les deux yeux fermés, en un soir chaud d'automne,
> Je respire l'odeur de ton sein chaleureux,
> Je vois se dérouler des rivages heureux
> Qu'éblouissent les feux d'un soleil monotone,

there is a relation of cause and effect between 'l'odeur de ton sein chaleureux' and 'des rivages heureux' which is reinforced by line 9:

> Guidé par ton odeur vers de charmants climats.

The perfume sets in motion the machinery of vision. It is a vision of the earthly paradise which recalls 'J'aime le souvenir'. In that poem he writes:

> Alors l'homme et la femme en leur agilité
> Jouissaient sans mensonge et sans anxiété . . .

and in *Parfum exotique*:

> Une île paresseuse où la nature donne
> Des arbres singuliers et des fruits savoureux;
> Des hommes dont le corps est mince et vigoureux,
> Et des femmes dont l'œil par sa franchise étonne.

In both poems the psychological qualities are more important than the physical qualities, or rather physical well-being reflects psychological well-being. For the most important words are 'sans anxiété' and 'franchise'. The poet is describing people who are free from the contemporary tensions and neuroses and whose lithe, slim bodies and clear gaze compare strangely with

> Des visages rongés par les chancres du cœur.

La Chevelure is a much more elaborate and impressive treatment of the same phase and is one of the greatest of all Baudelaire's poems. The woman's hair is the fetish which provides a release for the poet's feelings and starts the process of poetic creation:

O toison, moutonnant jusque sur l'encolure!
O boucles! O parfum chargé de nonchaloir!
Extase! Pour peupler ce soir l'alcôve obscure
Des souvenirs dormant dans cette chevelure,
Je la veux agiter dans l'air comme un mouchoir!

The spectacle of the poet shaking the woman's hair in order to bring forgotten memories to life is a good illustration of Baudelaire's personal imagery and of his method of exploring a situation until he seems to have extracted the last drop of feeling from it. It explains, too, why Proust regarded him as one of the discoverers of *la mémoire involontaire*. For in this poem the woman's hair performs the same function as the *petite madeleine* in Proust's celebrated experience. 'Souvenir' is used here in a positive and not in a negative sense as it is in *Le Voyage*, creating a feeling of expansion instead of the feeling of contraction which we found in that poem.[1] Forests, the sea, ships, the port, and the exotic countries come tumbling out of the hair in the same way that memories of Combray, M. Swann's park, the gardens, and the water-lilies seem to tumble out of Marcel's cup of tea in *A la Recherche du temps perdu*. It is natural that each of them should seem to take us further from the woman so that the handkerchief is almost a handkerchief waved in sign of farewell. For Baudelaire is using the 'analogical' method and substituting images or, as they have been called, 'emotional equivalences' for the direct statement of feelings.

When we read in the next verse:

La langoureuse Asie et la brûlante Afrique,
Tout un monde lointain, absent, presque défunt,
Vit dans tes profondeurs, forêt aromatique!
Comme d'autres esprits voguent sur la musique,
Le mien, ô mon amour! nage sur ton parfum,

we feel as though we are watching an image thrown by a magic lantern on a screen and flickering fitfully. It almost disappears in the dying fall of

Tout un monde lointain, absent, presque défunt . . .

[1] Aux yeux du souvenir que le monde est petit!

H

Then it comes to life again in the verb:

> *Vit* dans tes profondeurs . . .

The last two lines create a sense of relaxation, almost of dissolution, as though the poet were melting away into the perfume.
'Nage sur ton parfum' is the start of a fresh movement away
from the woman:

> J'irai là-bas où l'arbre et l'homme, pleins de sève,
> Se pâment longuement sous l'ardeur des climats;
> Fortes tresses, soyez la houle qui m'enlève!
> Tu contiens, mer d'ébène, un éblouissant rêve
> De voiles, de rameurs, de flammes et de mâts . . .

It is another vision of the earthly paradise, and in 'l'arbre et
l'homme, pleins de sève' the accent falls once more on physical
well-being as a reflection of the psychological well-being which
belongs to the man who is in harmony with nature. 'Se pâment'
heightens the sense of drowsy dissolution of the previous verse;
the 'forêt aromatique' melts into the images of 'la houle' and the
'mer d'ébène', while the movement suggested by 'nage sur ton
parfum' is prolonged by 'la houle qui m'enlève'. The 'éblouissant
rêve' prepares the way for the central experience of the poem.

It becomes apparent at this point that the woman is only a
means to an end and that the poet, in Mr. T. S. Eliot's words, is
'reaching out towards something which cannot be had *in*, but
which may be had partly *through* personal relations'.[1] For when
we reach the heart of the poem—the sense of beatitude described
in the fourth verse—we find that the woman has vanished from
the scene altogether:

> Un port retentissant où mon âme peut boire
> A grands flots le parfum, le son et la couleur;
> Où les vaisseaux, glissant dans l'or et dans la moire,
> Ouvrent leurs vastes bras pour embrasser la gloire
> D'un ciel pur où frémit l'éternelle chaleur.

The lines with their atmosphere of warmth and maturity, and
the superb image of the vessels 'glissant dans l'or et dans la
moire', are so beautiful that we are inclined to take them for

[1] *Op. cit.*, p. 376.

granted. It is only when we turn to the Cycle of Spleen that we are forced to the conclusion that Baudelaire is far more concrete and precise when describing negative states than when describing the realization of the 'Ideal'. If we look at the next verse:

> Je plongerai ma tête amoureuse d'ivresse
> Dans ce noir océan où l'autre est enfermé;
> Et mon esprit subtil que le roulis caresse
> Saura vous retrouver, ô féconde paresse,
> Infinis bercements du loisir embaumé!

we are able to appreciate the full force of Mr. Eliot's comment. 'Amoureuse d'ivresse' is, as Professor Hackett has observed, a 'significant inversion of the conventional "ivre d'amour" '.[1] It is significant because as surely as in *Les Bijoux*, Baudelaire's attention is fixed not on the *person*, but on the *state* that she may induce in him. A glance at this state confirms the doubts expressed earlier about the efficacity of Baudelaire's positives. His interest in perfumes, taste and touch was prompted, as M. Vivier remarks, by a determination to give his undivided attention to his own inner life; but it was not confined to that.[2] The truth is that his conception of the good life is little more than a general sense of euphoria, a riot of perfumes, sounds, and colours. The whole poem, indeed, is an *extase* or an *ivresse*, and in phrases like 'féconde paresse' or 'loisir embaumé' the poet is trying to express something which lies just beyond language.

Although the woman disappears in the fourth verse, we are dimly conscious of her presence in the 'noir océan' of the fifth verse and the 'Cheveux bleus' of the sixth:

> Cheveux bleus, pavillon de ténèbres tendues,
> Vous me rendez l'azur du ciel immense et rond;
> Sur les bords duvetés de vos mèches tordues
> Je m'enivre ardemment des senteurs confondues
> De l'huile de coco, du musc et du goudron.

The 'pavillon de ténèbres tendues' is rightly one of the most admired images in the whole of Baudelaire's poetry, but what needs emphasis is that in both these verses he is mediating be-

[1] *Op. cit.*, p. 191.   [2] *Op. cit.*, p. 79.

tween two states of mind. The *extase* is not complete and cannot
be complete for reasons that have already been suggested. The
word 'tendues', which is reinforced by 'tordues', reveals an effort
to break through the darkness and to become part of the 'éblouissant rêve'; but the 'ciel immense et rond' shows that there is no
true *vision*, only the sight of the vast, empty sky and the intoxi-
cating scents. The sense of effort that we have observed in
'tendues' and 'tordues' is extended in:

> Je m'enivre ardemment des senteurs confondues.

The poet is trying to preserve the sense of ecstasy, but it is
evident that the unified impression of the fourth verse is already
dissolving into its component parts which are the 'senteurs
confondues':

> De l'huile de coco, du musc et du goudron.

In the final verse we find the poet back at his starting-place
contemplating the 'crinière lourde':

> Longtemps! toujours! ma main dans ta crinière lourde
> Sèmera le rubis, la perle et le saphir,
> Afin qu'à mon désir tu ne sois jamais sourde!
> N'es-tu pas l'oasis où je rêve, et la gourde
> Où je hume à longs traits le vin du souvenir?

The woman has become a courtesan again whose favours must
be purchased by gifts of precious stones; the *extase* is no more than
a memory of the voyage to Mauritius; and the 'vin du souvenir',
echoing the 'souvenirs' of the first verse, completes the circle.

I have used the word 'beatitude' to describe Baudelaire's
experience in this poem. His own word is *extase*, but the distinction between *extase* and *volupté* vanishes in *La Chevelure*, which
is his most sustained attempt to define *volupté*. It is therefore
appropriate at this point to anticipate a little, to glance at some lines
from *Le Balcon*, and to make some general observations on *volupté*:

> Que les soleils sont beaux dans les chaudes soirées!
> Que l'espace est profond! que le cœur est puissant!
> En me penchant vers toi, reine des adorées,
> Je croyais respirer le parfum de ton sang.
> Que les soleils sont beaux dans les chaudes soirées!

·   ·   ·   ·   ·

Ces serments, ces parfums, ces baisers infinis,
Renaîtront-ils d'un gouffre interdit à nos sondes,
Comme montent au ciel les soleils rajeunis
Après s'êtres lavés au fond des mers profondes?
—O serments! ô parfums! ô baisers infinis!

Le Balcon is not a poem of the same calibre as *La Chevelure*, but it is to an even greater extent than that poem an example of *sorcellerie évocatoire*. Baudelaire does not hesitate to make liberal use of highly suggestive words, and he succeeds in inducing what has been called in the case of Proust an *état privilégié*. We exist for a moment in a luminous, trance-like atmosphere. We are separated from the everyday world. Time seems to have stopped. Everything is larger, more real than in 'ordinary life':

Je croyais *respirer le parfum de ton sang* . . .

Comme montent au ciel les soleils rajeunis
Après s'être *lavés au fond des mers profondes* . . .

We are conscious all the time of an immense sense of relaxation and well-being, of deliverance from the *ennuis* of normal life.

I shall have something to say later of parallels between Baudelaire and the English Metaphysical Poets. I merely want to draw attention here to the resemblance between Baudelaire's *volupté* or *extase* and Donne's 'extasie' in the poem of that name:

WHERE, like a pillow on a bed,
    A Pregnant banke swel'd up, to rest
The violets reclining head,
    Sat we two, one anothers best.

Our hands were firmely cimented
    With a faste balme, which thence did spring,
Our eye-beames twisted, and did thred
    Our eyes, upon one double string.

Donne's experience is more 'intellectual' than Baudelaire's and he keeps his eye on the woman, but there is the same luminous, trance-like atmosphere and the same element of hallucination. Donne imagines the 'Pregnant banke' swelling up like a pillow and uses the baroque images of the 'eye-beames' threaded 'upon one double string', reminding us of:

Je croyais respirer le parfum de ton sang

and the 'soleils rajeunis'.

When he writes thirty lines later:

> A single violet transplant,
> The strength, the colour, and the size,
> (All which before was poore, and scant,)
> Redoubles still, and multiplies,

the violet seems to perform a similar function to the hair in *La Chevelure*, and reality 'which before was poore, and scant' is transformed.

Finally, Donne's ecstasy like Baudelaire's is transitory:

> So must pure lovers soules descend
> T'affections, and to faculties,
> Which sense may reach and apprehend,
> Else a great Prince in prison lies.[1]

With the next poem the honeymoon is over and 'la vie commune' has begun. It is impossible in this cycle to make a clear distinction between 'la vie commune' and the 'premières désillusions'. For it is essentially the period of 'distance', 'coldness',

[1] Compare: Car à quoi bon chercher tes beautés langoureuses
Ailleurs qu'en ton cher corps et qu'en ton cœur si doux?
Baudelaire has analysed this sense of *volupté* in a remarkable account of his own state of mind while listening to a performance of Wagner:
'I remember that as soon as I heard the opening bars I experienced one of those delightful impressions which nearly all imaginative people have felt in dreams while asleep. I was freed from *the bonds of heaviness*, and through memory I felt again the extraordinary sense of *volupté* which belongs to *high places*. . . . Next, I found myself involuntarily conjuring up the delicious state of a man in the middle of a vast reverie in absolute solitude, but a solitude with an *immense horizon* and a *large diffused light*; *immensity* without any other décor except itself. Soon I experienced the sensation of a more vivid *light*, of an *intensity of light* which grew with such rapidity that the shades of meaning furnished by the dictionary would be insufficient to express *this continually increasing addition of ardour and whiteness*. At this point I was fully in possession of the idea of the soul moving in a luminous milieu, of an ecstasy *composed of volupté and knowledge*, floating above and far away from the natural world.' (*L'Art romantique*, p. 207. Italics in the text.)

'indifference', and 'cruelty'. There is a significant change of décor. The blazing tropical skies disappear and are replaced by the image of the night skies which dominate this phase of the poet's experience:

> Je t'adore à l'égal de la voûte nocturne,
> O vase de tristesse, ô grande taciturne,
> Et je t'aime d'autant plus, belle, que tu me fuis,
> Et que tu me parais, ornement de mes nuits,
> Plus ironiquement accumuler les lieues
> Qui séparent mes bras des immensités bleues.
>
> Je m'avance à l'attaque, et je grimpe aux assauts,
> Comme après un cadavre un chœur de vermisseaux,
> Et je chéris, ô bête implacable et cruelle!
> Jusqu'à cette froideur par où tu m'es plus belle!

The assertions contained in the third, fifth, ninth, and tenth lines should not be dismissed as the sort of conventional declaration that is found in traditional love poetry. Nor should we be misled by the reflex action of the hand straying towards 'ces grappes de ma vigne' in *Les Bijoux* or the imaginary 'assault' in this poem. A sense of distance between the man and the woman is a constant factor in Baudelaire's poetry, and except when they come to blows there is virtually no contact between them.[1]

This brings me to the essential characteristics of the Baudelairean woman which are apparent in a greater or lesser degree in all four love cycles. 'C'est à l'Idole ou à la Chienne qu'il s'adresse . . .' writes M. Decaunes. 'Jamais à l'amante, désir et spiritualité confondus.'[2] This illuminating comment calls for one reservation. I think that we must say not 'the Idol or the Bitch', but 'the Idol *and* the Bitch'. Baudelaire's sexual experience seems to have been confined to courtesans, and it is on this experience that he draws in his work. The Baudelairean woman is a simplified and, at the same time, a twofold being. She possesses the simplicity of the animal and the surface sophistication of the courtesan.

[1] Compare this comment on relations between men and women from the diaries: 'Le gouffre infranchissable, qui fait l'incommunicabilité, reste infranchi (*Journaux intimes*, p. 85).'

[2] *Charles Baudelaire*, Paris, 1952, p. 35.

She is the Bitch whose 'métamorphoses' are enjoyed in private and the imaginary Idol who is paraded before the world because she is the opposite of the Bitch. She is always cold and remote, either because she deliberately withholds herself sexually and emotionally, or because some psychological peculiarity prevents the poet from rousing her, or because the poet himself has placed her on a pedestal. For whether he is writing of Jeanne Duval or Marie Daubrun or even Mme Sabatier, he is the worshipper and the *voyeur* whose imagination alternates between the Idol and the Bitch. I think we can say that it is precisely on account of the strong contrast between her attributes that she fits into Baudelaire's conception of experience as a perpetual oscillation between opposite poles.

We must next examine the psychological reasons for Baudelaire's preoccupation with coldness and distance. When we look at the last two lines of 'Je t'adore à l'égal':

> Et je chéris, ô bête implacable et cruelle!
> Jusqu'à cette froideur par où tu m'es plus belle!

we cannot fail to notice the perverse element. It is clear that the woman's coldness is the cause of her attraction, that the poet does not want her to give herself or to rouse her. And we begin to suspect that the Idol is a defence-mechanism against the Bitch.

The perverse element is not confined to this poem. The fifth poem of the Cycle records the discovery of the first infidelity, and the woman is roundly denounced as 'Femme impure'. A possible clue to the nature of the infidelity is given in the sixth poem. The title of *Sed non satiata* is taken from a line of Juvenal's:

> Et lassiata viris, sed non satiata.

Although there is no certain proof, it is thought that Jeanne was a Lesbian and Nadar speaks of a pretty blonde servant who at one time accompanied her everywhere.[1] If this is true, it would

---

[1] The editors of the critical edition point out that Baudelaire was too good a Latinist to translate 'lassiata viris' as 'tired *of* men', but think that he may have had this possible mistranslation in mind. They declare, categorically, that 'Jeanne Duval sacrifiait certainement, à ses heures, au culte de la saphique Vénus' (p. 344).

explain many of the riddles of Baudelaire's relationship with her as well as the opening of the poem where she is addressed as 'Bizarre déité'. The imagery of the poem is obscure. I take the line,

Œuvre de quelque obi, le Faust de la savane

to be a poetic suggestion that Jeanne is the creation of some tribal magician, a Faust operating in the country from which she came.

In the quatrains she is treated as the passive object of the poet's contemplation, but there is a change in the first tercet:

Par ces deux grands yeux noirs, soupiraux de ton âme,
O démon sans pitié! verse-moi moins de flamme;
Je ne suis pas le Styx pour t'embrasser neuf fois . . .

The passive woman appears to have become too active, the cold woman too warm. She is 'unsatisfied' and turns her eyes towards the poet who at once recoils. The third line seems to contain a veiled statistical reference as though he were telling her, somewhat plaintively, that he is not capable of the feats of which Stendhal boasted.

Hélas! et je ne puis, Mégère libertine,
Pour briser ton courage et te mettre aux abois,
Dans l'enfer de ton lit devenir Proserpine!

The general sense of the lines is clear. The poet is attracted by his mistress's Lesbianism and wishes that he were a woman so that he could have relations with her. The wish is impossible. That is precisely its attraction. It enables the poet to dream of a strange satisfaction which can never be realized. The sense of the words 'briser ton courage' and 'te mettre aux abois' is less clear. I think that they mean to exhaust sexually and that the poet is saying: 'It is a pity that I am not a woman. If I were I could bring you to that extreme point of sexual exhaustion to which *men* have failed to bring you because you are a Lesbian, and to which I have failed to bring you partly because you are a Lesbian and partly because of my own inhibitions.'

I think we can conclude that her Lesbianism is at bottom a welcome protection against her 'flamme', against normal relations. He is free to indulge his imagination at a safe distance, and there is as usual no contact between the pair.

Coldness and cruelty are the theme of the seventh poem which describes the conflict between movements calculated to rouse desire and the refusal or inability of the woman to satisfy the desire that she has aroused:

> Avec ses vêtements ondoyants et nacrés,
> Même quand elle marche on croirait qu'elle danse,
> Comme ces longs serpents que les jongleurs sacrés
> Au bout de leurs bâtons agitent en cadence.

> Comme le sable morne et l'azur des déserts,
> Insensibles tous deux à l'humaine souffrance,
> Comme les longs réseaux de la houle des mers,
> Elle se développe avec indifférence.

> Ses yeux polis sont faits de minéraux charmants,
> Et dans cette nature étrange et symbolique
> Où l'ange inviolé se mêle au sphinx antique,

> Où tout n'est qu'or, acier, lumière et diamants,
> Resplendit à jamais, comme un astre inutile,
> La froide majesté de la femme stérile.

The opening of the poem is not merely one of the most famous of Baudelaire's images; the image of the slow lilting movement of women, skirts, and sails is a familiar method of recording the stirring of desire. The beginning of conflict is apparent in the first line. 'Ondoyants' is the word of invitation; 'nacrés', with its suggestion of stiffness, formality, decoration, stands for the resistance of the unyielding or the frigid woman. The movement of the skirt 'dissolves'—the cinematic term has an obvious relevance—into the movement of the snake responding to the snake-charmer's baton. The intention is to prolong the initial movement and to mark the transition from the cold woman to the traditionally cold reptile—its appearance points to the persistent note of sexual antagonism in Baudelaire's poetry of which I spoke in an earlier chapter—while the word 'sacrés' seems to be an allusion to the 'spell' cast by the beloved over the poet. Baudelaire was fascinated by snakes, snake-charmers and jugglers, and he draws on them more than once in the *Fleurs du mal* for his imagery. It cannot be said that they are among his happiest images. It is difficult to discover any compelling psychological reason for his choice of them. I think we must assume that he shared the taste of his age for oriental bric-à-brac and that they are simply a borrowing for the nineteenth-century lumber room.

The second quatrain conforms to a pattern which is familiar in Baudelaire. He proceeds logically in a downward direction from the woman to the reptiles and from the reptiles to inanimate nature. The 'longs réseaux' is a reference back to the 'longs serpents'. 'Se développe' links the movements of the woman, the snakes, and the sea. They are all symbols of 'indifference', but that is not their only common characteristic. The most striking thing about all these movements is their *pointlessness*. The 'pattern' of the dance is as meaningless as the pattern formed by the tide on the shore or the snakes following the baton. The woman rouses desires that she cannot satisfy; the snakes serve only to distract the idle spectator, and the rise and fall of the sea is mindless, mechanical, and unproductive.

The hard, unseeing, glassy eyes of the first tercet amplify the idea of coldness and indifference. The 'minéraux charmants' re-introduces the conflict between invitation and refusal, and the comparison between 'ange inviolé' and 'sphinx antique' repeats the theme of the woman and the reptile. For each in its way is 'étrange' and 'symbolique'. They appear 'inscrutable', but it is only a mask for emptiness. The idea of sterility is already implicit in the 'ange *inviolé*', and the poem seems to gather momentum in the last six lines as it moves towards its brilliantly ironical finale. The inclusion of 'steel'—the hard, base metal—among the gold and the diamonds may be a mocking retort to 'minéraux charmants', but it may also stand for the hard, base streak in the woman while the association of the gold and diamonds with the 'astre inutile' robs them of their value, suggests that in some way they are not genuine.

The poem has a wider reference than some of the other poems in the Cycle. The mechanical courtesan, who is a sister of the 'enchantress' of *Le Beau navire* and the heroine with the 'granite skin' of *Allégorie*, stands not merely for 'the new woman', but for the new civilization. She knows all the tricks for pleasing, is well versed in 'le savant amour', but beneath the brilliant exterior there is nothing. She is a machine for sexual intercourse and nothing more.[1] The climax is achieved by the contrast between 'froide majesté' and 'femme stérile'. The machine suddenly collapses, leaving only a tangled mass of shattered properties and broken springs. The judgment implied is a moral judgment, and by placing 'stérile' at the end of the last line Baudelaire makes us feel that the impact of the whole poem is behind this one word.

I must glance at two other variations on the theme of perversity before drawing some general conclusions. *Le Vampire* describes the attraction-and-repulsion which exists between the poet and his mistress. He derives a certain satisfaction from being treated badly and cannot break away from her. She is addressed as:

> —Infâme à qui je suis lié
> Comme le forçat à la chaîne.

In 'Une nuit que j'étais près d'une affreuse Juive' the poet, spurned by his mistress, consoles or rather tortures himself with the hideous Louchette and intensifies the horror by imagining that the beloved—M. Sartre thinks that she is 'the sexual incarnation of the Judge'—is watching the degrading performance.[2]

The common factor in all these poems is the obstacle—the unnatural obstacle—between the man and the woman. It lies in a double refusal. The woman withholds herself. The man clings to her because she does withhold herself and because his only satisfaction lies in the titillation of the senses followed by an ultimate refusal. This provokes his ingrained sexual antagonism, and his emotions are transformed into the negative and destructive emotions which find expression in other poems.

In *Une Charogne*, which has been compared to a medieval *memento mori*, the poet takes a grim delight in reminding his mistress of her mortality. His triumph, however, is short-lived, and in *De Profundis clamavi* it is he who is crying to her 'out of the depths' for mercy. *Remords posthume*, which follows 'Une nuit que j'étais près d'une affreuse Juive', is another reminder of

[1] Cf. *Machine* aveugle et sourde, en cruautés féconde!

[2] *Op. cit.*, p. 141. (I have analysed this poem in some detail on pp. 263–5 below.)

her mortality and he reflects with satisfaction on the time when she will sleep, a prisoner,

> Au fond d'un monument construit en marbre noir.

Duellum belongs to the period of 'rupture' and describes a battle royal between them. It is followed by *Le Balcon* which marks a temporary reconciliation and in which he tries to recapture the mood of the 'lune de miel'. The attempt is only partly successful —there is something half-hearted about it—and the change from the nocturnal landscape to the warm evening and the sunset is significant. The season is not mentioned, but the reference to

> Les soirs illuminés par l'ardeur du charbon

suggests that it is autumn. It is, indeed, a poem of the 'arrière-saison' and describes the reconciliation which precedes the final rupture. The four short poems grouped under the title of *Un Fantôme* were written after the illness which destroyed Jeanne's beauty, and they illustrate the way in which the poet's experience was modified between the publication of the first and second editions. This is a retrospective glance at the phase of 'décristallisation'. The poet has fallen out of love and tries to console himself with memories of the beauty of his mistress. He makes effective use of images drawn from painting and perfumes. The images borrowed from painting in particular underline the close connection which existed in his imagination between woman and art. One of the most arresting of these images occurs in the first poem of the sequence:

> Je suis comme un peintre qu'un Dieu moqueur
> Condamne à peindre, hélas! sur les ténèbres . . .

The themes of art, love, and memory are welded into a whole in the final poem of the sequence which he calls 'Le Portrait'. He reflects on the destructiveness of time and sickness which have left him only

> . . . un dessin fort pâle, aux trois crayons,

and he turns to defy Time:

> Noir assassin de la Vie et de l'Art,
> Tu ne tueras jamais dans ma mémoire
> Celle qui fut mon plaisir et ma gloire!

I have spoken of the Cycle as a drama and one of its most striking qualities is its variety of tone. There is the sly, oblique tone of *Les Bijoux*, the rapt adoration of the poems of the honeymoon period or of 'Je t'adore à l'égal' which switches to a tone of savage, proletarian invective in:

> Tu mettrais l'univers entier dans ta ruelle,
> Femme impure!

He reverts to the tone of adoration—a somewhat equivocal adoration—in *Sed non satiata*, but in *Une Charogne* he dwells with sardonic glee on the impending dissolution of his mistress. *De profundis clamavi* seems to contain an ironical reference to the liturgy, but the note of supplication is genuine and painful:

> J'implore ta pitié, Toi, l'unique que j'aime,
> Du fond du gouffre obscur où mon cœur est tombé.

Duellum closes on a note of violent hatred which dissolves in the soft caressing tone of *Le Balcon*:

> Mère des souvenirs, maîtresse des maîtresses,
> O toi, tous mes plaisirs! ô toi, tous mes devoirs!
> Tu te rappelleras la beauté des caresses,
> La douceur du foyer et le charme des soirs . . .

Le Possédé ends on a note of bravado:

> Sois ce que tu voudras, nuit noire, rouge aurore;
> Il n'est pas une fibre en tout mon cœur tremblant
> Qui ne crie: *O mon cher Belzébuth, je t'adore!*[1]

Un Fantôme sounds a fresh note. The sequence is written with a gravity and sorrow which distinguish it from any of the other poems of the cycle and which are strangely impressive:

> Charme profond, magique, dont nous grise
> Dans le présent le passé restauré!
> Ainsi l'amant sur un corps adoré
> Du souvenir cueille la fleur exquise.

[1] A letter written to Poulet-Malassis on 11 November 1858 contains an amused comment on an attempt by Baudelaire's publisher to interpret the poem in what today would be called Freudian terms:
'Il est possible, après tout, que la tournure subtile de votre esprit vous ait fait prendre Belzébuth pour le c . . . et le poignard charmant pour la p . . . Quand j'ai fait cette découverte, j'ai bien ri' (*Corr. gén.*, 2, p. 234).

The last poem of the cycle beginning

> Je te donne ces vers afin que si mon nom
> Aborde heureusement aux époques lointaines . . .

is written in a reflective mood and corresponds to the 'Envoi' of traditional love poetry in which the Poet expresses the hope that he has made the Lady immortal or congratulates himself on having done so, but even here Baudelaire contrives to give his farewell a fresh accent by describing her as

> Être maudit à qui, de l'abîme profond
> Jusqu'au plus haut du ciel, rien, hors moi, ne répond!

The Cycle of Madame Sabatier

The Cycle of Jeanne Duval is 'Spleen et Idéal' translated into erotic terms, and it provides an excellent illustration of the way in which the movement of the book is reflected in its separate parts. In the next two cycles Baudelaire tried, for reasons which have been mentioned, to separate *spleen* and *Idéal*. He did not succeed completely in eliminating conflict from them, but in the second cycle we watch him moving in the direction of the *Idéal* and in the third we see him slipping back into *spleen* with an occasional wistful glance over his shoulder at 'better things'.

The second cycle does not possess the force or the variety of the first and we do not see Mme Sabatier with the same clarity as Jeanne Duval. She is felt as a beneficent presence and the accent falls on what, for want of a better word, must be called the 'spiritual' qualities of the beloved. Jeanne is a 'bête implacable et cruelle', a 'vil animal', an 'amazone inhumaine', a 'démon sans pitié': Mme Sabatier an 'ange plein de gaieté', an 'ange plein de bonté', an 'ange plein de santé', an 'ange plein de beauté', and, finally, an 'ange plein de bonheur'. Jeanne's eyes are 'deux bijoux froids' or 'tes froides prunelles'; Mme Sabatier's 'yeux pleins de lumières'. The setting undergoes a similar transformation. The sultry atmosphere charged with passion and hatred clears and gives way to a more temperate atmosphere where there is 'laughter', 'gaiety', 'joy', 'happiness'. Night changes to day, darkness to light. Instead of the 'soleil monotone', 'soleil . . .

couvert d'un crêpe', 'soleil de glace', there is 'l'immortel soleil'
shining in a 'clear sky' with a 'fresh wind'. The sickening descent
into the 'gulf' is replaced by an upward movement:

> Que ce soit dans la nuit et dans la solitude,
> Que ce soit dans la rue et dans la multitude,
> Son fantôme dans l'air danse comme un flambeau.
>
> .   .   .
>
> Sur les débris fumeux des stupides orgies
> Ton souvenir plus clair, plus rose, plus charmant,
> A mes yeux agrandis voltige incessamment.

Only two changes were made in the second edition. *A Celle
qui est trop gaie* was omitted and *Semper eadem*—a significant title
—was added. It closes with the lines:

> Laissez, laissez mon cœur s'enivrer d'un *mensonge*,
> Plonger dans vos beaux yeux comme dans un beau songe,
> Et sommeiller longtemps à l'ombre de vos cils!

It is commonly assumed that Baudelaire underlined the word
'mensonge' in order to emphasize the disillusion which followed
the 'fiasco' of August 1857, and that the poem was placed at the
beginning of the cycle to show that it was a game of make-believe
which could no longer be taken altogether seriously. This was no
doubt his intention, but the view that he never entirely believed
in the role that he assigned to Mme Sabatier is strongly supported
by the internal evidence of the poems. He clearly found it a
considerable effort to keep the woman on the pedestal that he
had erected for her. Poems of 'uplift' and disillusionment alternate. *Le Flambeau vivant* is followed by *A Celle qui est trop gaie*,
Réversibilité by *Confession* where the 'ange plein de gaieté' is
transformed into the fashionable courtesan complaining about her
'dur métier' and the perpetual need to wear 'un sourire machinal'.
It is impossible not to feel that too much importance has been
attached to the famous lines:

> Me sauvant de tout piège et de tout péché grave,
> Ils conduisent mes pas dans la route du Beau.
>
> Rien ne vaut la douceur de son autorité.
>
> Je suis l'Ange gardien, la Muse et la Madone.

The lines stick out like pious texts hung on the wall, spurring the poet on to fresh efforts, reminding him constantly of the rewards of virtue and the penalties of sin. It can scarcely be pretended that they are impressive as poetry and this criticism applies to the cycle as a whole. The strain is apparent in the mechanical repetition of the words 'gaieté', 'santé', 'bonté', 'Ange', and 'fantôme', and in the images of light. The three most interesting poems are *Harmonie du soir*, where the woman is not seen at all, *A Celle qui est trop gaie* and *Le Flacon*, where the poet surrenders to his characteristic impulses.

François Porché has suggested that *A Celle qui est trop gaie* was indeed written in a moment of exasperation with her gaiety.[1] This view fails to take account of Feuillerat's theory that the poem was really written against Marie Daubrun, but it does not entirely invalidate it. I have suggested the reasons which may have prompted him to send it with his first letter to Mme Sabatier but he may well have included it in her cycle for very different reasons. In the first edition the cycles begin on a quiet note, rise to a crescendo, and close on a note of melancholy or resignation. The poems of exceptional violence are nearly always placed in the middle, and in the first edition *A Celle qui est trop gaie* was in fact the fourth poem of the cycle. It describes an imaginary assault on a woman as *Une Martyre* describes the imaginary murder and violation of a woman who was probably Jeanne Duval. In doing so it reflects those destructive impulses which were always lurking just beneath the surface of the poet's personality, which are liable to break out at any moment in man and which are often directed against his mistress for the time being. The poem opens in a tone of gentle badinage:

> Ta tête, ton geste, ton air
> Sont beaux comme un beau paysage;
> Le rire joue en ton visage
> Comme un vent frais dans un ciel clair ...
>
> Les retentissantes couleurs
> Dont tu parsèmes tes toilettes

[1] *Baudelaire et la Présidente*, Geneva, 1941, p. 209.

I

> Jettent dans l'esprit des poëtes
> L'image d'un ballet de fleurs.
>
> Ces robes folles sont l'emblème
> De ton esprit bariolé;
> Folle dont je suis affolé,
> Je te hais autant que je t'aime!

The image of 'un ballet de fleurs' suggests gay, light-hearted movement which is reflected in the gay, irresponsible movement of feeling. The 'robes folles' suggests that she is 'folle' and he 'affolé'. Then there is a startling change. The 'folie' is not good-natured, but dangerous:

> Je te hais autant que je t'aime!

The 'beau paysage' to which he compared her in the first verse reminds him of incidents in 'un beau jardin':

> Quelquefois dans un beau jardin
> Où je traînais mon atonie,
> J'ai senti, comme une ironie,
> Le soleil déchirer mon sein;
>
> Et le printemps et la verdure
> Ont tant humilié mon cœur,
> Que j'ai puni sur une fleur
> L'insolence de la Nature.

It will be seen that the destructive impulses are provoked by the very beauty of nature which is a taunt and a challenge to the poet, and that he slashes down the flower simply in order to destroy the peaceful landscape. He has moved from the 'beau paysage' represented by the woman to 'un beau jardin'. Now he moves back to the woman, wishing that he could repeat the outrage against the flower on her person, and the poem ends with a sadistic orgy:

> Ainsi je voudrais, une nuit,
> Quand l'heure des voluptés sonne,
> Vers les trésors de ta personne,
> Comme un lâche, ramper sans bruit,

Pour châtier ta chair joyeuse,
Pour meurtrir ton sein pardonné,
Et faire à ton flanc étonné
Une blessure large et creuse,

Et, vertigineuse douceur!
A travers ces lèvres nouvelles,
Plus éclatantes et plus belles,
T'infuser mon venin, ma sœur!

The poem strengthens the view that puritanism is, at any rate in some cases, a sign of overcompensation. There was certainly a genuine element of puritanism in Baudelaire's make-up, but the desire for pleasure—sexual pleasure—was equally strong. This not only makes the tension real and not simply formal; it shows that when a violent desire for pleasure becomes inhibited, it is inclined to seek an outlet in strange ways. We may not care for the sentiments expressed in the poem, but we can scarcely deny their power or the skill with which they are expressed. Once the word 'folle' has been mentioned, the poet falls under the sway of impulses that he is totally unable to control, and the poem which opened with a peaceful landscape ends with a gaping wound infected by his own disease.

Harmonie du soir is not a masterpiece, but it is a successful exercise in Baudelaire's Symbolist manner which deserves examining:

Voici venir les temps où vibrant sur sa tige
Chaque fleur s'évapore ainsi qu'un encensoir;
Les sons et les parfums tournent dans l'air du soir;
Valse mélancolique et langoureux vertige!

Chaque fleur s'évapore ainsi qu'un encensoir;
Le violon frémit comme un cœur qu'on afflige;
Valse mélancolique et langoureux vertige!
Le ciel est triste et beau comme un grand reposoir.

Le violon frémit comme un cœur qu'on afflige,
Un cœur tendre, qui hait le néant vaste et noir!
Le ciel est triste et beau comme un grand reposoir.
Le soleil s'est noyé dans son sang qui se fige.

Un cœur tendre, qui hait le néant vaste et noir,
Du passé lumineux recueille tout vestige!
Le soleil s'est noyé dans son sang qui se fige . . .
Ton souvenir en moi luit comme un ostensoir!

The drooping flowers might well have come from the strange enchanted gardens of the Symbolists. The poetical conceit comparing them to the wisp of smoke rising from a censer clearly looks forward to the movement of 1886, and the plaintive sounds of the violin will be heard again in Verlaine's *Chanson d'automne*. Although we do not see the woman, we are conscious of her presence in a line like

Les sons et les parfums tournent dans l'air du soir.

For in this poem Baudelaire seems to be giving a practical demonstration of the principle that Mallarmé was to enunciate in a letter written in 1864: 'Peindre, non la chose, mais l'effet qu'elle produit.' Sounds and perfumes merge into the movement of a dance, feelings into the sound of a violin, the sky into the image of an altar of repose. The words are immensely suggestive and their suggestiveness is heightened by the unusual refrains which bind perfumes, sounds, and colours until we have a unified impression of an impalpable presence which crystallizes in the final image:

Ton souvenir en moi luit comme un ostensoir!

If the style seems unlike Baudelaire's usual manner—it has none of its tautness and 'bite'—there is no doubt about the central experience. The poet is in an enclosed garden where everything suggests the woman's presence, but when he glances over the drooping flowers to see what lies beyond, he finds himself looking down into the abyss, into 'le néant vaste et noir'. His sudden sense of the void corresponds to the experience of the woman in *Confession* when she complains of the 'dur métier d'être belle femme' and expresses the realization:

Que bâtir sur les cœurs est une chose sotte;
Que tout craque, amour et beauté,
Jusqu'à ce que l'Oubli les jette dans sa hotte
Pour les rendre à l'Éternité.

Le Flacon is his 'Envoi' and performs the same function as the

BAUDELAIRE

A photograph by Nadar

final poem of the Cycle of Jeanne Duval. He uses the expanded image in the manner of *L'Albatros*, but in spite of its preciosity and its unevenness the poem is a much more elaborate and characteristic example of his mature style. The only difficulty lies in the interpretation of the complicated central image. The bottle stands not for the poet, but for his work. The perfume contained in the bottle is the love which is the subject of his poetry. He imagines someone coming across the bottle, which is also the 'tomb' of his love, in an oriental box or at the bottom of a wardrobe long after the deaths of the lovers, uncorking it, and releasing the exceptionally sharp perfume.

The opening is an admirable illustration not only of the care with which Baudelaire constructed his poems, but of his classical method of exposition:

> Il est de forts parfums pour qui toute matière
> Est poreuse. On dirait qu'ils pénètrent le verre.
> En ouvrant un coffret venu de l'Orient
> Dont la serrure grince et rechigne en criant,
>
> Ou dans une maison déserte quelque armoire
> Pleine de l'âcre odeur des temps, poudreuse et noire,
> Parfois on trouve un vieux flacon qui se souvient,
> D'où jaillit toute vive une âme qui revient.

The poet begins with a general proposition about the power of certain perfumes to penetrate solid bodies, and the first two lines —'rasant la prose'—demonstrate the flexibility of his verse. He goes on to illustrate his general proposition by a concrete example. What is remarkable about the poem is that the main theme is not simply described, but enacted. The penetration of solid bodies by perfumes is reflected in the alternation of the dense -*o* and -*ou* sounds and the thin i's and sharp nasals. Already in the peculiar felicity of 'grince' and 'rechigne' we hear the box opening or the door of the wardrobe creaking, and we have a vivid sensation of choking in the thick dusty atmosphere in

> Pleine de l'âcre odeur des temps, poudreuse et noire,

with its harsh, grating r's and the open and closed vowel sounds. But in the next two lines we feel the i's and the nasals cutting through the dense atmosphere and the 'âme' stirring, trying to force its way to the surface. This impression grows in the third verse :

> Mille pensers dormaient, chrysalides funèbres,
> Frémissant doucement dans les lourdes ténèbres,
> Qui dégagent leur aile et prennent leur essor,
> Teintés d'azur, glacés de rose, lamés d'or.

The perfume has not yet been identified with love, but the 'mille pensers' points the way to it. The unexpected conjunction of 'chrysalides funèbres'—the unborn and the dead—which looks forward to the funeral imagery of the fifth verse, prepares us for the feeling of life stirring again in 'frémissant' and struggling against the 'lourdes ténèbres'. In the next line the 'thoughts' break free and sail upwards into the air, and we find ourselves watching them trembling, blue, pink, and gold, in the clear atmosphere.

The fourth verse is marred by the unfortunate image of Vertigo grasping and pushing the soul with both hands, but it is a striking example of Baudelaire's power of presenting sensation at the moment it comes into being:

> Voilà le souvenir enivrant qui voltige
> Dans l'air troublé; les yeux se ferment; le Vertige
> Saisit l'âme vaincue et la pousse à deux mains
> Vers un gouffre obscurci de miasmes humains.

The sharp i's, the blunt v's, and the abrupt statement—'les yeux se ferment'—register the intense physical impact of the perfume which makes the person opening the bottle blink and catch his breath. The strength of the perfume produces a feeling of giddiness, and the thick heavy consonants in the last two lines reflect its compulsive force driving him to the verge of the gulf. When we look at the next verse:

> Il la terrasse au bord d'un gouffre séculaire,
> Où, Lazare odorant déchirant son suaire,
> Se meut dans son réveil le cadavre spectral
> D'un vieil amour ranci, charmant et sépulcral,

we see that the whole poem is built out of the double image of perfume and tomb. The perfume is entombed in an old bottle which in turn is entombed in an oriental box or a wardrobe. Its potency drives the person who opens the bottle to the edge of the 'tomb' from which it has escaped. The description of Lazarus rising from the dead is a reference back to the 'coffret venu de l'Orient'. The word 'odorant' is intentionally ambiguous. It stands for the perfumes used in eastern burial rites and for the smell of the corpse, looking forward to 'un vieil amour ranci, charmant et sépulcral' in the fourth line, and the 'aimable pestilence' in the final verse. Lazarus was raised from the dead by love, but here he is associated with a different kind of love—a poisonous love—which in rising from the dead drags the living down into the tomb where it was buried:

> Ainsi, quand je serai perdu dans la mémoire
> Des hommes, dans le coin d'une sinistre armoire
> Quand on m'aura jeté, vieux flacon désolé,
> Décrépit, poudreux, sale, abject, visqueux, fêlé,
>
> Je serai ton cercueil, aimable pestilence!
> Le témoin de ta force et de ta virulence,
> Cher poison préparé par les anges! Liqueur
> Qui me ronge, ô la vie et la mort de mon cœur!

The construction of the last two verses has caused some perplexity among Baudelaire's editors. The sixth verse does not present any particular difficulty. After developing his image of the perfume of a dead love poisoning the living, the poet returns to himself with 'Ainsi'; but, as I have said, the bottle is not so much the poet as the poet's work, the battered, dusty, greasy volume:

> Décrépit, poudreux, sale, abject, visqueux, fêlé.

The 'aimable pestilence', which has misled some editors, evidently refers back to the 'vieil amour ranci'. It can only be understood when we recognize that the volume of poems is the 'coffin' or 'tomb' of a love which has retained all its old power and virulence.

Technically, the close of the poem is as effective as the opening. The poet skilfully gathers all the threads together. He restates the theme of the perfume entombed in the bottle which is buried in an old wardrobe where it has been carelessly cast aside. The images of death and burial are repeated in 'cercueil', and the potency of the perfume in 'pestilence' and 'virulence'. The movement of putting things into cupboards and boxes, taking them out again, driving people into dark 'gulfs' and 'tombs', is also repeated. It will be seen that all Baudelaire's closest interests are represented in the poem, particularly his preoccupation with death, with intoxicants, and his ambivalent attitude towards love. For love is at once the source of life and death; a 'poison' but a 'cher poison préparé par les anges'; a 'liqueur' but a 'liqueur qui me ronge' and 'la vie et la mort de mon cœur!'

The Cycle of Marie Daubrun

We have seen that the Cycle of Jeanne Duval is a full-length study of a liaison lasting many years. The Cycle of Mme Sabatier is on a much smaller scale. It is no more than an interlude, and in spite of discordant notes concentrates almost exclusively on a single attitude. The Cycle of Marie Daubrun introduces a varia-tion into the pattern. It cannot be summed up, as we shall see, under the rubric of *tendresse*. It is more varied than the Cycle of Mme Sabatier because it reflects the vicissitudes of an 'affair'. A word must be said here about the chronology of the *Fleurs du mal*. Although Baudelaire was probably on intimate terms with Marie Daubrun before Mme Sabatier, they both belong to the same period of his life and some of the poems written to them may have been composed at the same time. It follows that by publishing the poems in separate groups instead of in the order in which they were written, Baudelaire modified the nature of his relationship with both women in the interests of his book. Instead of describing a succession of *moods* which alternate between 'sacred' and 'profane' love, he has deliberately divided his experience into separate *periods*. Although Jeanne Duval's cycle is dominated by a shuddering downward movement towards *spleen*, Mme Sabatier's by a faltering upward movement towards the *Idéal*, and Marie Daubrun's by the downward movement back to *spleen*, there are pronounced differences between the cycles of Jeanne Duval and Marie Daubrun. 'Le cycle de la femme aux yeux verts,' wrote Benedetto, 'ne marque pas seulement un retour aux plaisirs sensuels, mais aussi un art plus savant de la sensualité. . . . Combien la volupté est devenue plus compliquée, et plus froide, plus calme à la fois.'[1] Baudelaire speaks of her in one poem as 'Amante ou sœur', and in another as 'Mon enfant, ma sœur'. It is one of the signs of the refinement and complexity of the poet's attitude that she plays both parts—plays them in the same poem—is sometimes the 'sister-figure' who represents normality, and sometimes the sophisticated mistress who brings out the perverse impulses in the poet to almost the same extent as Jeanne Duval. I will anticipate a little by saying that the different moods of 'Spleen et Idéal' correspond to the different seasons—spring, summer, autumn, and winter—of man's life, and that the wintry autumn of this cycle is closely connected with its extreme refinement.

The Cycle of Marie Daubrun originally consisted of seven poems, but two poems were added to it in the second edition which reveal the changes that took place in the relationship between 1857 and 1861. *Chant d'automne* seems to mark the *rapprochement* which occurred in the autumn of 1859 and *A une Madone* the final rupture when Marie Daubrun abandoned Baudelaire at the end of the same year and went to live with Banville at Nice.

The theme of *Le Poison*, the first poem of the cycle, recalls that of *Le Flacon*. Love is compared to opium and wine as an antidote to *ennui*, but though it is superior to both it is nevertheless a 'poison'. The growing refinement of Baudelaire's conception of love and the way in which positive emotions are haunted by their opposites is apparent in the last verse:

> Tout cela ne vaut pas le terrible prodige
> De ta salive qui mord,
> Qui plonge dans l'oubli mon âme sans remord,
> Et, charriant le vertige,
> La roule défaillante aux rives de la mort![2]

[1] *Art. cit.*, p. 55.
[2] It will be seen that resemblances between *Le Poison* and *Le Flacon* are not confined to their themes, but extend to the image of 'le vertige' attacking the soul.

The refinement, which takes the form of an obstinate determination to be hurt, a desire for destruction, is still more evident in the final verse of *Ciel brouillé*:

> O femme dangereuse, ô séduisants climats!
> Adorerai-je aussi ta neige et vos frimas,
> Et saurai-je tirer de l'implacable hiver
> Des plaisirs plus aigus que la glace et le fer?

This poem introduces the autumn landscape which dominates the cycle, but it is very different from the mellow autumn of poems like *Parfum exotique* and *Le Balcon*. *Ciel brouillé* is the work of a man who feels that his emotional life has entered on a period of decline, that his senses have become blunted and are no longer capable of reacting to normal stimulation. He therefore wonders hopefully whether a hard, cold, calculating sensuality will provide the necessary stimulus. The sensation is so vividly apprehended in the fourth line, the opposition between 'plaisir' and 'la glace et le fer', with their suggestion of coldness and brittleness, so violent and the impact of 'aigus' so intense, that it is almost impossible to read the line without wincing.

There is a certain irony in the reference to winter. It appears to look forward to the winter landscape of the Cycle of Spleen, but it does so unconsciously. For his mistress will have abandoned him before he can taste the 'plaisirs plus aigus que la glace et le fer'.

Comparisons between women and landscapes or the seasons belong to traditional poetry. Baudelaire uses them extensively, but with considerable originality. The identification of the woman and the landscape is much closer than in the poetry of the past. It is an understatement to say that the woman melts into the landscape or even that the poet and the woman are figures in the landscape. They are rather part of an emotional situation of which the landscape becomes the 'symbol' in the fullest sense of that term. *Harmonie du soir* is in a sense the extreme example. Identification is so complete that the garden *is* the woman's presence which encloses the poet. The process, however, is similar in the lovely *Invitation au voyage*:

Mon enfant, ma sœur,
Songe à la douceur
D'aller là-bas vivre ensemble!
Aimer à loisir,
Aimer et mourir
Au pays quite ressemble!
Les soleils mouillés
De ces ciels brouillés
Pour mon esprit ont les charmes
Si mystérieux
De tes traîtres yeux,
Brillant à travers leurs larmes.

Là, tout n'est qu'ordre et beauté,
Luxe, calme et volupté.

Des meubles luisants,
Polis par les ans,
Décoreraient notre chambre;
Les plus rares fleurs
Mêlant leurs odeurs
Aux vagues senteurs de l'ambre,
Les riches plafonds,
Les miroirs profonds,
La splendeur orientale,
Tout y parlerait
A l'âme en secret
Sa douce langue natale.

Identification begins in the comparison between the woman's eyes and the autumn skies with their gentle melancholy and their veiled elusive colours. The second verse is a vision of order, security, tranquillity. The 'meubles luisants, polis par les ans' appear to stand for emotional and material stability, 'notre chambre' for the unity of the lovers, the 'plus rares fleurs' for the uniqueness and mysteriousness of their love. The 'splendeur orientale' introduces an exotic note, but there is not the slightest hint of perversity in this poem. On the contrary, words like 'sœur', 'natale', 'ordre', and 'calme' stress the normality of the lovers' feelings for one another. The scene is Holland and the 'miroirs profonds' were probably suggested by the mirrors which in Dutch painting seem to give the pictures another dimension. For the external physical changes of the first verse have become internal emotional changes, and the mirrors symbolize the gradual deepening of their love. The richness and maturity of the experience described here corresponds to the richness and maturity of *La Chevelure*, but devotion has taken the place of passion.

L'Invitation au voyage explains the emphasis that certain French critics place on *tendresse*, but the moment we look at it in relation to the other poems of the cycle we see how one-sided their emphasis is. The poems of the Cycle of Jeanne Duval alternate between passion and hatred, the poems of this cycle between a cold, brittle sensuality and a warm, calm tenderness, bringing home to us again the difference between the youthful love of the first cycle and the middle-aged love of the third. *Ciel brouillé* is followed by *Le Chat*, a slight, genial poem in which the mistress is compared to a cat who is 'l'esprit familier du lieu' and in which words like 'tendre' and 'discret' predominate. There is nothing sisterly or tender or discreet about *Le Beau navire*—a poem to which I shall return presently—and *L'Invitation au voyage* is followed by *L'Irréparable* which sounds a grimmer note than any of the preceding poems. It shows that love and tenderness are failing as an antidote, and when he writes of *ennui* as

> ce vieil ennemi,
> Destructeur et gourmand comme la courtisane,

the distinction between love as he knows it and *ennui* disappears, and they both become agents of destruction. The word 'irréparable' is a word of doom and it is followed by those other words of doom—'remords' and 'irrémissible' which echo and throb throughout the poem:

> Pouvons-nous étouffer le vieux, le long Remords . . .
> Pouvons-nous étouffer l'implacable Remords? . . .
> L'Espérance qui brille aux carreaux de l'Auberge
>   Est soufflée, est morte à jamais! . . .
> L'Irréparable ronge avec sa dent maudite!

The answer is reflected in the heavy, relentless thud of the verse and the emphasis on darkness and extinction. Nor should we overlook the force of 'ronge'. In Baudelaire destruction is seldom violent. It is stealthy, undermining and rotting away the very fibres of being until we suddenly find ourselves gazing into an abyss. The poem closes with some famous and beautiful lines that I cannot forbear to quote:

> —J'ai vu parfois, au fond d'un théâtre banal
> Qu'enflammait l'orchestre sonore,
> Une fée allumer dans un ciel infernal
> Une miraculeuse aurore;
> J'ai vu parfois au fond d'un théâtre banal
>
> Un être, qui n'était que lumière, or et gaze,
> Terrasser l'énorme Satan;
> Mais mon cœur, que jamais ne visite l'extase,
> Est un théâtre où l'on attend
> Toujours, toujours en vain, l'Être aux ailes de gaze!

It is evidently a nostalgic memory both of childhood and his first meeting with Marie Daubrun, and the switch from present horror to the past is characteristic of the finest poems of the cycle. We must admit that the poet's sense of the beauty and squalor of life—the city with its flickering *becs de gaz*, the small theatres with their flaming gas jets, their smell of sawdust and resin, and their tawdry trappings—has never been better expressed. Baudelaire uses the words 'banal', 'fané', and 'suranné' in a highly personal sense. In the 'théâtre banal' of this poem and the 'Eldorado banal' of *Un Voyage à Cythère*, the hopes raised by 'théâtre' and 'Eldorado' are crushed by the finality of 'banal', and the poet is left waiting for the miraculous dawn that he knows will never come.

The autumn landscape reappears in *Causerie*, where Marie Daubrun is compared to 'un beau ciel d'automne, clair et rose', and at a much more impressive level in the magnificent *Chant d'automne* where the poet makes admirable use of the heavy polysyllabic words, which are often derivations from the Latin, in order to convey the peculiar hopelessness and monotony of a *fin de saison* which foreshadows the end of himself and his hopes:

Bientôt nous plongerons dans les froides ténèbres;
Adieu, vive clarté de nos étés trop courts!
J'entends déjà tomber avec des chocs funèbres
Le bois retentissant sur le pavé des cours.

Tout l'hiver va rentrer dans mon être: colère,
Haine, frissons, horreur, labeur dur et forcé,
Et, comme le soleil dans son enfer polaire,
Mon cœur ne sera plus qu'un bloc rouge et glacé.

J'écoute en frémissant chaque bûche qui tombe;
L'échafaud qu'on bâtit n'a pas d'écho plus sourd.
Mon esprit est pareil à la tour qui succombe
Sous les coups du bélier infatigable et lourd.

The falling logs are the heralds of winter, and in the second
verse the poet looks beyond the present, almost imagining for a
moment that winter has come. This verse reveals very clearly the
way in which he identifies his mood with the seasons and the
process by which he becomes part of the winter landscape. The
first line describes the inward movement of the winter cold penetrating into him. The five substantives apply partly to man and
partly to nature. 'Colère' can be used literally of man and metaphorically of nature. The winter produces physical 'shivers' and
turns work into a 'labeur dur et forcé'. 'Horreur' and 'haine'
are subjective reactions to winter. In the last line the identification or transition is complete. Baudelaire uses the image of the
'sun' and the 'heart' in another place. The sun is the source of
heat which warms the world, the heart of emotion which should
warm life. But in winter the sun and the heart lose their natural
warmth. The 'bloc rouge et glacé' is the concrete embodiment of
the inhibited modern man whose emotions have withered.

The second part of the poem is a typical backward glance, but
this time he confesses that love has failed, and the memory of
summer adds poignancy to the falling autumn logs:

J'aime de vos longs yeux la lumière verdâtre,
Douce beauté, mais tout aujourd'hui m'est amer,
Et rien, ni votre amour, ni le boudoir, ni l'âtre,
Ne me vaut le soleil rayonnant sur la mer . . .

> Courte tâche! La tombe attend; elle est avide!
> Ah! laissez-moi, mon front posé sur vos genoux,
> Goûter, en regrettant l'été blanc et torride,
> De l'arrière-saison le rayon jaune et doux!

There are moments in reading Baudelaire when we suddenly become conscious that we are listening to the voice not of an individual, but of civilization. So it is in

> . . . rien, ni votre amour, ni le boudoir, ni l'âtre,
> Ne me vaut le soleil rayonnant sur la mer,

or in

> De l'arrière-saison le rayon jaune et doux!

For this is the voice of a man who seems to be weighed down by centuries of experience, who seems indeed to have traversed the whole range of human experience and to feel at the end of it only an immense lassitude. It is because the voice speaks for what Paul Bourget called 'une civilisation vieillissante' that Baudelaire's 'De l'arrière-saison le rayon jaune et doux' has a wider reference than Macbeth's 'the sear, the yellow leaf'.[1]

Le Beau navire is a remarkable poem which gives striking expression to the peculiarly refined sensuality of this cycle:

> Je veux te raconter, ô molle enchanteresse!
> Les diverses beautés qui parent ta jeunesse;
> Je veux te peindre ta beauté,
> Où l'enfance s'allie à la maturité.

Baudelaire's sensuous, flexible rhythms have a way of weaving themselves into our consciousness and by their power of incantation imposing the pattern of the poem. In *Le Beau navire* he adopts the tone of whispered confidence which he used with great effect and which gives his poetry its sense of intimacy. The focal word in the first verse is 'diverses'. The poem is a catalogue of the woman's varied charms and their very potent effect on the poet. In Baudelaire words are seldom purely descriptive; they nearly always have a moral connotation. 'Molle enchanteresse' is

---

[1] *Essais de psychologie contemporaine*, I, Ed. définitive, Paris, 1926, p. 19.

an example. 'Molle' illustrates his sensitiveness to tactile sensations. We feel the hand stretching out to caress the woman, but
it does so half-fearfully, hesitates, and withdraws as though
ashamed or expecting a rebuff. The conflict runs all through the
poem. 'Molle' describes the texture of the woman's skin, but it
also suggests the weakness of the man already half-yielding to
temptation. The characteristics of the Baudelairean woman begin
to emerge in the fourth line—the mixture of innocence and
experience, the person who is mentally a child but physically
mature, the animal beneath the sophisticated courtesan. In the
next verse he introduces the image of the ship:

> Quand tu vas balayant l'air de ta jupe large,
> Tu fais l'effet d'un beau vaisseau qui prend le large,
>   Chargé de toile, et va roulant
> Suivant un rhythme doux, et paresseux, et lent.

The erotic significance of the skirt in this verse is evident. It
reminds the poet naturally of a sail bellying before the wind, but
the image of the ship is more complex. Ships and the sea, as we
know, are usually symbols of liberation in Baudelaire, but the
balancing movement of ships nearly always has a sexual connotation. It offers him the prospect of escape from the oppressive
desires which crowd in upon him. The complexity lies in the
ambivalent feeling of rising sexual desire and the urge to escape
from its consequences. The intensity of the feeling increases in
the last two lines of the verse where the light airy movement of
the skirt merges into the heavy movement of the ship weighed
down under its sails. The motion of the ship—the 'rhythme doux,
et paresseux, et lent'—is also the slow heavy movement of the
blood which threatens to submerge the poet. The prospect of
escape begins to fade.

> Sur ton cou large et rond, sur tes épaules grasses,
> Ta tête se pavane avec d'étranges grâces;
>   D'un air placide et triomphant
> Tu passes ton chemin, majestueuse enfant.

The key to the third verse and, indeed, to the whole poem,
lies in the words 'se pavane'. They describe the proud turn of

the woman's head as she looks about her, but they also contain an allusion to dancing and we remember

> Même quand elle marche, on croirait qu'elle danse.

For the poem is a pavan—'a stately dance in which the dancers were elaborately dressed'—danced by the mistress, and the décor is carefully built up by the words 'large', 'lent', 'placide', 'triomphant', 'majestueuse', and 'nobles'. The movement of the third verse prolongs and develops that of the second; the roll of the heavily laden ship is transformed into a stately dance with the dancer 'elaborately dressed'.

The fourth verse is a repetition of the first. It is not a mere refrain or a restatement of the main theme. In the last line of the third verse the dancer seems, tantalizingly, about to pass across the stage and out of sight, cheating the poet's desires but also freeing him from the enchantress's toils. The refrain brings her back again, repeating part of the first movement of the dance as a prelude to a fresh movement and at the same time allowing the poet to continue his strange suit.[1] It is introduced after the third, sixth, and ninth verses, marking each time the end of one movement and the beginning of the next. Baudelaire does not use the same refrain; he draws on the first, second, and third verses in turn as this enables him to give greater variety to his poem. The tempo is continually changing: images 'fade' into one another—a skirt into a sail, a sail back into a skirt, breasts into a wardrobe, a wardrobe into shields. The refrain is the signal, too, for a change of angle. The dancer has been shown full-length. The focus suddenly shifts and, cinematograph-like, there follows a series of close-ups of different parts of the body. The dancer, who has been a remote figure, turns and advances towards the watching poet. Her charms at once become more potent:

> Ta gorge qui s'avance et qui pousse la moire,
> Ta gorge triomphante est une belle armoire

---

[1] 'Repetition and refrain are natural to Baudelaire. It is the form which is most suitable to an artist who is obsessed by fixed ideas, a victim of *spleen*, unceasingly preoccupied with himself and lost in dreams' (G. de Reynold, *Charles Baudelaire*, Paris and Geneva, 1920, p. 351).

Dont les panneaux bombés et clairs
Comme les boucliers accrochent des éclairs;

Boucliers provoquants, armés de pointes roses!
Armoire à doux secrets, pleine de bonnes choses,
De vins, de parfums, de liqueurs
Qui feraient délirer les cerveaux et les cœurs!

There is no need to stress the erotic symbolism of these lines. It will be noticed that though Baudelaire is considering different parts of the body, he has the same limited interest in the woman who is here a bedfellow and no more. The 'gorge triomphante' reinforces the 'placide et triomphante' of the third verse. The 'Boucliers provoquants, armés de pointes roses!' underlines once more the poet's conflicting feelings. The 'boucliers' stand for the serried ranks of the 'enemy' bearing irresistibly down on him. The whole force of the poem is behind them because it is a description of an attack on the poet—an attack concentrated on a single weak place in his defences. The curves of a breast swelling beneath the silken dress, suggesting at once the curves of the 'shields' or a 'cupboard', are weapons in the enemy's armoury. The 'boucliers' are 'provoquants' because the poet, conscious of the hopelessness of the struggle—there is a reference back to 'triomphante'—is constantly tempted to capitulate.

The cupboard with its 'good things', its wines and mysterious perfumes, is probably a reminiscence of the child's furtive pleasure in rummaging in his mother's cupboard and is connected with his early adoration of her. In this way it becomes an expression of the nostalgic longing of the grown man to return to a simpler age—there is another reference back to 'Où l'enfance s'allie à la maturité'—to escape from the problems of manhood and from the sense of sin which weighs so heavily on him.

The seventh verse is a repetition of the second and it shows how the sudden switch from the close-up to the long-shot lowers the tension of the poem as each movement comes to an end. In the eighth and ninth verses we proceed a stage further:

Tes nobles jambes, sous les volants qu'elles chassent,
Tourmentent les désirs obscurs et les agacent,

> Comme deux sorcières qui font
> Tourner un philtre noir dans un vase profond.
>
> Tes bras, qui se joueraient des précoces hercules,
> Sont des boas luisants les solides émules,
>   Faits pour serrer obstinément,
> Comme pour l'imprimer dans ton cœur, ton amant.

It is not unusual for Baudelaire to exhaust the feelings which can profitably be extracted from a situation before reaching the end of a poem. Although the intention of these two verses is clear enough, there is a pronounced falling off in their poetic quality. The legs make the skirt belly like sails, like breasts swelling, provocatively, beneath the 'moire'. The sorcerers with their phials are a familiar part of the furniture of the *Fleurs du mal*, but as we have already seen, they have not worn well. The turning of the jar is intended to prolong the movement of the poem, but it weakens instead of strengthening its appeal, diffuses instead of concentrating emotion. The gap between intention and execution in the ninth verse is so palpable that it does not call for detailed comment.

The tenth and last verse is a repetition of the third verse. At the close of the poem we are left watching the woman who is about to pass from the stage. We know that she never will and that she will never satisfy the poet's desires. For the poem is an allegory of the sexual act, but of a sexual act which never takes place or, to use M. Sartre's phrase, a blank sexual act. This explains the sense of frustration that we feel in the repeated descriptions of the uncompleted movements which are the subject of the poem.

The cycle has no 'Envoi' in the accepted sense. *A une Madone*, the last poem, is the expression of a 'rupture consommée' and is used as the vehicle for the mixture of distress and hatred caused by Marie Daubrun's abandonment of the poet. Her Christian name naturally suggested the title and the form of the poem; he takes a delight in emphasizing that she is a 'mortelle Madone'; and the word 'rôle' in line 37 is a reference to her profession and to the curious part that she plays here. Baudelaire called the poem an 'Ex-voto dans le Goût Espagnol', and the sub-title reveals his intention. When he said 'Spanish taste', he meant the Spanish taste of the Baroque seventeenth century. It will be remembered that it was the moment when the man and the age imposed their pattern on religious practice and religious art. The religious emotion of a Bernini or a Crashaw is not pure; it contains a marked erotic element. In choosing a seventeenth-century model Baudelaire deliberately set out to exploit the mingling of religious and erotic elements. He made his model 'Spanish' because he wished to underline the savagery and the ferocity of the emotions expressed. The result is not merely a remarkable poem, but a remarkable *tour de force*. It opens with an arresting image:

> Je veux bâtir pour toi, Madone, ma maîtresse,
> Un autel souterrain au fond de ma détresse,
> Et creuser dans le coin le plus noir de mon cœur,
> Loin du désir mondain et du regard moqueur,
> Une niche, d'azur et d'or tout émaillée,
> Où tu te dresseras, Statue émerveillée.

The poem is at once an invocation and an incantation which creates the object that the poet is invoking. It is written in a mood of religious solemnity, but the tone is highly complex. The 'Je veux' contains a threat and a supplication; the persistent use of the second person singular adds to the general ambiguity of the tone. The mingling of religious and erotic elements is apparent in 'Madone' and 'maîtresse', 'autel' and 'cœur'. The woman is Idol and Mistress, but this time the Idol is a religious idol. The same ambivalence surrounds 'autel' and 'niche'. They belong to the place of prayer where the Madonna is invoked, but it is also the 'dark corner' where the mistress will receive very different treatment. 'Noir' is a reference to the perverse emotions—the mixture of love and hate, awe and contempt—that fill his heart and are contrasted with the fragile blue and gold of the 'mortal Madonna' whom he intends to destroy.

The poem goes on:

> Avec mes Vers polis, treillis d'un pur métal
> Savamment constellé de rimes de cristal,
> Je ferai pour ta tête une énorme Couronne;
> Et dans ma Jalousie, ô mortelle Madone,

> Je saurai te tailler un Manteau de façon,
> Barbare, roide et lourd, et doublé de soupçon,
> Qui, comme une guérite, enfermera tes charmes;
> Non de Perles brodé, mais de toutes mes Larmes!

The poet is not merely constructing an 'Ex-voto'; he is trying to take possession of the mistress. The 'énorme Couronne' and the 'Manteau' are a prison

> Qui, comme une guérite, enfermera tes charmes.

M. Decaunes speaks of an 'opposition constante entre une sorte de violence contenue et la faiblesse d'un enfant désarmé'.[1] The violence is evident in the 'Jalousie', in the rugged r's and t's, and in the choking rage of

> Je saurai te tailler un Manteau, de façon
> Barbare, roide et lourd, et doublé de soupçon . . .

But there is a sense of weakness in the last line of the passage:

> Non de Perles brodé, mais de toutes mes Larmes!

It becomes still more evident in the next fourteen lines:

> Ta Robe, ce sera mon Désir, frémissant,
> Onduleux, mon Désir qui monte et qui descend,
> Aux pointes se balance, aux vallons se repose,
> Et revêt d'un baiser tout ton corps blanc et rose.
> Je te ferai de mon Respect de beaux Souliers
> De satin, par tes pieds divins humiliés,
> Qui, les emprisonnant dans une molle étreinte,
> Comme un moule fidèle en garderont l'empreinte.
> Si je ne puis, malgré tout mon art diligent,
> Pour Marchepied tailler une Lune d'argent,
> Je mettrai le Serpent qui me mord les entrailles
> Sous tes talons, afin que tu foules et railles,
> Reine victorieuse et féconde en rachats,
> Ce monstre tout gonflé de haine et de crachats.

The woman has clearly gained the upper hand. The accent shifts from his 'Jealousy' to his 'Respect', but even his respect is a humiliation for her 'pieds divins'. He still wishes to imprison

[1] *Op. cit.*, p. 72.

her, but she is now to be a prisoner held in a 'molle étreinte'.
He had begun by seeking refuge from the 'regard moqueur'
of the world in the darkest corner of his heart where he could
gloat over his perverse feelings, but the note of exultation
vanishes. He lays the perverse feelings, which are symbolized
by the serpent, at her feet:

> afin que *tu foules et railles*,
> Reine victorieuse et féconde en rachats,
> Ce monstre tout gonflé de haine et de crachats.

'Reine victorieuse' is an explicit admission of her victory over
him. The next eight lines are an act of submission:

> Tu verras mes Pensers, rangés comme les Cierges
> Devant l'autel fleuri de la Reine les Vierges,
> Étoilant de reflets le plafond peint en bleu,
> Te regarder toujours avec des yeux de feu;
> Et comme tout en moi te chérit et t'admire,
> Tout se fera Benjoin, Encens, Oliban, Myrrhe,
> Et sans cesse vers toi, sommet blanc et neigeux,
> En Vapeurs montera mon Esprit orageux.

The poet is on his knees in the double role of the worshipper,
burning metaphorical candles and incense in front of the completed Idol, and the lover secretly 'cherishing' the Mistress. Only
the 'Esprit orageux' prepares us for what is to come:

> Enfin, pour compléter ton rôle de Marie,
> Et pour mêler l'amour avec la barbarie,
> Volupté noire! des sept Péchés capitaux,
> Bourreau plein de remords, je ferai sept Couteaux
> Bien affilés, et, comme un jongleur insensible,
> Prenant le plus profond de ton amour pour cible,
> Je les planterai tous dans ton Cœur pantelant,
> Dans ton Cœur sanglotant, dans ton Cœur ruisselant!

The allusion to the well-known image of the Madonna with
her heart transfixed by seven swords maintains the religious
décor, but it is evident that the poet and the mistress are playing
new parts, and the word 'rôle' acquires a fresh overtone. The
worshipper is transformed into a 'juggler'—in the present con-

text a knife-thrower—and the Mistress into his partner. For what we are witnessing is a music-hall turn which is at the same time the sacrilegious destruction of the image of the Madonna by the worshipper. There is a calculated cruelty in the 'Enfin'. We watch the knife-thrower poising the first of his weapons and taking aim. We know that this knife-thrower is an executioner—'an executioner filled with remorse'—who intends his act to end in tragedy. The poem closes in a breathless sadistic orgy. In the last two lines we hear the speaker half-sobbing, half-choking in the intensity of his emotion, and we hear the knives hissing towards the target:

> Je les planterai tous dans ton Cœur pantelant,
> Dans ton Cœur sanglotant, dans ton Cœur ruisselant!

The pattern of the poem is familiar. It begins and ends with the image of the 'heart' or, more accurately, it starts with one heart and finishes with two—the hearts of the poet and his mistress. The irony of the close is not confined to the image of the Madonna. There is an allusion to another and much more plebeian emblem of love—an emblem that would certainly appeal to a music hall audience—the two hearts transfixed by Cupid's arrow. The arrow is no doubt a sexual symbol, but a positive symbol which stands for union and fruitfulness. The knives are a negative symbol. They are aimed not merely at the woman's life, but at her sexual life:

Prenant *le plus profond de ton amour* pour cible . . .

The whole of the drama, including the final act, takes place in the poet's 'heart' which is seen as the source and centre of the emotional life, and 'au fond de ma détresse' is answered by 'le plus profond de ton amour.' 'The Spanish taste' of the sub-title was certainly an invitation to unleash savage impulses, but the sumptuous ornate style has another function. It enables the poet to transmute into art and give a curious dignity to feelings which would otherwise be unbearable.

Not the least of the poem's attractions is the contrast between the perverse feelings and the rich images. The mingling of the religious and the erotic motifs gives it its dialectical movement.

There is a continual switch from one set of feelings to another: from 'Jealousy' to 'Respect', from 'Respect' to 'Humility', from 'Humility' to 'Adoration', from 'Adoration' to 'Volupté noire'. Baudelaire follows the example of his seventeenth-century predecessors in making liberal use of capital letters. The words with capitals—'Madone', 'Statue`, 'Jalousie , 'Manteau , 'Perles , 'Désir , 'Respect , 'Souliers , 'Serpent , 'Lune , 'Pensers`, 'Péchés', 'Couteaux', and 'Cœur'—weave themselves into obsessive patterns. The perverse emotions— erotomania and sado-masochism—in the religious setting, the extraordinary collection of fetishes and the hideous knives give the impression that we are reading a fantastic illustrated case-history from the library of a Des Esseintes.

The Cycle of the 'héroines secondaires' originally consisted of four poems: *L'Héautontimorouménos, Franciscæ meæ laudes, A une Dame créole,* and *Mœsta et errabunda.* Feuillerat has compared the last three to a 'joli bouquet d'amours printanières', and they certainly illustrate Baudelaire's habit of ending each section on a gentle note.[1] Considerable alterations were made in the second edition. *L'Héautontimorouménos* became the last poem but two in the Cycle of Spleen; four poems were introduced before the 'joli bouquet' and three after it. Fueillerat describes their subjects as 'ces peu vertueuses personnes', and the words are apposite.[2] We must, however, understand the poet's intention. The three main love affairs were over. In the third he was already a prey to *spleen.* In the fourth cycle he set out to show how dissipation with a succession of women taken by chance led to the final collapse of all his hopes of finding some remedy against the invading *spleen.*

The effect of the alterations is interesting. 'Tout poëte lyrique,' said Baudelaire, 'en vertu de sa nature, opère fatalement un retour vers l'Éden perdu.'[3] In *Mœsta et errabunda,* one of his loveliest poems, we see the poet as a traveller in the middle way, some-times transfixed with horror at his surroundings, sometimes gazing hopefully at what lies beyond, and sometimes glancing

[1] *Studies,* p. 299.   [2] *Ibid., loc. cit.*   [3] *L'Art romantique,* p. 355.

wistfully over his shoulder at the childhood paradise which lies
behind him:

> Dis-moi, ton cœur parfois s'envole-t-il, Agathe,
> Loin du noir océan de l'immonde cité,
> Vers un autre océan où la splendeur éclate,
> Bleu, clair, profond, ainsi que la virginité?
> Dis-moi, ton cœur parfois s'envole-t-il, Agathe?
>
> La mer, la vaste mer, console nos labeurs!
> Quel démon a doté la mer, rauque chanteuse
> Qu'accompagne l'immense orgue des vents grondeurs,
> De cette fonction sublime de berceuse?
> La mer, la vaste mer, console nos labeurs!
>
> Emporte-moi, wagon! enlève-moi, frégate!
> Loin! loin! ici la boue est faite de nos pleurs!
> —Est-il vrai que parfois le triste cœur d'Agathe
> Dise: Loin des remords, des crimes, des douleurs,
> Emporte-moi, wagon, enlève-moi, frégate?
>
> Comme vous êtes loin, paradis parfumé,
> Où sous un clair azur tout n'est qu'amour et joie,
> Où tout ce que l'on aime est digne d'être aimé,
> Où dans la volupté pure le cœur se noie!
> Comme vous êtes loin, paradis parfumé!
>
> Mais le vert paradis des amours enfantines,
> Les courses, les chansons, les baisers, les bouquets,
> Les violons vibrant derrière les collines,
> Avec les brocs de vin, le soir, dans les bosquets,
> —Mais le vert paradis des amours enfantines,
>
> L'innocent paradis, plein de plaisirs furtifs,
> Est-il déjà plus loin que l'Inde et que la Chine?
> Peut-on le rappeler avec des cris plaintifs,
> Et l'animer encor d'une voix argentine,
> L'innocent paradis plein de plaisirs furtifs?

The three colours represent what might be called the three
distances of the poem. Green—always a symbol of peace in Baudelaire as in Rimbaud—stands for the calm and absence of tension
of childhood; black for the present horror; blue with its religious

associations for something that lies beyond the horror. The poet appears in the first verse to be trying to transcend the present and reach the mysterious region symbolized by blue, but there is a change of direction in the second verse. It is the least attractive verse in the poem, but the part it plays is interesting. It corresponds to a 'mix' in films. The visual images of the first verse are replaced by sound images. In the midst of the confused roar of the waves, we hear the voice of the poet pleading with the sea to perform its traditional function—its 'fonction sublime'—of bringing consolation and liberation. The atmosphere clears in the third verse. The vision of religious peace has vanished. The poet turns away from the present. The 'wagon' and the 'frégate' carry him back in imagination to the childhood paradise.

> Comme vous êtes loin, paradis parfumé!

is one of the most magically evocative lines in French poetry. There is an immense wistfulness behind the 'loin' and the line seems to go on echoing in the mind, continually sending out fresh ripples. There are resemblances between the beatitude of this poem and the beatitude of *La Chevelure*. The prominence given to perfumes is the most striking of the similarities—the 'paradis parfumé' matches the 'loisir embaumé' of the earlier poem—but perfumes, sounds, and colours are common to both. The paradise of *Mœsta et errabunda*, however, is a specifically childhood paradise with children's games and décors:

> Les courses, les chansons, les baisers, les bouquets.

There is also a strong emphasis on 'purity' and 'innocence' in 'l'innocent paradis', 'la volupté pure', and the declaration that all that is loved is worthy to be loved.

Its music is among the most impressive of the poem's qualities. The words 'loin', 'plein' and 'plaintif' answer and echo one another, reminding us that childhood, which is 'plein de plaisirs furtifs', is also 'plus loin que l'Inde et que la Chine'. But the sharp sounds melt into the soft sounds of the words ending in *-ine(s)*. Although it is not specifically mentioned until the last line but one, the silvery voice runs like a thread through the closing verses.

It is heard for the first time in 'enfantines' at the beginning of the fifth verse, is picked up by 'colline', repeated in the second 'enfantines', relayed by 'Chine', and finally crystallizes in 'voix argentine'.

When the poet asks:

> L'innocent paradis, plein de plaisirs furtifs,
> Est-il déjà plus loin que l'Inde et que la Chine?

the answer of a poem like *Chanson d'après-midi* seems to be that it certainly is. For we are very far from the 'innocent paradise' where 'all that is loved is worthy to be loved', and the 'volupté' that it describes is not precisely 'pure':

> Je t'adore, ô ma frivole,
> Ma terrible passion!
> Avec la dévotion
> Du prêtre pour son idole.

The passion with its mixture of perfumes and religious imagery is highly sophisticated:

> Sur ta chair le parfum rôde
> Comme autour d'un encensoir;
> Tu charmes comme le soir,
> Nymphe ténébreuse et chaude . . .
>
> Quelquefois, pour apaiser
> Ta rage mystérieuse,
> Tu prodigues, sérieuse,
> La morsure et le baiser.

In the final verse we are furthest of all from the 'vert paradis' when he speaks of the woman as

> Explosion de chaleur
> Dans ma noire Sibérie!

In *Sonnet d'automne*—one of the poems which follows *Mœsta et errabunda*—he deliberately puts innocence and idealism behind him and sighs for 'la candeur de l'antique animal'. He no longer wants a vigorous love, but a gentle titillation:

> Je hais la passion et l'esprit me fait mal!
> Aimons-nous doucement.

Tristesses de la lune, which was originally one of the last three poems in 'Spleen et Idéal', was turned into the last poem of the 'héroines secondaires', and it leaves us with a glimpse of the courtesan caressing her breasts before going to sleep.

We can see now what Baudelaire has done. In the first edition the freshness and fragrance of the three poems came like a breath of spring after the sultry atmosphere and the exotic perfumes of the sophisticated summer and autumnal loves of the earlier cycles. The spring fragrance is preserved in the second edition, but it is no more than a distant memory entirely surrounded by a 'noire Sibérie' in which we watch a performance of the complicated rite of 'le savant amour' with its 'morsures', 'douleurs', and 'remords'.

When we look at the love cycles as a whole, we can scarcely fail to be impressed by their originality. The originality lies principally in the new pattern that the poet has woven out of traditional feelings and in the way in which he has arranged his experience. For the effect is cumulative. It is the story of his emotional life. It begins with a 'passion' which looks different from any passion that we have ever seen before, passes on to the strangest form of 'pure' love, and closes with an experience which is a mixture of devotion and depravity. 'I have a horror of passion', Baudelaire had said. I think we must take the words literally. The core of his experience is an attitude of passionate refusal. It was not for nothing that he compared love to a 'poison'. It was the indispensable antidote to *spleen*, but it was an antidote which corroded and destroyed. That was his predicament. That is why he was continually using poetry itself to neutralize love, why he sought desperately for 'spiritual' love and for the protective love of certain poems in the third cycle.

The Cycle of Spleen

The Cycle of Spleen opens in both editions with *Les Chats* and *Les Hiboux*. The cats and owls are totem figures which will watch over the poet as he sinks more and more deeply into the mood of *spleen*. Once again there is a significant change in the order of the poems in the second edition. In the first edition 'Spleen et Idéal' ended with *Tristesses de la lune*, *La Musique*, and *La Pipe*. We have already seen that *Tristesses de la lune* was transferred to the 'héroines secondaires' in the second edition. We now find that *Les Hiboux* is followed by *La Pipe* and *La Musique*. The reasons for the change are clear. *La Pipe*, which is one of Baudelaire's weakest poems, describes the soothing effects of the poet's pipe. The pipe was intended as another and more homely antidote to *spleen* and the cycle originally closed with the 'miasmes' of *spleen* being dispersed in its friendly smoke. This was in keeping with the poet's practice of ending on a note of calm and relaxation after the storms of passion and the debilitating effects of *spleen*. The process was reversed in the second edition where cycles and chapters are inclined to end on a note of violence and despair. The position of *La Pipe* was altered and we have the impression of the poet walking into his room, protected by the totem figures on either side of the entrance, where he will meditate on the ravages of *spleen* in solitude. The alteration is ingenious, but not completely successful. It indicates very well the poet's exit from the world of women and love and his entry into solitude, but the suggestion that his pipe will 'cure his mind of its weariness' is scarcely a preparation for what is to come.

Once we enter the Cycle of Spleen the landscape changes. It is no longer autumn with its gentle melancholy and falling leaves or even its frosts, but midwinter. The poet's mood is identified with the season. He succeeds in a remarkable way in penetrating further and further into himself and in showing the destructive forces at work beneath the surface of life. This does not mean that the poems are faultless. The macabre décor and the images of worms, spiders, snakes, snails, bats, skeletons, tombstones, and 'lakes of blood' have not worn well, and the successes are achieved in spite of them. It is important, however, not to let this undergrowth obscure the brilliance with which the poet uses the images of bells, clocks, and prisons. The sound of bells and clocks gives the cycle its peculiar resonance. The 'song' of bells mocks the poet's despair; their 'lamentation' reflects it; their 'hurlements' express the violence of his rebellion while the ticking of clocks stands for the relentless passage of time as he sits, a prisoner in his sordid attic, unable to write.

The poems define and elaborate the *ennui* which was described in *Au Lecteur* or an early piece like *La Vie antérieure* and which pervades even the love poems. When he speaks in *La Vie antérieure* of the naked slaves

> . . . dont l'unique soin était d'approfondir
> Le secret douloureux qui me faisait languir,

the 'secret douloureux' looks suspiciously like the Romantic malaise, but is not. The Romantic malaise was vague, adolescent, an illusion which depended in the last resort upon failure to analyse the mood and resolve it into its component parts. Baudelaire's malaise was neither vague nor immature. It was capable of exact—sometimes of uncomfortably exact—definition, as we can see from some lines in *Ciel brouillé*:

> Tu rappelles ces jours blancs, tièdes et voilés,
> Qui font se fondre en pleurs les cœurs ensorcelés,
> Quand, agités d'un mal inconnu qui les tord,
> Les nerfs trop éveillés raillent l'esprit qui dort.

The drama of the exhausted mind unable to grapple with its problems and the shattered, vibrating nerves which leave it no rest echoes and re-echoes all through this part of the *Fleurs du mal*. Baudelaire's aim was the total analysis of states of mind which are variously described as *ennui*, *spleen*, *tristesse*, and *mélancolie*. When we compare his

> L'ennui, fruit de la morne incuriosité

with Racine's

> Dans l'Orient désert quel devint mon ennui!

it may appear that his method does not differ materially from that of Racine and a number of other French masters. It is true that he possessed Racine's power of translating obscure perceptions into language which has something of the precision of a mathematical formula and that his material is the same, but the material had been modified by changes which had taken place in civilization. New feelings had emerged; old feelings had been broken up and had formed fresh combinations like the pieces in a kaleidoscope.

Racine limited himself to the great primary emotions: love, hate, fear, jealousy, anger, revenge. Baudelaire analysed not only the great primary emotions, but the many subsidiary feelings contained within them. This accounts for the difference of method. The line from *Bérénice* is not unlike a geometrical proposition or, if one prefers, a syllogism. A man who has been disappointed in love goes into exile: but Antiochus has been disappointed in love: therefore Antiochus goes into exile: therefore he feels *ennui*. It will be seen that the term is a precise definition. It consists of the pain of separation which is intensified by isolation. In seven words Racine gives us an incomparable picture of the East with its vast empty spaces and huge vistas of desolation open before us. We know exactly how Antiochus felt and why he felt as he did. There is nothing to add.

Racine's method is compression; Baudelaire's amplification. In Racine feelings are stripped to their bare essentials; in Baudelaire we find the same accumulation of sense-perceptions as in English poetry, the same marshalling of concrete objects and the same use of suggestion. In Racine's poetry the great primary emotions are at bottom the same. The plays are variations on a theme, and the variations are mainly due to different characters and situations. Baudelaire used the words *spleen* and *ennui* to describe moods which certainly bear a strong resemblance to one another, but though they have common characteristics their component parts are by no means identical, and each of the finest poems in the cycle is a fresh approach to the central mood from a fresh angle. This means that instead of being variations on a theme or a series of separate definitions like Racine's plays their effect is cumulative. When we put them together, we find that they are all part of a single definition.

In Baudelaire *ennui* is not a precise definition as it is in Racine, nor is it intended to be. It is a portmanteau word which contains a large number of different possible combinations. Racine describes a situation or formulates a proposition which leads logically to *ennui* as its final term. Baudelaire seems to work in the opposite direction, to move inwards and downwards. He starts with *ennui* and proceeds to peel away the outer layers and to resolve it into its elements. All the best poems in the cycle might very well have been called 'alchimie de la douleur'. Loneliness and apathy are common to them all, but we shall see that in *La Cloche fêlée* the mood springs from contrasted sounds and from the poet's doubts about his vocation; in the first *Spleen* from loneliness arising from disappointed love; and in the third *Spleen* from the conflicting feelings of richness and sterility which crystallize in the image of the prematurely aged monarch.

In the poems that I have been discussing *ennui* does not spring from a clear-cut situation. It proceeds from another *feeling*—from 'morne incuriosité'—which in turn is the result of the long succession of 'boiteuses journées'. Nor is that all. The physical succession of the long, empty days produces a sensation of complete helplessness, of unending, unchanging monotony, and we have

> L'ennui, fruit de la morne incuriosité,
> Prend les proportions de l'immortalité.

This brings us to a further difference. Racine extracts only those elements from a situation which are strictly necessary for his purpose and he knows where he is going. With Baudelaire every poem is a voyage—an interior voyage—of discovery and he does not know where he is going until the end of the journey. He therefore extracts one feeling from another feeling without limit, and he sometimes pushes analysis to the point at which the feeling is destroyed. In *Le Voyage* he writes of

> Une oasis d'horreur dans un désert d'ennui,

and the line illustrates very well the process of extracting one feeling from another like a series of Chinese boxes. 'Horreur' destroys the normal associations of 'oasis'; the feeling of horror is concentrated, pin-pointed *inside* the surrounding feeling of desolation which throws it into high relief, so that there is a striking interplay between the two without their merging into one another.

When we look at his style more closely, we find that Baudelaire uses three different methods of presenting feeling. The first is direct description:

Morne esprit, autrefois amoureux de la lutte . . .

There are times when this approaches clinical observation as it does in the line from *Ciel brouillé*:

> Les nerfs trop éveillés raillent l'esprit qui dort.

The second is indirect description when he compares himself to a mythical figure or an animal:

> Je suis comme le roi d'un pays pluvieux,
> Riche, mais impuissant, jeune et pourtant très-vieux . . .

'Riche' stands for the potential richness of his poetic genius and 'impuissant' for the apathy which prevents him from writing. Under cover of describing the life of the king at his court, he goes on to elaborate his own mood. Nothing can distract him from his gloom:

> Rien ne peut l'égayer, ni gibier, ni faucon,
> Ni son peuple mourant en face du balcon.

The wiles of the ladies of the court—the poet may be thinking of his mistresses—are equally ineffectual:

> Et les dames d'atour . . .
> Ne savent plus trouver d'impudique toilette
> Pour tirer un souris de ce jeune squelette.

The next two lines are less easy to interpret:

> Le savant qui lui fait de l'or n'a jamais pu
> De son être extirper l'élément corrompu.

I think that 'savant' must stand for the transforming power of his poetic genius which has never been able to root out the 'corrupt element' that blights his life, or it may refer to his failure to reach the *Idéal*.

The third method is the description of scenes or objects of experience:

> Un gros meuble à tiroirs encombré de bilans,
> De vers, de billets doux, de procès, de romances,
> Avec de lourds cheveux roulés dans des quittances,
> Cache moins de secrets que mon triste cerveau.
> C'est une pyramide, un immense caveau,
> Qui contient plus de morts que la fosse commune.

L

The word order and the matter-of-fact tone differ little from prose, but the lines are not a trivial catalogue of bric-à-brac. Each of the objects mentioned—inventories, verses, love letters, lawsuits, songs, heavy locks of hair rolled up in receipts which significantly links love and money—stands for some experience in the poet's life, for one of the emotional strands out of which his mood is composed. The words 'morts', 'pyramide', 'caveau', and 'fosse commune' in the last two lines should not be over-looked. What Baudelaire is describing are not *living* but *dead* emotions dragged up from the past, reminding us of specimens in a museum labelled, docketed, and pinned to cards, or of funeral urns with neat inscriptions carefully arranged in a mausoleum. It is precisely from the contemplation of these exhibits that the suffocating sense of weariness and monotony arises. The 'pyra-mide', with its suggestion of immense size, accentuates the sense of monotony, while the 'fosse commune' reduces the poet and his feelings to the condition of the anonymous pauper whose body is flung into the common grave.

It is not for nothing that the poem opens with a direct state-ment:

J'ai plus de souvenirs que si j'avais mille ans,

or that the catalogue leads back to 'mon triste cerveau'. For there is both analysis and synthesis. The poet begins with a general proposition about his mood; the catalogue resolves it into its component parts; the 'triste cerveau' puts them together again, and the last two lines quoted introduce further qualifications. I think we should add that the lines are a particularly good example of the structure of the image in Baudelaire. They illustrate not merely his gift of finding concrete equivalents for intangible feelings, and his skill in blending the different strands of feeling which is only achieved by the analogical method; the image of the piece of furniture with its drawers corresponds very closely to Baudelaire's psychic structure and to the labyrinthine nature of the mood that he is analysing.

The three methods that I have described might be used in isolation, but the poems are usually a combination of two, or in the case of the first *Spleen*, of all three of them. He also uses three methods of describing his physical environment. There is direct notation:

> . . . sur les faubourgs brumeux.

There is the notation of the impression that a scene makes on him:

> Rien n'égale en longueur les *boiteuses* journées,
> Quand sous les lourds flocons des *neigeuses* années . . .

Finally, there is the atmosphere of hallucination and nightmare when the figures on a pack of cards seem to come to life:

> Le beau valet de cœur et la dame de pique
> Causent sinistrement de leurs amours défunts.

It is noticeable that his normal practice—particularly in the Cycle of Spleen—is to begin with a direct transcription of the surface of life and to work inwards:

> Quand le ciel bas et lourd pèse comme un couvercle
> Sur l'esprit gémissant en proie aux longs ennuis,
> Et que de l'horizon embrassant tout le cercle
> Il nous verse un jour noir plus triste que les nuits.

He sees himself a prisoner in a shrinking world under a low sky with a circumscribed horizon. The image of the 'lid' in line 1 shows that direct transcription is already being transformed into an impression. In the verses that follow, the transformation is completed—the words 'changée' and 'imite' are significant— and we reach the next level where the image of the prison predominates:

> Quand la terre est *changée* en un cachot humide . . .

> Quand la pluie étalant ses immenses traînées
> D'une vaste prison *imite* les barreaux . . .

This is the final verse:

> —Et de longs corbillards, sans tambours ni musique,
> Défilent lentement dans mon âme; l'Espoir,
> Vaincu, pleure, et l'Angoisse atroce, despotique,
> Sur mon crâne incliné plante son drapeau noir.

The spectacle of the silent, interior funeral procession belongs to a still deeper level and the last two lines take us into the world of the nightmare.

La Cloche fêlée and the first *Spleen* not only provide an interesting study in contrast, they show how the poet employs the various devices that I have been examining.[1]

> Il est amer et doux, pendant les nuits d'hiver,
> D'écouter, près du feu qui palpite et qui fume,
> Les souvenirs lointains lentement s'élever
> Au bruit des carillons qui chantent dans la brume.
>
> Bienheureuse la cloche au gosier vigoureux
> Qui, malgré sa vieillesse, alerte et bien portante,
> Jette fidèlement son cri religieux,
> Ainsi qu'un vieux soldat qui veille sous la tente!
>
> Moi, mon âme est fêlée, et lorsqu'en ses ennuis
> Elle veut de ses chants peupler l'air froid des nuits,
> Il arrive souvent que sa voix affaiblie
>
> Semble le râle épais d'un blessé qu'on oublie
> Au bord d'un lac de sang, sous un grand tas de morts,
> Et qui meurt, sans bouger, dans d'immenses efforts.

The poem is constructed out of a series of sound-images which alternately blend and clash. It is of some importance to notice that the scene opens *inside* the poet's dwelling. He is sitting in front of the flickering fire. His feelings are mixed—'Il est amer et doux'—but the atmosphere is comfortable and the word 'doux' softens the implications of 'amer'. When the poem was first published in a magazine, he used the word 'sentir' in the second line, but changed it in the *Fleurs du mal* to 'écouter' in order to emphasize the significance of sound and in fact to transform the 'memories' into auditory memories. For it is the sound of bells coming from outside which sets the mechanism of memory in motion. The sharp i's and the nasals reflect the clear, harmonious chime coming without any blur through the thick 'brume'.

In the second quatrain he enlarges on the nature of the sound.

[1] It is interesting to notice that both poems were first published in *Le Messager de l'Assemblée* on 9 April 1851 and were both entitled *Le Spleen*.

Although 'chantent' seems at first to reinforce 'doux', its real effect is to stir up 'bitter' memories, to point to something which is lacking in the poet. The word 'bienheureuse' introduces the religious motif. In spite of old age the sound of the bell is clear and 'faithful' because it is associated with religion. The 'cri religieux' stands for a definite unchanging message coming out of the darkness and the mists to the doubting poet. It is supported by an example of 'fidelity' on the human plane in the somewhat conventional figure of the 'old soldier' at his post.

In the first tercet the poet turns on himself. He is the 'cloche fêlée' of the title. He contrasts his 'âme fêlée' with the 'gosier vigoureux' of the church bell, his 'chant', which is enfeebled by the foggy night air, with its 'song' and his 'ennuis' with its clear message. The 'voix affaiblie' appears to be a reference to his doubts about his poetic vocation which we have already met in *La Muse malade* and *L'Ennemi*—it is another illustration of the tightness of the structure of the *Fleurs du mal*—the darkness and the fog to the tragic situation which gave rise to his doubts. The contrast between the song of the bells and the 'voix affaiblie' shows that the poet is moving away from certainty and plunging more deeply into doubt and despair. His 'feeble voice' merges into the 'death rattle' of the wounded man who is abandoned among the dead when the battle is over because there is no 'old soldier' to look after him. It will be apparent that the scene has changed from indoors to outdoors, from the spectacle of the poet sitting quietly in front of the gently flickering fire to the nightmare vision of himself as one of the anonymous mass of the dead —the outcasts—who have presumably been destroyed in the 'battle of life'. The 'râle épais' repeats the motif of the thick symbolical fog which stifles his 'voice'. The 'immenses efforts' produce no poetry; they are the sterile convulsions of death. The agreeable feelings described by 'doux' have been eliminated; his mood has been transformed into one of unmixed bitterness caused by the doubt and sterility which enfeeble his 'voice' and his 'song'.

> Pluviôse, irrité contre la ville entière,
> De son urne à grands flots verse un froid ténébreux

Aux pâles habitants du voisin cimetière
Et la mortalité sur les faubourgs brumeux.

Mon chat sur le carreau cherchant une litière
Agite sans repos son corps maigre et galeux;
L'âme d'un vieux poëte erre dans la gouttière
Avec la triste voix d'un fantôme frileux.

Le bourdon se lamente, et la bûche enfumée
Accompagne en fausset la pendule enrhumée,
Cependant qu'en un jeu plein de sales parfums,

Héritage fatal d'une vieille hydropique,
Le beau valet de cœur et la dame de pique
Causent sinistrement de leurs amours défunts.

La Cloche fêlée opens inside the poet's room, *Spleen* in the foggy streets outside. The first poem begins on a quiet note which reflects the comfortable, almost 'cosy' atmosphere of the room; the second in the grand manner with figures drawn from legend. 'Pluviôse'—the fifth month of the republican calendar corresponding to the period 20 January to 18 February—is a personification in the classical manner, and the 'urn' from which he pours 'un froid ténébreux' one of the commonest of classical stage properties. No nineteenth-century poet was more successful than Baudelaire in combining the grand manner and the intimate manner, poetic and prosaic, abstract and concrete. François Porché has drawn attention to the effectiveness in line 4 of the contrast between the abstract 'mortalité', used as a collective noun to describe the pedestrians and maintain the note struck by 'pâles habitants', and the precisely observed 'faubourgs brumeux'.[1] Sound-images play the same part in this poem as in *La Cloche fêlée*, but greater use is made of visual images for reasons that will be apparent presently. 'Irrité' is a key-word which sets the tone of the poem. It suggests the exasperation and the frayed nerves of the sensitive modern man trapped in the great industrial city.

[1] See his interesting analysis of the poem in *Baudelaire: Histoire d'une âme*, pp. 198–200, to which I am indebted for some of the suggestions in what follows.

In the second quatrain the scene shifts to the interior of the poet's room. We notice at once the precise observation in the picture of the cat with its 'corps maigre et galeux' and later in 'le bourdon se lamente' and the 'bûche enfumée'. The condition of the cat and the uncarpeted floor ('carreau') are signs of the poet's poverty. The restless movements of the cat 'cherchant une litière' reflect the spiritual restlessness of the poet who also finds himself without a family ('litière') like a ghost 'wandering in the gutter'. The 'triste voix' is a repetition of the 'voix affaiblie' of *La Cloche fêlée*. This time it blends with the sad tolling of the bell—'le bourdon se lamente'—which suddenly strikes the poet's ear, bringing a message not of hope but of doom, and reminding the 'fantôme frileux' that he will soon be one of the 'pâles habitants du voisin cimetière'. This is reinforced by the hissing of the damp wood on the fire which contrasts with the cheerful crackle of the fire in the previous poem and is, according to Porché, another sign of the poet's poverty, as well as by the falsetto sound of the clock. 'La pendule enrhumée' is an example of Baudelaire's impressionism. It marks the transition from actuality to hallucination, and shows that the poem is moving towards its climax which in Baudelaire's sonnets usually occurs in the last two lines. The 'sales parfums' are a symbol of prostitution. The use of the word 'fatal' applied to a pack of cards points to fortune-telling. The 'sale parfums' and the fact that it is an ordinary pack and not, for example, a Tarot pack which might be used by a professional clairvoyante, suggests that the 'vieille hydropique' is a retired prostitute turned fortune-teller. We are presented with the ugly image of the obese old woman who has paid a visit to the poet's garret, possibly at the request of the vanished mistress or possibly to act as a procuress for her. I think that the Knave of Hearts must be the poet and the Queen of Spades Jeanne Duval. He is called 'le beau valet de cœur' which turns him into the Knight of Chivalry who has made advances to the Lady. The colours of the cards and the words 'cœur' and 'pique' are important. Red stands for love. Black is no doubt a reference to Jeanne's colouring, but it probably stands for refusal. *Spleen* is a malady that attacks the heart which is traditionally the seat of the emotions.

There may be a play on the word 'pique' meaning the ill-humoured refusal of the Lady. The poem closes not with the customary shock, but in a whispered undertone. The poet and his mistress become the grotesque gesticulating figures in a night-mare, discussing a love that is over and done with, and reduced to an unending futile bickering.

The poem works at three different and contrasted levels: the legendary 'poetic' level of Pluviôse and his urn; the level of actuality with the scraggy cat, the uncarpeted floor and the damp wood, and the level of hallucination. It moves relentlessly from a level which is deliberately remote and faintly unreal to the level of actuality, and from actuality to the level of the heightened reality of the nightmare. The first level is the level of silence, the second of the realistic sounds of the bell and the burning wood, and the third of the obsessive sound of the wheezing clock and the sinister undertone. The grandiose gesture of Pluviôse empty-ing his urn changes to the restless nervous movements of the cat which give way to the strained jerky movements of the figures in the nightmare.

When we reread the poem we can see with equal clarity the logical sequence of the images. Baudelaire begins by evoking death, passes on to the ailing condition of himself and his cat, to the ghost with its 'sad voice' blending into the funereal tolling of the bell, to the sound of the 'ailing' clock and leading, finally, to another image of death—'leurs amours défunts'. The pack of cards is a complex image of superstition, squalor, degradation, apathy and death, which stands for the poet's life and his state of mind.

Feuillerat speaks of 'the skilfully graduated horror' of the seven poems which composed the cycle in the first edition, but this attitude is not without danger.[1] It is important not to allow a taste for measure and proportion to obscure the peculiar merits of the new poems or prevent us from recognizing the validity of the mood they express. Their violence and despair are admittedly very different from the lassitude and resignation of the original cycle. In the fourth *Spleen* he had written:

[1] *Studies*, p. 265.

> l'Espoir,
> Vaincu, pleure . . .

The word 'vaincu' occurs in *Obsession* and *Le Goût du néant*, but this time it is not merely 'hope', but the poet himself who is defeated. When he speaks in *Obsession* of

> ce rire amer
> De l'homme vaincu,

we hear the strident, hysterical scream of despair. The word is used in the same sense in *Le Goût du néant*, where he addresses himself as

> Esprit vaincu, fourbu!

What is new in these poems is not merely their more sombre tone, but an attitude of deliberate nihilism which is brilliantly expressed in the bare sober line:

> Car je cherche le vide, et le noir, et le nu!

In *Horreur sympathique* he interrogates himself savagely:

> Quels pensers dans ton âme vide
> Descendent? Réponds, libertin.

In the last two words we seem to feel him shaking himself in fury, and in fact the answer is jerked out of him:

> —Insatiablement avide
> De l'obscur et de l'incertain,
> Je ne geindrai pas comme Ovide
> Chassé du paradis latin.

The poems in the first edition sometimes struck a note of violence and we remember the bells in the fourth *Spleen*:

> Des cloches tout à coup sautent avec furie
> Et lancent vers le ciel un affreux hurlement,
> Ainsi que des esprits errants et sans patrie
> Qui se mettent à geindre opiniâtrement.

It is very different, however, from the violence of the later poems. 'Je ne geindrai pas comme Ovide', he has said. Nor does he:

> Je te hais, Océan! tes bonds et tes tumultes,
> Mon esprit les retrouve en lui; ce rire amer
> De l'homme vaincu, plein de sanglots et d'insultes,
> Je l'entends dans le rire énorme de la mer.
>
> Comme tu me plairais, ô nuit! sans ces étoiles
> Dont la lumière parle un langage connu!
> Car je cherche le vide, et le noir, et le nu!

It is apparent that in these poems a growing disorder of the spirit is reflected in the brusqueness of the transitions and in a sort of *décousu* in the sequence of the images. The best example is *Le Goût du néant* which is remarkable for the highly effective use of only two rhymes:

> Morne esprit, autrefois amoureux de la lutte,
> L'Espoir, dont l'éperon attisait ton ardeur,
> Ne veut plus t'enfourcher! Couche-toi sans pudeur,
> Vieux cheval dont le pied à chaque obstacle butte.
>
> Résigne-toi, mon cœur; dors ton sommeil de brute.
>
> Esprit vaincu, fourbu! Pour toi, vieux maraudeur,
> L'amour n'a plus de goût, non plus que la dispute;
> Adieu donc, chants du cuivre et soupirs de la flûte!
> Plaisirs, ne tentez plus un cœur sombre et boudeur!
>
> Le Printemps adorable a perdu son odeur!
>
> Et le Temps m'engloutit minute par minute,
> Comme la neige immense un corps pris de roideur;
> Je contemple d'en haut le globe en sa rondeur,
> Et je n'y cherche plus l'abri d'une cahute!
>
> Avalanche, veux-tu m'emporter dans ta chute?

The dominant images of these poems are death by drowning, by suffocation under avalanches, or by being 'engulfed' in the void. In *Le Goût du néant* the poet seems to be sliding down into a pit, tantalized by flashes of light and by sounds from the world that he is leaving. The poem opens on a quiet note as he addresses himself, sorrowfully, as 'Morne esprit' and compares himself to an aged horse longing for sleep. In the sixth line the tone changes to bitter mockery:

> Esprit vaincu, fourbu!

He hears the disappearing 'chants du cuivre' and the 'soupirs de la flûte' which are followed by the maddening memory of the 'Printemps adorable'. Then comes the sense of being swallowed up as he falls like a stiffening corpse 'pris de roideur':

> Et le Temps m'engloutit minute par minute.

The isolation of the fifth and tenth lines may be intended to mark pauses in the downward movement or those moments when time seems to stand still and the doomed man sees where he is really going. There is another pause at lines 13 and 14 as he surveys 'le globe en sa rondeur' before making his final appeal for extinction:

> Avalanche, veux-tu m'emporter dans ta chute?

The whole poem leads, appropriately, to the final word—'chute'.

The unusual rhyme-scheme and the vocabulary deserve special attention. With the possible exception of line 10, the end words divide into three groups. The words of the first group suggest violence or conflict; those of the second gentleness or repose, and those of the third the clash with an obstacle or some form of internal or external inhibition. To the first belong 'lutte-brute-dispute-chute', 'ardeur-maraudeur'; to the second, 'flûte-cahute', 'pudeur-odeur-rondeur'; to the third, 'butte', 'boudeur-roideur'. The rhyme-scheme produces a continual alternation between words belonging to the three groups which either reinforce or cancel one another out. We have, for example, 'lutte-butte-brute' where violence breaks out in 'lutte', is checked in 'butte', then breaks out again in 'brute'. We find the same effect in 'ardeur-pudeur-maraudeur' where 'ardeur' is attenuated by 'pudeur' and reinforced by 'maraudeur'. It will further be seen that in the first two quatrains the pattern is identical: 'lutte-ardeur-pudeur-butte' and 'maraudeur-dispute-flûte-boudeur', which corresponds in terms of groups to the pattern 1, 1, 2, 3. I have said enough to show that the different possible combinations are considerable, and I need only add that to read the poem properly we must be conscious of each of these possible combinations.

We know that *L'Héautontimorouménos* originally formed part of the Cycle of the 'héroines secondaires', but the Cycle of Spleen seems to be its proper place.[1] The word means to be one's own executioner. The poet appears in the first three verses to be hurting himself indirectly by beating the woman—another example of the 'bourreau plein de remords'—but in the last four he turns on himself with the words:

> Ne suis-je pas un faux accord
> Dans la divine symphonie,
> Grâce à la vorace Ironie
> Qui me secoue et qui me mord?
>
> Elle est dans ma voix, la criarde!
> C'est tout mon sang, ce poison noir!
> Je suis le sinistre miroir
> Où la mégère se regarde.
>
> Je suis la plaie et le couteau!
> Je suis le soufflet et la joue!
> Je suis les membres et la roue,
> Et la victime et le bourreau!
>
> Je suis de mon cœur le vampire,
> —Un de ces grands abandonnés,
> Au rire éternel condamnés,
> Et qui ne peuvent plus sourire!

When we look at the cycle as a whole, I think that we have to admit that the tone of *Le Goût du néant* or *Obsession* is closer to that of *L'Héautontimorouménos* than it is to that of the four poems called *Spleen* or *La Cloche fêlée*. There is the same savage grating note in 'la vorace Ironie', 'la criarde', and 'rire éternel'. There is also a new limpidity in the verse beginning:

> Je suis la plaie et le couteau!

[1] The poem like *Les Paradis artificiels* is dedicated to 'J.G.F.' The dedication has puzzled Baudelaire's editors and was thought to refer to Jeanne Duval. (*Vide* the ingenious speculations in the critical edition of the *Fleurs du mal*, pp. 432–3.) It has, however, recently been suggested that the woman was Juliette Gex-Fagon. See *Corr. gén.*, 3, p. 105 n., and Porché, *Baudelaire: Histoire d'une âme*, pp. 253–6.

But it is the limpidity of a man who has seen through everything and is caught in that final prison from which there is no escape— the prison of the self.

L'Irrémédiable seems to be a renunciation of his poetic ambitions, particularly his ambition to reach the 'Ideal':

> Une Idée, une Forme, un Être
> Parti de l'azur et tombé
> Dans un Styx bourbeux et plombé
> Où nul œil du Ciel ne pénètre;
>
> Un Ange, imprudent voyageur
> Qu'a tenté l'amour du difforme,
> Au fond d'un cauchemar énorme
> Se débattant comme un nageur,
>
> Et luttant, angoisses funèbres!
> Contre un gigantesque remous
> Qui va chantant comme les fous
> Et pirouettant dans les ténèbres;
>
> Un malheureux ensorcelé
> Dans ses tâtonnements futiles,
> Pour fuir d'un lieu pleins de reptiles,
> Cherchant la lumière et la clé . . .

The critical edition contains the usual ingenious speculations about the origin and identity of the 'Idée', 'Forme', and 'Être'. It seems possible, however, that whatever the sources of his imagery Baudelaire is here referring to his poetic theories and to himself, is saying that his lofty theories and his lofty ambitions alike have come to rest in 'un Styx bourbeux'. The Angel who has been tempted by 'l'amour du difforme' appears to be the poet whose ambition, as he puts it in one of the draft prefaces, was to 'extract beauty from evil', and who now finds himself 'chantant comme les fous . . . dans les ténèbres'. I think that he is also the 'malheureux ensorcelé Dans ses tâtonnements futiles' who had been seeking 'la lumière et la clé', that 'lumière' means the 'Ideal' or the experience which transcends all other experiences and that the 'clé' is the theory by which it was to have been reached.

The second part of *L'Irrémédiable*, which consists of only two

verses, possesses the same limpidity as *L'Héautontimorouménos*,
and the word 'limpide' is actually used:

> Tête-à-tête sombre et limpide
> Qu'un cœur devenu son miroir!
> Puits de Vérité, clair et noir,
> Où tremble une étoile livide,
>
> Un phare ironique, infernal,
> Flambeau des grâces sataniques,
> Soulagement et gloire uniques,
> —La conscience dans le Mal!

The poet traces the failure described in the first part of the
poem back to a moral cause, but he is not to be left brooding on
what appears to him to be the reasons for the failure of his poetic
theory or the cause of the victory of *spleen*. The sound of the
clock calls him back to the world and to the final reckoning. We
hear the desperate, panting note in:

> Horloge! dieu sinistre, effrayant, impassible,
> Dont le doigt nous menace et nous dit: *Souviens-toi!* . . .'
>
> Trois mille six cents fois par heure, la Seconde
> Chuchote: *Souviens-toi!*—Rapide, avec sa voix
> D'insecte, Mainteant dit: Je suis Autrefois,
> Et j'ai pompé ta vie avec ma trompe immonde!

The 'voix d'insecte', echoing the ticking of the clock, drives
itself into the mind, endlessly repeated like a maddening refrain.
The figures become an obsession. The sense of time slipping
away with the poet's work unwritten is familiar in Baudelaire, but
in this poem a fresh feeling is introduced. Time does not merely
slip away; every instant

> te dévore un morceau du délice
> A chaque homme accordé pour toute sa saison.

This leads up to the image—an image which is used with
considerable effect in the poems of the fourth chapter—of life
itself being 'pumped away', running into the sand, and of the
poet's life blood draining away:

> Et j'ai pompé ta vie avec ma trompe immonde!

> Souviens-toi que le Temps est un joueur avide
> Qui gagne sans tricher, à tout coup! c'est la loi.
> Le jour décroit; la nuit augmente; la clepsydre se vide.

He is left waiting for the moment when 'le divin Hasard', 'l'auguste Vertu', and 'le Repentir' will unite in the cry:

> Meurs, vieux lâche! il est trop tard!

2. 'Tableaux Parisiens'

I have already suggested that the 'Tableaux Parisiens' are not incidental glimpses of the city, but an attempt by the poet to re-establish contact with the world of common experience, to escape from the self. The attempt naturally fails, but it produces some of his finest and most original poetry.

The chapter contains eighteen poems. They record a 'circular tour' of the city lasting twenty-four hours, and three of them—*Le Soleil*, *Le Crépuscule du soir*, and *Le Crépuscule du matin*—mark the changes from morning to night, from night to dawn.

The first poem is a panorama of the city. The poet imagines himself in the traditional garret and adopts, ironically, the pastoral tone:

> Je veux, pour composer chastement mes églogues,
> Coucher auprès du ciel, comme des astrologues,
> Et, voisin des clochers, écouter en rêvant
> Leurs hymnes solennels emportés par le vent.

He looks down across

> Les tuyaux, les clochers, ces mâts de la cité,

but decides to shut out the world and write. The storms may thunder outside, but he will not care:

> Car je serai plongé dans cette volupté
> D'évoquer le Printemps avec ma volonté,
> De tirer un soleil de mon cœur, et de faire
> De mes pensers brûlants une tiède atmosphère.

I think we can take it that the seventeen poems which follow
are in fact the vision that he sets to work to 'evoke' in the fast-
ness of his garret, but his picture of Paris turns out to be very
different from the one that he suggests in these lines. It will be
an autumn and not a spring landscape, nor will it be sunlight—we
note the recurrence of the image—that he draws from his 'heart'.

Le Soleil—originally the second poem of 'Spleen et Idéal'—
describes his aims very neatly:

> Je vais m'exercer seul à ma fantasque escrime,
> Flairant dans tous les coins les hasards de la rime,
> Trébuchant sur les mots comme sur les pavés,
> Heurtant parfois des vers depuis longtemps rêvés.

He goes on to compare the sun and the poet:

> il descend dans les villes,
> Il ennoblit le sort des choses les plus viles,
> Et s'introduit en roi, sans bruit et sans valets,
> Dans tous les hôpitaux et dans tous les palais.

It is, indeed, the relation between 'words' and 'paving-stones',
'dream' and 'reality' which gives the 'Tableaux' their special
fascination. The poet imagines himself leaving his attic, going
down into the city and recording his impressions of it, finding
his way into palaces, poor-houses, and hospitals, and transforming what he sees into something unique. For he has succeeded
better than any other modern poet in conveying the atmosphere
of the great city—the mists rising over the Seine at dawn, the
sun beating remorselessly down on the dry dusty pavements at
noon, and the winter fogs blotting out the city at dusk; the
sinister procession of beggars, murderers, drunkards, prostitutes,
and rag-pickers slinking through the twilight. His verse catches
the sounds as well as the sights. We hear the bugle in the barracks
at dawn, the rattle of the traffic in the 'rue assourdissante', the
medley of sounds as night-life begins:

> les cuisines siffler,
> Les théâtres glapir, les orchestres ronfler . . .

the music of a military band:

> ces concerts, riches de cuivre,
> Dont les soldats parfois inondent nos jardins . . .

or the haunting melody of a street song:

> Que des nœuds mal attachés
> Dévoilent pour nos péchés
> Tes deux beaux seins, radieux
>   Comme des yeux;
>
> Que pour te déshabiller
> Tes bras se fassent prier
> Et chassent à coups mutins
>   Les doigts lutins . . .
>
> Tu compterais dans tes lits
> Plus de baisers que de lis
> Et rangerais sous tes lois
>   Plus d'un Valois! . . .
>
> Tu vas lorgnant en dessous
> Des bijoux de vingt-neuf sous
> Dont je ne puis, oh! pardon!
>   Te faire don.

A une Mendiante rousse is based on a combination of two traditional metres, and the use of the word *lois* is a charming archaism. The careful blending of tradition and innovation that we find in the poem is a good indication of Baudelaire's approach to his material and of the way in which he achieves his effects in this part of his work.

'Impressionism', writes Arnold Hauser, 'is an urban art, and not only because it discovers the landscape quality of the city and brings painting back from the country to the town, but because it sees the world through the eyes of the townsman and reacts to external impressions with the overstrained nerves of modern technical man. It is an urban style, because it describes the changeability, the nervous rhythm, the sudden sharp but always ephemeral impressions of the city.'[1]

This passage throws considerable light on the 'Tableaux Parisiens'. It seems to me to be misleading to suggest, as Vivier does, that the poems are in some way 'objective'.[2] Baudelaire's

[1] *The Social History of Art*, London, 1952, Vol. II, p. 871.
[2] *Op. cit.*, p. 23.

M

pictures are traditional in the sense that they are carefully composed and contain a pronounced formal element which we shall not find in Laforgue's much more impressionistic pictures of Paris life; but his main concern is to give a personal 'impression' and not a realistic study of the city and its inhabitants. Nor can it be denied that he brings out to the full 'the overstrained nerves of modern technical man . . . the changeability, the nervous rhythm, the sudden sharp but always ephemeral impressions of the city'. The poems are highly stylized, their imagery a mixture of exact observation and impressionism of the kind that we find in:

> Le long du vieux faubourg, où pendent aux masures
> Les persiennes, abri des secrètes luxures . . .
>
> La Prostitution s'allume dans les rues;
> Comme une fourmilière elle ouvre ses issues;
> Partout elle se fraye un occulte chemin,
> Ainsi que l'ennemi qui tente un coup de main;
> Elle remue au sein de la cité de fange . . .

In these lines there is not simply a mixture of exact observation and impression; the impression takes the form of comment or criticism such as we find in 'secrètes luxures', 'Comme une fourmilière' and 'cité de fange'.

When he writes:

> Fourmillante cité, cité pleine de rêves,
> Où le spectre en plein jour raccroche le passant!

we see that the city of swarming multitudes is also the city of dreams where the apparition clutches us by the arm in broad daylight. 'Tout pour moi devient allégorie', he said in *Le Cygne*. 'Rêve', 'cauchemar', 'mythe', and 'allégorie' are among the words to which Baudelaire has given a special resonance and they are key-words for an appreciation of the 'Tableaux Parisiens'. For these 'pictures' have the sharpness and the intensity of a dream. The dream is a *dédoublement* which enables us to contemplate life simultaneously under two aspects, giving us the sensation of the dream world with its strange shapes continually breaking in on the 'real' world. 'Il aime le mot charmant appliqué aux choses équivoques', said Laforgue.[1] He did so because the use of this and similar words enabled him to render perfectly 'the ecstasy of life and the horror of life':

> Dans les plis sinueux des vieilles capitales,
> Où tout, même l'horreur, tourne aux *enchantements*,
> Je guette, obéissant à mes humeurs fatales,
> Des êtres singuliers, décrépits et *charmants*.
>
> Aurais-je, sans mourir, contemplé le huitième,
> Sosie inexorable, *ironique* et fatal . . .

I have said sufficient to give some idea of 'the landscape quality of the city', but we can only grasp the significance of the landscape when it is provided with figures, and this leads to a consideration of the general meaning of the chapter. The centre of the 'Tableaux Parisiens' is a group of four poems which follows *A une Mendiante rousse*. The theme of all four is exile. *Le Cygne*, which forms the prologue, deals both with the general idea of exile and with the poet's personal sense of exile. The three remaining poems—*Les Sept vieillards*, *Les Petites vieilles*, and *Les Aveugles*—are concerned with specific examples of those modern exiles and outcasts, old men, old women, and the blind.

Le Cygne begins with an example of exile taken from classical times, with the image of the widowed Andromache weeping beside the river:

> Andromaque, je pense à vous! Ce petit fleuve,
> Pauvre et triste miroir où jadis resplendit
> L'immense majesté de vos douleurs de veuve,
> Ce Simoïs menteur qui par vos pleurs grandit,
>
> A fécondé soudain ma mémoire fertile,
> Comme je traversais le nouveau Carrousel.
> Le vieux Paris n'est plus (la forme d'une ville
> Change plus vite, hélas! que le cœur d'un mortel);
>
> Je ne vois qu'en esprit tout ce camp de baraques,
> Ces tas de chapiteaux ébauchés et de fûts,
> Les herbes, les gros blocs verdis par l'eau des flaques,
> Et, brillant aux carreaux, le bric-à-brac confus.

---

[1] *Entretiens Politiques et Littéraires, art. cit.*, p. 111. *Mélanges posthumes*, p. 115.

It seems probable that the memory of Andromache—'memory' is a crucial word in this poem—was recalled by the sight of the 'classical' buildings in the centre of Paris. When the poem was first published it had an epigraph from the Third Book of Virgil's *Æneid*: 'Falsi Simonentis ad undam'. For Baudelaire evokes the image of Andromache at the time when she was an exile in Pyrrhus's capital and had made a river there 'in imitation of the river Simois of Troy to remind her of her native land'.[1]

The image of Andromache stirs the poet's personal memories. In the last two lines of the second verse the 'classical' tone, which was admirably suited to the opening of the poem, changes to a more colloquial tone; but though the reference to the changing face of Paris seems almost an aside, we shall find that the contrast between change and the unchanging is one of the central themes of the poem. The poet remembers the swan that he himself had seen many years before when passing through the same part of Paris:

> Là s'étalait jadis une ménagerie;
> Là je vis, un matin, à l'heure où sous les cieux
> Froids et clairs le Travail s'éveille, où la voirie
> Pousse un sombre ouragan dans l'air silencieux,
>
> Un cygne qui s'était évadé de sa cage,
> Et, de ses pieds palmés frottant le pavé sec,
> Sur le sol raboteux traînait son blanc plumage.
> Près d'un ruisseau sans eau la bête ouvrant le bec
>
> Baignait nerveusement ses ailes dans la poudre,
> Et disait, le cœur plein de son beau lac natal:
> 'Eau, quand donc pleuvras-tu? quand tonneras-tu, foudre?'
> Je vois ce malheureux, mythe étrange et fatal,
>
> Vers le ciel quelquefois, comme l'homme d'Ovide,
> Vers le ciel ironique et cruellement bleu,
> Sur son cou convulsif tendant sa tête avide,
> Comme s'il adressait des reproches à Dieu!

I shall discuss Baudelaire's syntax in some detail later on and need only remark here on the effectiveness with which he builds

---

[1] Hackett, *op. cit.*, p. 191.

up the confused and sordid background and delays the appearance of the swan, who is the object of 'je vis' in line 2, until the beginning of the next verse. What are mainly interesting, however, are the similarities and contrasts between the images of Andromache and the swan. The word 'mythe' applies to both of them. Andromache belongs to a classical myth, the swan to a new myth which the poet is creating. He is a 'symbol' in the same sense as Baudelaire's albatross, but in this poem the symbol is worked out with consummate skill.[1]

Andromache has been taken from her native land and brought as a captive to Pyrrhus's capital where she stands weeping beside an imitation river. The swan, too, has been taken from his 'beau lac natal' and imprisoned in a 'ménagerie' where he becomes like the weeping Andromache a spectacle for strangers to gaze on. He escaped from his cage, but it was an escape into a fresh 'exile', and he remains an incongruous figure with his white plumage set against the dim background of the city amid the clatter of the refuse bins. The skies, which are 'froids et clairs', remind him tantalizingly of his native lake as the false river reminds Andromache of the real river in her native land. Her tears swell the imitation river, but they cannot make it anything but 'ce petit fleuve'. The swan is deprived of water altogether. The sight of him scratching the dry stones, and dipping his wings into the dust near the 'ruisseau sans eau', appears to be an ironical allusion to 'ce Simoïs menteur' because the swan is lamenting beside a stream which is a caricature of the 'beau lac natal' in the same way that Andromache's river is a caricature of the real Simois.

An American critic suggests that there is a parallel between these verses and the fifth section of *The Waste Land*.[2] Baudelaire certainly uses absence of water as a symbol not merely of frustration, but of *stagnation*, in the same way that Mr. Eliot does in *What the Thunder Said* and *Gerontion*. This explains the appeal:

'Eau, quand donc pleuvras-tu? quand tonneras-tu, foudre?'

[1] He is also an immediate ancestor of Mallarmé's swan in 'Le vierge, le vivace et le bel aujourd'hui'.

[2] Joseph D. Bennett, *Baudelaire: A Criticism*, Princeton and London, 2nd ed., 1946, pp. 103–4.

It is an appeal for water to provide him with another lake, but it is more than that. It is an appeal for a convulsion of nature which will bring water that is literally and metaphorically life-giving to a stagnant civilization.

I have said that the description of the changing face of Paris in the second verse is one of the main themes of the poem. Andromache is a symbol of the unchanging sense of exile which remains in the human heart in spite of the changes that take place in the 'form' of life. 'Le cœur d'un mortel', therefore, stands for something permanent, for something that belongs to the human condition; 'la forme d'une ville' stands for the impermanent, the transitory. In other words, the changes in the face of Paris mark the change from the classical to the modern symbols of exile. The futile, ineffectual movements of the swan scratching 'feverishly', bathing his wings 'nervously', and darting his neck 'convulsively' are contrasted with

> L'immense majesté de vos douleurs de veuve.

Andromache's grief is classical, restrained, majestic. The swan is the symbol of the unrest of the modern exile—the unrest which torments the poet himself.

This brings us to the end of the first part of the poem. The opening verse of the second part reintroduces the theme of the changing face of Paris and the unchanging 'melancholy' of the human heart:

> Paris change! mais rien dans ma mélancolie
> N'a bougé! palais neufs, échafaudages, blocs,
> Vieux faubourgs, tout pour moi devient allégorie,
> Et mes chers souvenirs sont plus lourds que des rocs.

The sight of the new 'palaces', the scaffolding, and the blocks of stone in the midst of the 'vieux faubourgs' brings home to us the confusion and the shapeless indifference of the modern city. The rocks to which he compares his memories are another symbol of sterility and frustration.

The images of the swan and Andromache reappear and are woven together:

Aussi devant ce Louvre une image m'opprime:
Je pense à mon grand cygne, avec ses gestes fous,
Comme les exilés, ridicule et sublime,
Et rongé d'un désir sans trêve! et puis à vous,

Andromaque, des bras d'un grand époux tombée,
Vil bétail, sous la main du superbe Pyrrhus,
Auprès d'un tombeau vide en extase courbée;
Veuve d'Hector, hélas! et femme d'Hélénus!

The comparison between the classical and the modern exile is maintained, but the sequence of the images is reversed which has the effect of stressing the peculiar position of the modern exile with his frayed nerves and his 'gestes fous'. 'Rongé d'un désir sans trêve' seems to refer to the longing to find a way home. It leads back to the spectacle of Andromache. The words 'vil bétail' introduce a fresh motif. Andromache is an exile and a captive, but 'vil bétail' turns her into a chattel, a commodity to be bought and sold as the swan was bought and sold and put into a cage. She is bent 'in ecstasy' over an empty tomb—the tomb that she had built beside the imitation Simois in honour of the dead Hector—which apparently stands for the impossibility of any return. 'Ridicule et sublime' seems to identify the poet unmistakably with the swan and recalls that other poem of exile— *L'Albatros*—where we leave the poet

Exilé sur le sol au milieu des huées
Ses ailes de géant l'empêchent de marcher.

In the last three verses we have a brief glimpse of other exiles and outcasts: the consumptive negress lost in the jostling throng of the modern city, the orphans, the weepers, the shipwrecked mariners. There are continual references back to the two main images. The negress thinking longingly of the coconut trees of her native Africa is Andromache longing for the Simois of her native Troy; the weepers are Andromache weeping into the imitation Simois; the orphans 'séchant comme des fleurs' the swan beside the dried-up stream; and the shipwrecked sailors remind us that the sea, though so often a symbol of liberation, is the greatest barrier between the exile and home.

In the closing verses the poet's own role undergoes a change. We find that he has taken the place of the mourning Andromache, as he stands watching the anonymous procession of the lesser exiles which passes rapidly across the stage and fades away in the 'bien d'autres encor' of the last line. His tone changes to a tone of lamentation and each type of exile is introduced by the words, 'Je pense à . . .' It strikes a note of despair in

> Je pense . . .
> A quiconque a perdu ce qui ne se retrouve
> Jamais, jamais!

In the final moving verse he identifies himself with exiles everywhere:

> Ainsi dans la forêt où mon esprit s'exile
> Un vieux Souvenir sonne à plein souffle du cor!
> Je pense aux matelots oubliés dans une île,
> Aux captifs, aux vaincus! . . . à bien d'autres encor!

'Souvenir' recalls the 'mémoire fertile' of the second verse, and the poem reminds us even more strongly than *La Chevelure* of the close connection between Baudelaire's memory and Proust's *mémoire involontaire*. The sight of an object in the external world sets the machinery in motion, stirring 'forgotten' memories. Emotions buried in the depths of the unconscious float to the surface of the conscious mind, attach themselves to *visual* images, and crystallize in a fresh experience.[1] The whole poem, in fact, is a reverie constructed out of memories, and the word 'Souvenir' completes the familiar 'circle'.

The 'symphonic' construction of this superb poem has been highly praised. It is probable that music did suggest the method of introducing the main images, but the source does not perhaps greatly matter. What does matter is that Baudelaire is using with complete mastery one of the most important and influential *poetic* devices of the century. The recurring image, which was later used with extreme brilliance by Laforgue in his *Derniers vers*, has

---

[1] 'Certes, ce qui palpite ainsi au fond de moi, ce doit être l'image, le souvenir visuel, qui, lié à cette saveur, tente de la suivre jusqu'à moi' (*A la Recherche du temps perdu*).

added enormously to the subtlety and complexity of modern poetry.[1] It was the outcome of that other discovery—the 'analogical' method or the method of 'emotional equivalences'. For once the poet used an image to symbolize an emotion instead of describing emotion or using the image as a mere illustration, he found himself in possession of a sort of poetic shorthand. When this is extended to the recurring image, themes and emotions can be made to weave in and out of one another, sometimes blending and sometimes clashing, in a way that gives the pattern of the poem its new complexity, and is particularly effective in the dream atmosphere of this poem. In *Le Cygne* it does not stop at the main images. It is applied to individual words so that they reinforce and add to the cohesion not merely of the main images, but of the whole poem. When we look back we find that there is in fact a series of words or subsidiary images suggesting fecundity, water, drought, and nervousness—'grandit', 'féconde', 'fertile', 'eau', 'ruisseau', 'sec', 'séchant', 'nerveusement', 'convulsif', 'fous'—which elaborate and prolong the principal themes. Baudelaire 'works' these words so that they all become symbols of frustration in a manner that looks forward to Mallarmé. Andromache's tears 'swell' the river, but it is an imitation river which stands for her frustration at being exiled from Troy. The recollection of her 'fertilizes' the poet's memory, but it leads to the other great image of frustration—the swan and the dried-up stream. The image of drought leads, finally, by way of the 'orphelins séchant comme des fleurs', to the sea which cuts the shipwrecked sailors off from their homes.

The poem possesses an impressive variety of tone which ranges not only from the grand manner to the colloquial style, but includes the ironic-heroic tone in which the swan is described:

> Comme s'il adressait des reproches à Dieu!

and the sorrowful tone of the close with its repeated 'Je pense'. We find a similar variety in the continually changing décors

[1] I have discussed Laforgue's use of the recurring image in 'The Poetry of Jules Laforgue', *Scrutiny*, Vol. V. No. 2, September 1936, and 'Jules Laforgue: Observations on the Theory and Practice of Free Verse,' *The Cornhill*, No. 973, Winter, 1947–8.

seen through the poet's unchanging 'melancholy'. The scene moves to and fro between the classical landscape of Greece and the rubble of Louis-Philippe's Paris, passes on to a fleeting glimpse of an exotic Africa and the islands lost in the middle of the ocean. The figures sometimes harmonize with their background and sometimes clash with it. Andromache is in harmony with hers; the swan clashes with his, but one of the most vivid moments in the poem is the silhouette of the shattered negress caught, as it were, between 'les cocotiers absents de la superbe Afrique' and 'la muraille immense du brouillard'.

The editors of the critical edition point out that we are not prevented from seeking a symbolical interpretation of *Les Sept vieillards* and suggest, tentatively, that this number may be an allusion to the seven deadly sins. Their observation is equally applicable to *Les Petites vieilles* and *Les Aveugles*. The symbolism of all three poems appears to be twofold. The old men, the old women, and the blind are, as we know, specific examples of the modern exile and they proceed logically from the exiles described in the closing verses of *Le Cygne*. I think that the seven old men, who are described significantly as 'ces sept monstres hideux', stand for the seven deadly sins and that there is a parallel between them and the seven kinds of animal and reptile mentioned in *Au Lecteur*. I suspect that there is a further parallel between the allegorical figure of 'Ennui' in that poem and the eighth old man. For the poet is so appalled at the idea that 'the eighth' may appear that he turns tail, goes back to his lodging, and shuts himself in. The introduction of names from classical legend in *Les Petites vieilles* suggests another contrast between classical and modern times in the manner of Andromache and the swan, while the spectacle of the blind men in *Les Aveugles* turning their sightless eyes to heaven is probably an allusion to contemporary unbelief—the exiles have no faith to sustain them—and to the poet's own religious doubts.[1]

Although the poet had gone down into the city in the hope of re-establishing contact with other people he remains imprisoned

[1] See the editors' note on p. 459 of the critical edition.

in his own loneliness, an exile among exiles. The sense of distance between himself and the other exiles—the sympathetic desire to enter into their lives and the impossibility of doing so—is accentuated by his irony. He proceeds to give an account of their plight in a tone in which pity and irony are blended and which gives the poems their distinctive quality.

Whether or not the seven old men represent the seven deadly sins, they are essentially sinister figures. The poet treats them as examples of the exile who has turned sour, and in order to convey the impression that they make on him he uses the words 'méchanceté', 'fiel', 'hostile', 'infâme', 'infernal', 'sinistre'. The poem begins with a general description of the frightening impression caused by the apparition which suddenly clutches the arm of the pedestrian in broad daylight. This creates a tense, uneasy atmosphere which prepares us for the entry of the procession, and the 'spectre' in line 2 looks forward to 'ces spectres baroques' in the eighth verse. The scene is set and the poet goes on to give an account of a personal experience:

> Un matin, cependant que dans la triste rue
> Les maisons, dont la brume allongeait la hauteur,
> Simulaient les deux quais d'une rivière accrue,
> Et que, décor semblable à l'âme de l'acteur,
>
> Un brouillard sale et jaune inondait tout l'espace,
> Je suivais, roidissant mes nerfs comme un héros
> Et discutant avec mon âme déjà lasse,
> Le faubourg secoué par les lourds tombereaux.

There is a deliberate lowering of the tension in these two verses. The poet puts the 'spectre' out of his mind, fixes our attention on the physical details of the scene—the street, the houses, the fog, and the vibration of the dust-carts. The sight of the changing shapes of the houses introduces the element of distortion which is of capital importance in this and the poems that follow. For the *physical* distortion, or the illusion of physical distortion, caused by the fog is the prelude to the *psychological* distortion which belongs to the machinery of the nightmare. In spite of the emphasis on physical details, the atmosphere remains equivocal.

We are not sure—the poet does not mean us to feel sure—whether we are awake and a supernatural apparition is about to arrive or whether we are in the middle of a 'bad dream'. The fourth line seems to me to be obscure. The word 'décor' must mean stage scenery—theatres always suggest a mixture of tawdriness and glamour in Baudelaire's poetry—but it is not certain whether the poet is speaking of the way in which the actor's life is divided between the real world and the world of illusion, or whether he himself is for the time being an actor whose mood reflects the confused foggy scene. I think that logically 'l'âme de l'acteur' must mean actors in general, though Baudelaire was probably conscious of the two possible interpretations. In any case 'actor' looks forward to 'a hero' which is clearly an ironical reference to the poet. He is about to relate the 'part' that he played in the comedy of the old men, but we shall see from the close of the poem that his conduct turns out to be very unheroic.

The procession is introduced in the next verse:

> Tout à coup, un vieillard dont les guenilles jaunes
> Imitaient la couleur de ce ciel pluvieux,
> Et dont l'aspect aurait fait pleuvoir les aumônes,
> Sans la méchanceté qui luisait dans ses yeux,
>
> M'apparut.

His appearance is a careful blending of the matter of fact and the sinister. The comparison between the colour of his rags and the colour of the rainy skies marks a very adroit transition from physical to psychological distortion, and we remain uncertain whether we are sleeping or waking. 'Imitaient' is the crucial word. It refers back to 'simulaient' and reinforces the image of the actor and of the poet himself suspended between the real world and the world of make-believe. The poem goes on:

> On eût dit sa prunelle trempée
> Dans le fiel; son regard aiguisait les frimas,
> Et sa barbe à longs poils, roide comme une épée,
> Se projetait, pareille à celle de Judas.
>
> Il n'était pas voûté, mais cassé, son échine
> Faisant avec sa jambe un parfait angle droit,

> Si bien que son bâton, parachevant sa mine,
> Lui donnait la tournure et le pas maladroit
>
> D'un quadrupède infirme ou d'un juif à trois pattes.
> Dans la neige et la boue il allait s'empêtrant,
> Comme s'il écrasait des morts sous ses savates,
> Hostile à l'univers plutôt qu'indifférent.
>
> Son pareil le suivait: barbe, œil, dos, bâton, loques,
> Nul trait ne distinguait, du même enfer venu,
> Ce jumeau centenaire, et ces spectres baroques
> Marchaient du même pas vers un but inconnu.
>
> A quel complot infâme étais-je donc en butte,
> Ou quel méchant hasard ainsi m'humiliait?
> Car je comptai sept fois, de minute en minute,
> Ce sinistre vieillard qui se multipliait!

The sober, prosaic tone is brilliantly successful in maintaining our doubts about the nature of the old men and in preventing the scene from becoming sensational or melodramatic. The sense of distortion is produced by the contrast between the inhuman geometrical images and the images of the shattered human beings:

> Il n'était pas voûté, mais *cassé*, son échine
> Faisant avec sa jambe *un parfait angle droit* . . .
>
>   son bâton, parachevant sa mine,
> Lui donnait la tournure et le pas maladroit
>
> D'un quadrupède *infirme* ou d'un juif à trois pattes.

The impression is heightened by words and images with intangible or disturbing associations. The old man's beard,

>   roide comme une épée,
> Se projetait, pareille à *celle de Judas*.

He is 'hostile', 'sinistre'; his fellows are 'spectres baroques'. The impression is completed by the inexplicable sight of seven identical old men coming relentlessly forward as though the image of the first were 'multiplied', making the poet wonder whether he is seeing double. He appeals to the reader for sympathy:

> Que celui-là qui rit de mon inquiétude,
> Et qui n'est pas saisi d'un frisson fraternel,
> Songe bien que malgré tant de décrépitude
> Ces sept monstres hideux avaient l'air éternel!

The poem is moving towards its climax. 'Monstres hideux' is stronger than any of the previous expressions that he has used of the old men and is a sign of fear. There is a contrast between 'décrépitude' and 'éternel', between their battered appearance and the violence of its impact on the poet. The word 'éternel' also looks back to 'simulaient' and 'imitaient'. The poet is really beginning to believe that he is faced with a supernatural apparition. The impression is driven home in the next verse by the words 'sosie inexorable, ironique et fatal'. For the last three verses describe the poet very unheroically 'going to pieces':

> Exaspéré comme un ivrogne qui voit double,
> Je rentrai, je fermai ma porte, épouvanté,
> Malade et morfondu, l'esprit fiévreux et trouble,
> Blessé par le mystère et par l'absurdité!

The words 'épouvanté', 'malade', 'fiévreux', and 'trouble' reflect the poet's growing panic. They are helped by the jerky movement of the versification and the double cæsura in lines 1 and 2 which isolates the word 'épouvanté':

> Exaspéré—comme un ivrogne—qui voit double,
> Je rentrai,—je fermai ma porte,—épouvanté.

Although the poet has left the scene, the impression of horror not only remains; it becomes more intense and he thinks that he must be 'ill'. 'Ivrogne' like 'malade' refers to a psychological impression; 'porte' to the physical action of banging the door in the vain attempt to blot out the spectacle. His doubts about the nature of the apparition also remain:

> Blessé par le mystère et par l'absurdité!

It is horrible, mysterious, but also absurd. 'Mystère' refers back to 'Les mystères partout coulent commes des sèves' in the first verse; 'l'absurdité' to the images drawn from acting in verses 2 and 3 and to 'ironique et fatal' in verse 12. The final verse beginning

> Vainement ma raison voulait prendre la barre,

describes a state of complete nervous collapse.

Baudelaire displays more sympathy for the old women in *Les Petites vieilles*; but though they are not intrinsically evil like the old men, they too have been turned by their environment into 'monsters' who are repugnant to the poet:

> Ces monstres disloqués furent jadis des femmes,
> Éponine ou Laïs! Monstres brisés, bossus
> Ou tordus, aimons-les! ce sont encor des âmes.
> Sous des jupons troués et sous de froids tissus
>
> Ils rampent, flagellés par les bises iniques,
> Frémissant au fracas roulant des omnibus,
> Et serrant sur leur flanc, ainsi que des reliques,
> Un petit sac brodé de fleurs ou de rébus;
>
> Ils trottent, tout pareils à des marionnettes;
> Se traînent, comme font les animaux blessés,
> Ou dansent, sans vouloir danser, pauvres sonnettes
> Où se pend un Démon sans pitié! Tout cassés . . .

The distortion provides a comment on the civilization which had produced such creatures. Baudelaire was specially concerned with the destructive nature of contemporary life, and the accent falls on the words 'brisés', 'bossus', 'tordus', 'disloqués', 'cassés'. The drama is not so much described as enacted. We hear the snap of breaking bone in 'brisés' and 'cassés', and the queer shuffling tread of the down-and-outs in 'disloqués'. Civilization has reduced these exiles to mindless, inhuman robots moving jerkily across the stage 'towards an unknown goal'.

Baudelaire's use of theological terms is not always free from ambiguity, but words like 'âme', 'ange', 'péché', and 'mal' are often used in a strictly orthodox sense. When he says:

> . . . aimons-les! ce sont encor des âmes,

or in another poem:

> Dans la brute assoupie un ange se réveille,

'âme' and 'ange' represent positive values. It was Baudelaire's consciousness of the worth of the individual soul which was being destroyed that makes his view of the modern world a tragic one, and the tragedy is heightened by the ironical 'Éponine ou Laïs!' Yet the total effect of the three poems is one of macabre comedy which is peculiarly Baudelaire's own. It is apparent in the assumed naïveté of:

> —Avez-vous observé que maints cercueils de vieilles
> Sont presque aussi petits que celui d'un enfant?

A few lines later he enlarges on the idea:

> Il me semble toujours que cet être fragile
> S'en va tout doucement vers un nouveau berceau;
>
> A moins que, méditant sur la géométrie,
> Je ne cherche, à l'aspect de ces membres discords,
> Combien de fois il faut que l'ouvrier varie
> La forme de la boîte où l'on met tous ces corps.

In *Les Aveugles* the irony becomes still more cruel:

> Contemple-les, mon âme, ils sont vraiment affreux!
> Pareils aux mannequins; vaguement ridicules;
> Terribles, singuliers comme des somnambules;
> Dardant on ne sait où leurs globes ténébreux.

Baudelaire was sometimes decidedly slapdash in his use of adjectives, but in these poems almost every adjective—even the most commonplace—fits its noun exactly and conveys the impression that he is trying to render. The blind are pitiful, but their mechanical gestures irritate the poet. The mixture of pity and irritation is expressed in the colloquial phrase, 'ils sont vraiment affreux', and by the combination of 'ridicules', 'terribles', 'singuliers'. 'Pareils aux mannequins' significantly recalls 'tout pareils à des marionnettes' in *Les Petites vieilles*. It is reinforced by the wicked 'comme des somnambules' and 'leurs globes ténébreux'. In the next verse:

> Leurs yeux, d'où la divine étincelle est partie,
> Comme s'ils regardaient au loin, restent levés
> Au ciel; on ne les voit jamais vers les pavés
> Pencher rêveusement leur tête appesantie

the effect depends on a mingling of the mock-heroic—'la divine
étincelle'—exact observation:

> Leurs yeux . . .
> Comme s'ils regardaient au loin, restent levés
> Au ciel . . .

and assumed surprise. But the final shot is the studied casualness
of the question in the last line:

> Je dis: Que cherchent-ils au Ciel, tous ces aveugles?

What is most striking in all these poems is the absence of any
sense of community. It is a world of stagnation and confusion, a
world of 'memories', 'dreams', 'shadows', and 'ghosts'. The
inhabitants are completely rootless. They stumble blindly through
the mud and fog and confusion of the 'ant-like' modern city:

> Traversant de Paris le *fourmillant* tableau.

> Telles vous cheminez, stoïques et sans plaintes,
> A travers le *chaos* des vivantes cités.

The poet has completed his daylight tour of the city and goes
on to explore its night-life. *Le Crépuscule du soir* describes night-
fall. The restaurants are full; the theatres open; the man who has
worked well looks back with satisfaction on his day; the exhausted
workman—'l'ouvrier courbé'—goes home to bed. But it is not
this that interests the poet most. For Baudelaire night is primarily
the time of sin and crime when thieves and prostitutes emerge
from their lairs. A stealthy, furtive note is apparent in the play
of the hissing c's and s's and the liquid l's of the opening lines,
giving the impression of whispered confidences:

> Voici le soir charmant, ami du criminel;
> Il vient comme un complice, à pas de loup; le ciel
> Se ferme lentement comme une grande alcôve,
> Et l'homme impatient se change en bête fauve.

He employs the same device to give us a glimpse of the
criminals in action:

N

Les tables d'hôte, dont le jeu fait les délices,
S'emplissent de catins et d'escrocs, leurs complices,
Et les voleurs, qui n'ont ni trêve ni merci,
Vont bientôt commencer leur travail, eux aussi,
Et forcer doucement les portes et les caisses
Pour vivre quelques jours et vêtir leurs maîtresses.

He pauses for a moment to reflect on the condition of the sick and dying in the hospitals:

C'est l'heure où les douleurs des malades s'aigrissent!
La sombre Nuit les prend à la gorge; ils finissent
Leur destinée et vont vers le gouffre commun . . .

But here the hissing sibilants are a sign of life slipping away.

Le Jeu and *Danse macabre* are both pictures of night-life. The subject is inevitably a temptation rather than an opportunity for Baudelaire, but *Le Jeu* contains some effective vignettes of the gamblers. These are the ageing courtesans:

Autour des verts tapis des visages sans lèvre,
Des lèvres sans couleur, des mâchoires sans dent,
Et des doigts convulsés d'une infernale fièvre,
Fouillant la poche vide ou le sein palpitant . . .

The 'doigts convulsés' and the 'sein palpitant' convey, a little melodramatically no doubt, the feverish futile passion of the players and the poet feels himself

Enviant de ces gens la passion tenace,
De ces vieilles putains la funèbre gaieté . . .

In the same poem he comments:

Voilà le noir tableau qu'en un rêve nocturne
Je vis se dérouler sous mon œil clairvoyant.

These poems are followed by a group of five pieces containing personal memories and reflexions. He has described prostitution in the city. In *L'Amour du mensonge*, which is thought by Crépet and Blin to have been addressed to Marie Daubrun, he describes

a personal relationship with a courtesan.[1] The theme is similar
to that of *Semper eadem*. In the middle of his tour the poet is
overcome by the horror of his situation. He knows that there is
no way out, but he is prepared to try make-believe again and
expresses it in the splendid final verse:

> Mais ne suffit-il pas que tu sois l'apparence,
> Pour réjouir un cœur qui fuit la vérité?
> Qu'importe ta bêtise ou ton indifférence?
> Masque ou décor, salut! J'adore ta beauté.

'Je n'ai pas oublié, voisine de la ville' and 'La servante au
grand cœur dont vous étiez jalouse' are both addressed to his
mother and recall, nostalgically, his childhood days with her.
The desire to escape is also the subject of *Brumes et pluies* with
its lovely opening:

> O fins d'automne, hivers, printemps trempés de boue,
> Endormeuses saisons! je vous aime et vous loue . . .

This time the choice seems to lie between insensibility and the
prospect of lulling himself by a chance encounter:

> par un soir sans lune, deux à deux,
> D'endormir la douleur sur un lit hasardeux.

Rêve parisien, the final poem of this group, is an outstanding
success. He is back in his attic and the poem purports to describe
a real dream as compared with the 'rêveries' and 'allégories' of
the earlier poems in the chapter. Superficially, it may sound like
a prophetic vision of the future, but what Baudelaire is really
doing is to give expression by a highly original use of language,
which was to have a decisive influence on the Rimbaud of the
Illuminations, to his sense of being trapped in a hostile universe:

> . . . peintre fier de mon génie,
> Je savourais dans mon tableau
> L'enivrante monotonie
> Du métal, du marbre et de l'eau.

[1] The internal evidence seems to me to point strongly to Jeanne Duval.
Expressions like 'ma chère indolente', 'ton allure harmonieuse', and 'l'ennui
de ton regard profond' are the sort of terms that he uses to describe her in
her cycle. Nor do I think that he would have used the word 'bêtise' of
anyone but Jeanne.

> Babel d'escaliers et d'arcades,
> C'était un palais infini,
> Plein de bassins et de cascades
> Tombant dans l'or mat ou bruni;
>
> Et des cataractes pesantes,
> Comme des rideaux de cristal,
> Se suspendaient, éblouissantes,
> A des murailles de métal.

The natural propensity of water is to flow, but in this world it loses its natural properties and is suspended, motionless, 'comme des rideaux de cristal'.

We know that Baudelaire detested nature—wild, untamed nature—and that one of his aims was to banish what he calls contemptuously 'le végétal irrégulier'; but in doing so he starved his own senses of the scents, sounds, and colours for which they craved. The laconic, sober style of this poem describes wonderfully the desolation of a soundless world:

> Nul astre d'ailleurs, nuls vestiges
> De soleil, même au bas du ciel,
> Pour illuminer ces prodiges,
> Qui brillaient d'un feu personnel!
>
> Et sur ces mouvantes merveilles
> Planait (terrible nouveauté!
> Tout pour l'œil, rien pour les oreilles!)
> Un silence d'éternité.

The poem expresses an element of capital importance in Baudelaire's experience and it cannot be treated in isolation. We have seen that in the first chapter he came to feel that he was the prisoner of his own mood and tried to break out of the *emotional* circle. *Rêve parisien* is really the answer to this attempt. For the prison is a twofold one. He escapes from himself simply to find that he has become a prisoner in an inhuman world which can only drive him back into the self from which he has escaped with the realization that all the exits are blocked and that there is no way out. For this reason *Rêve parisien* is the reply to *L'Héautontimorouménos* and *L'Irrémédiable*. When we look at the last two verses of part one of the second of these poems:

> Un navire pris dans le pôle,
> Comme en un piège de cristal,
> Cherchant par quel détroit fatal
> Il est tombé dans cette geôle;
>
> —Emblèmes nets, tableau parfait
> D'une fortune irrémédiable,
> Qui donne à penser que le Diable
> Fait toujours bien ce qu'il fait!

we cannot fail to be struck by the similarity of the imagery and that of *Rêve parisien*, particularly the 'piège de cristal', the 'rideaux de cristal', and the 'geôle'.

The final poem marks the end of the journey and the awakening from dreams:

> La diane chantait dans les cours des casernes,
> Et le vent du matin soufflait sur les lanternes.
>
> C'était l'heure où l'essaim des rêves malfaisants
> Tord sur leurs oreillers les bruns adolescents;
> Où, comme un œil sanglant qui palpite et qui bouge,
> La lampe sur le jour fait une tache rouge;
> Où l'âme, sous le poids du corps revêche et lourd,
> Imite les combats de la lampe et du jour.
> Comme un visage en pleurs que les brises essuient,
> L'air est plein du frisson des choses qui s'enfuient,
> Et l'homme est las d'écrire et la femme d'aimer.
>
> Les maisons çà et là commençaient à fumer.
> Les femmes de plaisir, la paupière livide,
> Bouche ouverte, dormaient de leur sommeil stupide;
> Les pauvresses, traînant leurs seins maigres et froids,
> Soufflaient sur leurs tisons et soufflaient sur leurs doigts.
> C'était l'heure où parmi le froid et la lésine
> S'aggravent les douleurs des femmes en gésine;
> Comme un sanglot coupé par un sang écumeux
> Le chant du coq au loin déchirait l'air brumeux;
> Une mer de brouillards baignait les édifices,
> Et les agonisants dans le fond des hospices
> Poussaient leur dernier râle en hoquets inégaux.
> Les débauchés rentraient, brisés par leurs travaux.

L'aurore grelottante en robe rose et verte
S'avançait lentement sur la Seine déserte,
Et le sombre Paris, en se frottant les yeux,
Empoignait ses outils, vieillard laborieux.

Although *Le Crépuscule du matin* is an early work, it is a brilliant performance which is greatly superior to its companion piece and a superb illustration of the skill with which Baudelaire uses his verbs. It is a panorama of the ravages of the night which began in *Le Crépuscule du soir*. We see the tormented adolescents tossing on their beds, the weary poet—this seems a backward glance at *Paysage*—throwing down his pen, women exhausted by love, prostitutes sprawling in their dens, the poor in their hovels trying to light the fire, the dying in the hospitals, and debauchees, ironically, 'brisés par leurs travaux'. The verbs give the poem its movement and life, but the cumulative effect depends very largely on the alternation of sound and visual images. There are two main sounds—the bugle which is answered from afar by the strident crowing of the cock presented in one masterly line:

Le chant du coq au loin déchirait l'air brumeux.

They are thrown into relief by the undertones: the sighing of the breeze in one of Baudelaire's loveliest couplets:

Comme un visage en pleurs que les brises essuient,
L'air est plein du frisson des choses qui s'enfuient.

It is followed by the snores of the sleeping prostitutes, the sound of the poor blowing on their fires and their frozen fingers —repeating the image of the wind 'blowing' on the lamps—and the 'hoquets inégaux' of the death-rattle in the hospitals.

The moment between sleeping and waking is caught by the sound of the bugle blending into the trembling of the street lamp. The movement of the fading light battling with the growing day reflects the flickering consciousness of the 'bruns adolescents':

Où l'âme, sous le poids du corps revêche et lourd,
Imite les combats de la lampe et du jour.

The movement of the lamp melts into the smoke drifting from the chimneys. At this point there is a pause. We are given a *static* picture of the sleeping prostitutes which is contrasted with the uneasy sleep of the adolescents. Movement begins again with the women going about their houses. The 'douleurs des femmes en gésine' is emphasized by 'un sanglot coupé par un sang écumeux'. The smoke from the chimneys disappears into the fog which leads naturally to the choking of the dying whom we saw in the first *Crépuscule* and whose agonies look back to

> Tord sur leurs oreillers les bruns adolescents,

and forward to

> Les débauchés rentraient, brisés par leurs travaux.

The final image is a careful piece of stylization. The disorders of the night are over; the city is going back to work. 'L'ouvrier courbé qui regagne son lit' of *Le Crépuscule du soir*, who has spent a restful night, shoulders his tools and sets out. The 'vieillard laborieux' stands for honest toil—the sound element in a corrupt civilization—in contrast to the 'travaux' of the prosperous debauchees.

3. 'Le Vin'

I have shown that the present placing of this chapter effectively neutralizes its effect in the architecture of the *Fleurs du mal*. The intrinsic value of the five poems that it contains is not great. We need only notice for future reference, when discussing the last chapter in the book, that the poems introduce the figures of the poor, lovers, the lonely man, and the murderer.

4. 'Fleurs du Mal'

'Many a time in front of these samples of the feelings of all and sundry, I have found myself wishing that the poet, the person interested in such things, the philosopher could enjoy the pleasure of a museum of love where everything would have a place from the tenderness of a Saint Teresa which had

no proper outlet to the serious debauches of the ages of boredom. No doubt the distance is immense which separates *Le
Départ pour l'île de Cythère* from the wretched coloured daubs
which hang in the bedrooms of harlots above a cracked jug
and a rickety console-table; but with a subject of such importance nothing should be neglected. And besides, genius sancti-
fies everything. If these subjects were treated with the necessary
care and composure, they would not be soiled by that revolt-
ing obscenity which is a form of bravado rather than of
truth.'
                                        Curiosités esthétiques

The fourth chapter of the *Fleurs du mal* has been described as
the heart of the volume. The choice of title shows that Baudelaire
attached particular importance to it, but we must not exaggerate
the intrinsic value of the individual poems. They are for the most
part early work and though some of them are impressive, only
Un Voyage à Cythère ranks among Baudelaire's greatest work.

The architectural importance of the chapter is not in doubt. It
originally contained twelve poems, but three of them were condemned by the court and in the second edition the section was
reduced to nine poems. Baudelaire made no attempt to replace
them because they were irreplaceable, or could only have been
replaced by poems which might have led to further trouble with
the authorities. For the section is in some ways more carefully
constructed than any of the others and its internal unity more
pronounced.

The poems, as we know, describe the poet's descent into the
world of pure evil. Their content explains not merely the main
title of the book, but the two rejected titles—*Les Lesbiennes* and
Les Limbes. The chapter is 'un musée de l'amour', but 'un
musée de l'amour perverti'. For the poems are all studies of the
principal forms of sexual perversion—homosexuality, sadism,
prostitution, necrophilia, and possibly onanism—which separate
the sinner from the rest of the world and condemn him to 'limbo'.
The sense of *ostracism* is a recurring motif. In the first poem he
speaks of himself as

                loin du regard de Dieu,
        Haletant et brisé de fatigue, au milieu
          Des plaines de l'Ennui, profondes et désertes;

in *La Béatrice*, as banished.

> Dans des terrains cendreux, calcinés, sans verdure.

At the close of one of the Lesbian poems, the poet turns on the women, crying:

> Loin des peuples vivants, errantes, condamnées,
> A travers les déserts courez comme les loups . . .

This sense of ostracism is different from the isolation and exile of the other chapters because it is at bottom religious and the emphasis falls on separation from God.

The flowers and the trees—the ranunculus, roses, myrtles, and cypresses—are all monstrous blooms which symbolize sex and death.[1] The connection is heavily underlined in *Les Deux bonnes sœurs*:

> Quand veux-tu m'enterrer, Débauche aux bras immondes?
> O Mort, quand viendras-tu, sa rivale en attraits,
> Sur ses myrtes infects enter tes noirs cyprès?

The title of the poem contains an ironic reference to nuns ('bonnes sœurs'). 'Myrtles' are traditionally Venus's flower and stand for love; but the abuse of love transforms them into 'myrtes infects' which are only fit for fertilizing the cypresses.

Over the whole picture of crime and perversity hangs an immense sense of guilt. As the panorama unfolds before us, we continually hear cries of lamentation and denunciation:

> —Ah! Seigneur! donnez-moi la force et le courage . . .

> —Descendez, descendez, lamentables victimes . . .

These are not the only notes. We hear in a remarkable line of

> De terribles plaisirs et d'affreuses douceurs

and

> Des rires effrénés mêlés aux sombres pleurs.

[1] Bracquemond was to have produced a design for the title-page of the second edition showing 'the flowers of evil', which were emblems of sins and vices, attacking the tree of Knowledge and Goodness. He was, however, unable to grasp the poet's intention, and the design was eventually executed by a Belgian artist for *Les Épaves*.

For mingled with the sense of guilt is an undeniable element of complicity which deserves investigation.

'The sympathy for the prostitute,' writes Arnold Hauser, 'which the decadents share with the romantics, and in which Baudelaire is again the intermediary, is the expression of the same inhibited, guilt-laden relationship to love. It is, of course, above all the expression of the revolt against bourgeois society and the morality based on the bourgeois family. The prostitute is the *déracinée* and the outlaw, the rebel who revolts not only against the institutional bourgeois form of love, but also against its "natural" spiritual form. She destroys not only the moral and social organization of the feeling, she destroys the bases of the feeling itself. She is cold in the midst of the storms of passion, she is and remains the superior spectator of the lust that she awakens, she feels lonely and apathetic when others are enraptured and intoxicated—she is, in brief, the artist's female double.'[1]

What Hauser says of the prostitute is true of all the perversions described in this chapter. For Baudelaire, sexual perversion is a symbol of revolt against the bourgeois world; a revolt which undermines not only bourgeois institutions, but also 'the bases of feeling itself'. The poet is naturally on the side of revolt, but far from diminishing his sense of guilt his complicity heightens it.

Four words recur constantly in the poems—'destruction', 'débauche', 'volupté', 'mort'—and their relevance is plain. The poet is engaged in a revolt which is directed at the very foundations of the bourgeois world, but his aim can only be achieved by participation in the 'débauche' and the 'volupté'—the word is used in an excluvisely sexual sense in this chapter—which are the weapons of this particular form of revolt. Now the theme of the cycle is the destruction of the human being by his own excesses. The poet cannot therefore escape the 'destruction' which is the consequence of revolt or 'death' which is the final outcome and which is in a sense its expiation.

'Destruction' is the most important of the four words and it gives its name to the opening poem.[2] This poem has been a source of some speculation among Baudelaire's editors and bio-

[1] *Op. cit.*, p. 888.

[2] When it was first published in 1855 its title was *La Volupté*.

graphers. The sin to which it refers is nameless, but is thought to be onanism. Now onanism, whether in its solitary or its communal form, may be an adolescent phase or an ingrained adult habit. The psychological evil lies in its sterility, in the gap it creates between the individual and the community and in the individual's weakened sense of reality. When it becomes a habit it also becomes a breeding ground for other forms of sexual perversion, principally for homosexuality. It is therefore a reasonable inference that Baudelaire had onanism in mind when he wrote the first poem of 'Fleurs du Mal'. In the last three lines he describes a diabolical vision—there may be a reference to the Temptation in the Desert—which comes to him in the 'plaines de l'Ennui':

> Des vêtements souillés, des blessures ouvertes,
> Et l'appareil sanglant de la Destruction!

The garments are soiled by blood, but also probably by sexual practices. The 'blessures ouvertes' point to the murders, executions and flagellations which occur in the later poems, while the 'appareil sanglant', which is made more horrible by its generality, seems to include the whips and knives that cause the wounds. It marks the transition to the next poem. In *La Destruction* the scene is set

> au milieu
> Des plaines de l'Ennui, profondes et désertes . . .

in *Une Martyre*

> Au milieu des flacons, des étoffes lamées
> Et des meubles voluptueux,
> Des marbres, des tableaux, des robes parfumées
> Qui traînent à plis somptueux.

The poem is a description of a sex-crime—the murdered courtesan is presumably 'love's martyr'—and we cannot fail to admire the skill with which the poet creates the rich, sumptuous atmosphere:

> Dans une chambre tiède où, comme en une serre,
> L'air est dangereux et fatal,
> Où des bouquets mourants dans leurs cercueils de verre
> Exhalent leur soupir final.

The dying flowers prepare us for the picture of the truncated courtesan:

> Un cadavre sans tête épanche, comme un fleuve,
>   Sur l'oreiller désaltéré
> Un sang rouge et vivant, dont la toile s'abreuve
>   Avec l'avidité d'un pré . . .
>
> La tête, avec l'amas de sa crinière sombre
>   Et de ses bijoux précieux,
>
> Sur la table de nuit, comme une renoncule,
>   Repose . . .

The luxury of the décor is a deliberate piece of stylization which is used to heighten the erotic attraction of the scene. It becomes more explicit when the poet turns to the torso:

> Sur le lit, le tronc nu sans scrupules étale
>   Dans le plus complet abandon
> La secrète splendeur et la beauté fatale
>   Dont la nature lui fit don.

There is a characteristically grim irony about the 'sans scrupules' and 'le plus complet abandon'. In the next verse we find an element of fetishism:

> Un bas rosâtre, orné de coins d'or, à la jambe,
>   Comme un souvenir est resté . . .

The poem ends with a suggestion of necrophilia:

> L'homme vindicatif que tu n'as pu, vivante,
>   Malgré tant d'amour, assouvir,
> Combla-t-il sur ta chair inerte et complaisante
>   L'immensité de son désir?
>
> Réponds, cadavre impur! et par tes tresses roides
>   Te soulevant d'un bras fiévreux,
> Dis-moi, tête effrayante, a-t-il sur tes dents froides
>   Collé les suprêmes adieux?

From *Une Martyre* we pass to the three Lesbian poems which form a triptych. Baudelaire's interest in Lesbianism is something of a mystery and no one has yet accounted satisfactorily for the prominence given to it in his poetry. We know that it was a fashionable topic in the first half of the last century and had been the subject of Gautier's *Mademoiselle de Maupin* and Balzac's *Fille aux yeux d'or*. We also know that the three poems were early ones. But neither fashion nor youthful bravado is sufficient to account for Baudelaire's interest, nor is there the slightest evidence for Proust's assertion that the poet was a homosexual and presumably using Lesbianism as a disguise for his own vices.[1] There is, however, another possible explanation. Since Baudelaire had decided to include a cycle of perversions in his work he obviously could not omit homosexuality. Now it is an undisputed fact that homosexuality in women has never aroused the same repugnance in the public—particularly the male public—as homosexuality in men.[2] It follows from this that it is easier for the poet not merely to write about Lesbianism with greater detachment, but to give it an exotic attractiveness which would have been impossible in the case of male homosexuality. That seems to me to be the explanation of the mystery.

Lesbos, the first of the three poems, is a general picture of the island, its atmosphere, its rites, and its history. When we remember the strong note of moral condemnation in the other two poems, it is interesting to observe that in this poem the poet seems to be on the side of the *femmes damnées*:

> Car Lesbos entre tous m'a choisi sur la terre
> Pour chanter le secret de ses vierges en fleurs,
> Et je fus dès l'enfance admis au noir mystère
> Des rires effrénés mêlés aux sombres pleurs;
> Car Lesbos entre tous m'a choisi sur la terre.

The form of the poem is a matter of some moment. *Lesbos* is a *ritual*. The poet becomes the celebrant of a perverse religious cult —the words 'rite', 'culte', 'secret', and 'mystère' are continually recurring—and the repetition of the first line of each verse at the

[1] As reported by Gide in *Journal 1889–1939*, 2nd ed., Paris, 1948, p. 692.
[2] It is an interesting fact that under present English law homosexual relations between women are not a criminal offence provided that they take place in private. I suspect that this is a survival of the code of chivalry. Officially, we do not admit that such things happen.

end of the verse gives the impression of an invisible congregation repeating the words after the celebrant. The poem is in fact an exposition and defence of the 'rites' from which the note of condemnation is completely absent:

> Qui des Dieux osera, Lesbos, être ton juge
> Et condamner ton front pâli dans les travaux . . .

> Que nous veulent les lois du juste et de l'injuste?
> Vierges au cœur sublime, honneur de l'Archipel,
> Votre religion comme une autre est auguste,
> Et l'amour se rira de l'Enfer et du Ciel!
> Que nous veulent les lois du juste et de l'injuste?

The tragedy of Lesbos—the explanation of its 'rivages déserts'—is seen to lie in the faithlessness of Sappho who abandoned the 'rite' and gave herself to a man.

Although *Lesbos* is a prologue to the other two poems it deals with the period when all was over. The scene is empty. We see no one; we have only a glimpse of 'les filles aux yeux creux' and catch only an echo of the 'rires effrénés'. The two other poems are 'flashbacks' which present Lesbos in its heyday. As a contrast to *Lesbos*, *Femmes damnées* (Delphine et Hippolyte) is a miniature *drama* which, as Vivier has pointed out, possesses a classic perfection of form.[1] It begins with a prologue in which we see the two women eyeing one another—the 'despotic' Delphine and the 'timid' Hippolyte:

> Beauté forte à genoux devant la beauté frêle.

There follows a monologue in which Delphine expounds the same arguments already used in *Lesbos* warning her companion against men. There is a *réplique* by Hippolyte and a further exchange between them. Hippolyte's second speech seems to become a sort of chorus. Then the poet breaks in with what is in fact the epilogue:

> —Descendez, descendez, lamentables victimes . . .

With the exception of *Le Voyage* this is the longest poem in the *Fleurs du mal*. Baudelaire's longer poems, as I have already

[1] *Op. cit.*, p. 25.

suggested, do not possess the density and punch of the finest of the shorter pieces, and his inspiration is inclined to flag before he reaches the end of the poem. In spite of the praise that Vivier gives it, *Femmes damnées* is decidedly diffuse and in places is only held together by the powerful formal structure. It does, however, contain some of Baudelaire's most striking images and we cannot fail to admire the contrast between the *physical* and *psychological* imagery used in the argument, particularly the concrete images used by Delphine in stating the case against heterosexual relationships:

'Mes baisers sont légers comme ces éphémères
Qui caressent le soir les grands lacs transparents,
Et ceux de ton amant creuseront leurs ornières
Comme des chariots ou des socs déchirants;

Ils passeront sur toi comme un lourd attelage
De chevaux et de bœufs aux sabots sans pitié . . . '

According to one commentator, the last four lines suggest the ravages of 'lust' on the human body, the 'constant, brutal wear and deterioration . . . the impression of casual, transient use of the body is set up'.[1] There is certainly an opposition between the gentleness of Delphine and the brutality of the male, but I do not think that the word 'lust' is exact. The humdrum, earthy images of the 'chariot', 'soc', 'attelage', 'ornières', 'chevaux', 'bœufs', and 'sabots' are admittedly 'brutal'—the conjunction of 'ornières' and the human body makes us shudder—and their brutality is heightened by the adjectives 'déchirants' and 'lourd'. It is clear, however, that all these images are symbols of *normality*. They are drawn from agriculture, and they suggest the activity of a peasant family or a farming community. If 'lust' is an incorrect term, so is 'love'. What is described is the rough peasant or farmer who 'uses' his wife with the same insensitiveness as his plough and the body being worn out in the process which is still a *natural* process. (We recall 'toutes les hideurs de la fécondité' in 'J'aime le souvenir'.)

The description of the physical effect of natural relationships

[1] Bennett, *op. cit.*, p. 52.

is followed by a description of the psychological effects of unnatural relationships:

> 'Tourne vers moi tes yeux pleins d'azur et d'étoiles!
> Pour un de ces regards charmants, baume divin,
> Des plaisirs plus obscurs je lèverai les voiles
> Et je t'endormirai dans un rêve sans fin!'

The images that I have just examined are drawn from the open-
air life: the 'plaisirs plus obscurs' and the 'voiles' take us back
to the 'rite', the 'culte', the 'alcôve'. It is in these terms that
Hippolyte replies:

> 'Ma Delphine, je souffre et je suis inquiète,
> Comme après un nocturne et terrible repas.
>
> 'Je sens fondre sur moi de lourdes épouvantes
> Et de noirs bataillons de fantômes épars,
> Qui veulent me conduire en des routes mouvantes
> Qu'un horizon sanglant ferme de toutes parts.'

The 'nocturne et terrible repas' introduces the atmosphere of
the orgy. The 'lourd attelage' is replaced by 'lourdes épouvantes',
the procession of horses and oxen by phantoms from the unconscious—'noirs bataillons de fantômes épars'—the 'ornières' cut
in the firm earth by the 'routes mouvantes' which brilliantly
expresses the acute sense of psychological instability. I spoke
earlier of the sense of moral ostracism of this chapter, of the
characters' feeling of being cut off from the rest of the world.
The veils which Delphine promises to lift in order to reveal the
mysterious refinements of homosexual love are matched by the
vision of the 'horizon sanglant [fermé] de toutes parts'. In other
words, the vision of the open fields and skies implicit in the
farming imagery is replaced by a sense of constriction, imprison-
ment, a vision of a bloody horizon closing in on the speaker who
already feels the earth giving way under her feet ('des routes
mouvantes').

The next verse contains these astonishing lines:

> 'Avons-nous donc commis une action étrange?
> Explique, si tu peux, mon trouble et mon effroi:
> Je frissonne de peur quand tu me dis: "Mon ange!"
> Et cependant je sens ma bouche aller vers toi.'

where we experience the immense psychological compulsion exercised by the 'beauté forte'.

The third poem has been compared to a series of tableaux, but in reality it is a *composite picture* showing four different stages in a 'rake's progress'. It opens with a general view of the women lying in the sand and the stirrings of desire:

> . . . leurs pieds se cherchant et leurs mains rapprochées
> Ont de douces langueurs et des frissons amers,

where we find again the mixture of pleasure and fear. Some of the women make their way to the woods:

> Les unes, cœurs épris de longues confidences,
> Dans le fond des bosquets où jasent les ruisseaux,
> Vont épelant l'amour des craintives enfances
> Et creusant le bois des jeunes arbrisseaux.

This is a comparatively innocent picture of a convent girl's 'crush' with the girls indulging in 'longues confidences' and romantically carving their names on the trees.

> D'autres, comme des sœurs, marchent lentes et graves
> A travers les rochers pleins d'apparitions,
> Où saint Antoine a vu surgir comme des laves
> Les seins nus et pourprés de ses tentations.

The opening has a deceptive air of innocence suggested by the words 'sœurs', 'lentes', and 'graves', while the cæsura at the hemistich in the first line gives the impression of a school procession with the girls walking decorously two by two. The next two lines, however, express an uprush of very unsisterly emotions. The rocks haunted by 'apparitions' are very different from the 'bosquets où jasent les ruisseaux'. St. Anthony introduces the dual theme of mysticism and sexual temptation.[1] The word 'surgir' stands for the eruption of subterranean desires as well as phantoms rising from the underworld and 'laves', with its suggestion of a sudden violent upheaval of nature, intensifies the impres-

[1] '. . . la vue de ces dessins m'a mis sur des pentes de rêverie immenses, à peu près comme un livre obscène nous précipite vers les océans mystiques du bleu' (*Curiosités esthétiques*, pp. 123–4).

O

sion. In the fourth line we come to the vision and see not the whole woman, but the most exciting parts of her which are heightened by the word 'pourprés'. It is not for nothing that the verse ends with 'tentations'. Although it records the second stage in the 'rake's progress', it is still the stage of 'temptation'. In the next stage they have evidently yielded to temptation:

> Il en est, aux lueurs des résines croulantes,
> Qui dans le creux muet des vieux antres païens
> T'appellent au secours de leurs fièvres hurlantes,
> O Bacchus, endormeur des remords anciens!

The 'lueurs' and the 'antres païens' introduce the theme of the 'rite'; but the innocent rite of carving names on trees has given way to a pagan orgy; the 'longues confidences' have merged into 'fièvres hurlantes'. It is the constant theme of these poems that the women are a prey to desires which cannot be assuaged. They are not yet 'hardened sinners', but try to escape from their 'remorse' through wine. The fifth verse records the final stage in their downfall. The pleasant 'bosquets' give way to a 'bois sombre':

> Et d'autres, dont la gorge aime les scapulaires,
> Qui, recélant un fouet sous leurs longs vêtements,
> Mêlent, dans le bois sombre et les nuits solitaires,
> L'écume du plaisir aux larmes des tourments.

Cries of remorse turn to cries of pleasure mixed with pain, names carved on trees to the weals raised by whips on naked flesh.

When the poet enters the scene to address the 'victims', we observe another change of emphasis. They are 'vierges' and 'démons', 'monstres' and 'martyres', 'dévotes' and 'satyres':

> Pauvres sœurs, je vous aime autant que je vous plains,
> Pour vos mornes douleurs, vos soifs inassouvies . . .

I have spoken of the sense of guilt which broods over this section of the *Fleurs du mal*, but it is evident that the poet's attitude varies. In *Lesbos* he appears as the apologist of unnatural love; in *Delphine et Hippolyte* it is summarily condemned; but here we find the idea of justice tempered with mercy. The women are 'dévotes' as well as 'satyres', are 'sisters' whom he pities. We come to realize that this division applies to the other poems. There are the sinners who deserve pity and the brazen sinners who neither want nor deserve sympathy. For the first, sin is its own punishment:

> . . . votre châtiment naîtra de vos plaisirs.

In other places, the excessive nature of the sin is seen to be in a sense a justification:

> Tu tires ton pardon de l'excès des baisers.

This is the theme of *Allégorie* where the splendid harlot 'rit à la Mort et nargue la Débauche', for

> la beauté du corps est un sublime don
> Qui de toute infamie arrache le pardon.

I think that we must conclude that these inconsistencies are the outcome of changes of mood on the part of the poet. The dominating theme, as we shall see when we come to *Un Voyage à Cythère*, is unnatural vice and its punishment.

The poems in this cycle divide broadly into two groups. There are descriptions of sin like *Une Martyre* or the two *Femmes damnées*, where the poet is not himself actively engaged, but is either a mere spectator or makes his entry at the close to deliver his moral exhortation. The other poems are more personal and are thought like *La Destruction* to imply a personal *aveu*. In *Les Deux bonnes sœurs* we read:

> Au poëte sinistre . . .
> Tombeaux et lupanars montrent sous leurs charmilles
> Un lit que le remords n'a jamais fréquenté.

While the main theme of the poem is the connection between death and debauchery, 'lupanars' introduces prostitution, and it is the first of the five poems which deal mainly with it. It turns up again in the last lines of the next poem, *La Fontaine de sang*. He has sought in wine, he says, an escape from 'la terreur qui me mine' and in love 'un sommeil oublieux':

> Mais l'amour n'est pour moi qu'un matelas d'aiguilles
> Fait pour donner à boire à ces cruelles filles!

A 'cruelle fille' is the heroine of *Allégorie* and we are given a vivid glimpse of her sprawling across the table at a café:

> C'est une femme belle et de riche encolure,
> Qui laisse dans son vin traîner sa chevelure.

In the poem ironically called *La Béatrice* she is the 'reine de mon cœur' who appears in the midst of demons jeering at the poet:

> . . . cette ombre d'Hamlet imitant sa posture,
> Le regard indécis et les cheveux au vent.

In the last poem of the sequence she is a vampire claiming to know

> la science
> De perdre au fond d'un lit l'antique conscience,

but intending to destroy the customer.

The theme and movement of *Un Voyage à Cythère* bear a marked resemblance to those of *Le Voyage*. The poems both describe the vain quest for an Eldorado; they both deal with the conflict between aspiration and reality; and in both the opening movement of expansion is followed by a movement of sudden contraction which leads finally to a mood of resignation or despair.

The subject of *Un Voyage à Cythère* is an imaginary voyage to Cythera which turns out to be not the sexual Eldorado of legend, but a place of punishment and expiation for sexual sins. Its immense technical effectiveness lies largely in the contrast between two sets of images and the brilliant use of the dramatic form. It opens with a highly stylized description of the poet's 'heart' flying joyously among the rigging of the ship like a rococo bird:

> Mon cœur, comme un oiseau, voltigeait tout joyeux
> Et planait librement à l'entour des cordages;
> Le navire roulait sous un ciel sans nuages,
> Comme un ange enivré d'un soleil radieux.

The radiant sunlight suddenly clouds. A voice—possibly the poet's—asks abruptly:

> Quelle est cette île triste et noire?

Another voice answers:

> —C'est Cythère,
> Nous dit-on, un pays fameux dans les chansons,
> Eldorado banal de tous les vieux garçons.
> Regardez, après tout, c'est une pauvre terre.

The word *banal* had special associations for the generation of Baudelaire. It stood for that sense of staleness and drabness which seemed to belong peculiarly to a bourgeois utilitarian age. Cythera with its elegantly licentious frolics in the bushes is transformed into the brothel with its inelegant 'fun and games' among the red plush which haunted the imagination of the nineteenth century as Watteau's island had haunted the imagination of the eighteenth century. 'Tous les vieux garçons', remarks Mr. Joseph Bennett caustically, are 'the old goats of the Jockey Club, or the comfortably-off retired bourgeois when they can escape from wife and family for an evening'.[1]

A third voice chimes in, repeating the lyrical note of the opening verse in the attempt to dissipate the uncomfortable impression created by the 'île triste et noire' and to restore the island of legend:

> —Ile des doux secrets et des fêtes du cœur! . . .
>
> Belle île aux myrtes verts, pleine de fleurs écloses,
> Vénérée à jamais par toute nation,
> Où les soupirs des cœurs en adoration
> Roulent comme l'encens sur un jardin de roses
>
> Ou le roucoulement éternel d'un ramier!

The poet's voice cuts in with:

> —Cythère n'était plus qu'un terrain des plus maigres,
> Un désert rocailleux troublé par des cris aigres.

The strident 'aigres', 'maigres', and 'rocailleux' shatter the

---

[1] *Op. cit.*, p. 68.

impression of langorous peace built up in the preceding lines with
their flowers, incense, and adoration, and come into violent conflict with the soft 'soupirs', the liquid l's and the warbling note of
the -*ou*'s in 'roulent' and 'roucoulement'. The next line creates a
sense of expectation:

> J'entrevoyais pourtant un objet singulier!

In order to prolong it, we are told what the 'objet singulier'
was not, enabling the poet to restore for a moment the voluptuous atmosphere while preparing a still greater shock:

> Ce n'était pas un temple aux ombres bocagères,
> Où la jeune prêtresse, amoureuse des fleurs,
> Allait, le corps brûlé de secrètes chaleurs,
> Entre-bâillant sa robe aux brise passagères . . .

The picture of the priestess of Venus is flashed on the screen
like an erotic postcard, but though the half-parted dress is intentionally inviting and draws attention to genital organs, it is not
gratuitous. It hints at what is to come. When the ship nears the
coast, it is apparent that the vision of the sylvan temple and of
the 'Eldorado banal' is equally far from the truth:

> Mais voilà qu'en rasant la côte d'assez près
> Pour troubler les oiseaux avec nos voiles blanches,
> Nous vîmes que c'était un gibet à trois branches,
> Du ciel se détachant en noir, comme un cyprès.

There is a spectacular contrast between the white sails and the
black gibbet, but the contrast between the different kinds of bird
which appear in the poem is not less striking. The amiable bird
of the first verse and the wood-pigeon of the fifth are replaced
by nameless birds of prey:

> De féroces oiseaux perchés sur leur pâture
> Détruisaient avec rage un pendu déjà mûr,
> Chacun plantant, comme un outil, son bec impur
> Dans tous les coins saignants de cette pourriture;

> Les yeux étaient deux trous, et du ventre effondré
> Les intestins pesants lui coulaient sur les cuisses,
> Et ses bourreaux, gorgés de hideuses délices,
> L'avaient à coups de bec absolument châtré.

The poet presents us with the spectacle of the human body ripped to pieces by lust. 'Pâture' and 'mûr' usually stand for richness and ripeness, but in their present context they assume a destructive ironical force which is stressed by rhyming them with 'impur' and 'pourriture'. The hideous mechanical movement of the birds pecking and tearing at the corpse is reflected in the use of the double cæsura in the third line:

> Chacun plantant,—comme un outil,—son bec impur.

The crux comes in the lines:

> Et ses bourreaux, gorgés de hideuses délices,
> L'avaient à coups de bec absolument châtré.[1]

The sin of the hanged man was sexual, was to have paid too much attention to priestesses of Venus, half-parted dresses and 'l'organe de l'amour'.

> Sous les pieds, un troupeau de jaloux quadrupèdes,
> Le museau relevé, tournoyait et rôdait;
> Une plus grande bête au milieu s'agitait
> Comme un exécuteur entouré de ses aides.

With the mention of the word 'exécuteur' in this verse the idea of justice becomes explicit. The birds of prey have already been described as 'bourreaux'. Now though 'bourreau' can mean a 'torturer' or 'tormentor', it must be interpreted here in the sense of 'executioner', or rather it should be given the double sense of tormentor and executioner. The birds are the instruments of justice who have removed the eyes through which temptation came and the organ by which it was satisfied. The nameless, indescribable animals, which seem to have come out of the medieval menagerie, are the representatives of justice. The poet's attitude towards them is evidently ambivalent. The hanged man, who later in what he calls 'cette allégorie' becomes identified with himself—

> Ridicule pendu, tes douleurs sont les miennes!

[1] When the poem was first published in a magazine in 1852 this line read:
> L'organe de l'amour avait fait leurs délices.

—has sinned, has been guilty of 'cultes infâmes', but he is at the same time the victim of an *unjust* justice, a 'judicial murder'. For the 'jaloux quadrupèdes' are somehow of the same nature as the birds mindlessly and remorselessly rending 'un pendu déjà mûr'. They are mechanical, but not detached. The birds are 'gorgés de hideuses délices' and the animals are 'jaloux' because each seems eager to 'get at' the corpse.

The identification of the poet with the hanged man is the signal for a change of tone. In the closing verses the contrasted tones of the first six verses blend to form a fresh tone:

> —Le ciel était charmant, la mer était unie;
> Pour moi tout était noir et sanglant désormais . . .

The real and the imaginary Eldorado, the 'ramier' and the 'féroces oiseaux', belong alike to the 'allegory' and have disappeared. The word 'unie' gives the impression of wounds closing, but the scene is bathed in darkness and blood. The calm is the calm of despair. For the poet has seen in the allegory what he really is and can only pray for the strength and the courage

> De contempler mon cœur et mon corps sans dégoût!

The appearance of the word 'cœur' in the first and last lines is characteristic. It is the close of another circular tour which has been particularly abundant in destructive self-knowledge.

This brings me back to the particular degree of internal coherence of the chapter. The underlying theme is the destruction of man by sin. The destruction may be violent like the imagined murder of the prostitute in *Une Martyre* or the imagined execution of the poet in *Un Voyage à Cythère*, or it may take the form of the gradual sapping of his vitality. In *La Fontaine de sang* the poet describes himself as bleeding to death from an invisible wound:

> Il me semble parfois que mon sang coule à flots,
> Ainsi qu'une fontaine aux rhythmiques sanglots.
> Je l'entends bien qui coule avec un long murmure,
> Mais je me tâte en vain pour trouver la blessure.

When he goes on:

> A travers la cité, comme dans un champ clos,
> Il s'en va, transformant les pavés en îlots,
> Désaltérant la soif de chaque créature,
> Et partout colorant en rouge la nature,

he looks back to *Une Martyre*:

> Un sang rouge et vivant, dont la toile s'abreuve
> Avec l'avidité d'un pré,

and forward to *Les Métamorphoses du vampire*:

> Quand elle eut de mes os sucé toute la moelle . . .

The blood clearly stands for life draining away, but it has a sexual overtone. Man is wasting his substance in the indulgence of his vices. In commenting on *Les Bijoux*, I suggested that the word 'métamorphoses' implied the absence of any centre in the woman. The title of the last poem from which I quoted is not without interest. For all the poems in this chapter do indeed record the metamorphosis of man, those destructive physical changes which are the outcome of moral collapse. The close relation between them is brought out in the final poem. He imagines an allegorical Love perched on the skull of Humanity and blowing bubbles with its 'brain, blood, and flesh', doing in fact what the vampire does to the poet and what the poet does to himself. There has been some discussion about the sources of the poem. It is thought that it may have been suggested by an engraving or more probably that it is a personal adaptation of a traditional theme. It is not a good poem, but it makes a curiously effective ending like a design at the end of the chapter of a book. Some of the imagery reminds us of Baudelaire's account of a very Freudian dream in a letter written to Asselineau on 13 March 1856,[1] and it is scarcely necessary to enlarge on the symbolism of the pipe or the bursting bubbles in the poem:

> Le globe lumineux et frêle
> Prend un grand essor,
> Crève et crache son âme grêle
> Comme un songe d'or.

[1] *Corr. gén.*, I, pp. 372–7.

J'entends le crâne à chaque bulle
   Prier et gémir:
—'Ce jeu féroce et ridicule,
   Quand doit-il finir?

Car ce que ta bouche cruelle
   Éparpille en l'air,
Monstre assassin, c'est ma cervelle,
   Mon sang et ma chair!'[1]

5. 'Révolte'

'Révolte' is the weakest of the six chapters. The reasons for its inclusion are evident, but it is too short and the quality of the three poems that it contains is too poor for it to fulfil the poet's purpose. *Le Reniement de Saint Pierre* is the best of the three poems. It contains one impressive couplet:

—Certes, je sortirai, quant à moi, satisfait
D'un monde où l'action n'est pas la sœur du rêve . . .

And there is the famous shock ending:

Saint Pierre a renié Jésus . . . il a bien fait!

Abel et Cain and *Les Litanies de Satan* appear to me to be the two silliest poems in the book.

6. 'La Mort'

The last chapter originally contained only three poems, but their number was doubled in 1861. The first three poems were called *La Mort des amants*, *La Mort des pauvres*, and *La Mort des artistes*. The titles reflect the special place occupied in the *Fleurs du mal* by artists, lovers, and the poor for whom Baudelaire had a genuine feeling. They are also the subject of three of the poems in 'Le Vin', but the resemblances between the two chapters do not go very deep and the parallel is not extended by the three

[1] Compare *L'Horloge*:
       Et j'ai pompé ta vie avec ma trompe immonde!

poems added to 'La Mort' in the second edition. In this chapter
lovers come first instead of last as they do in 'Le Vin':

> Nous aurons des lits pleins d'odeurs légères,
> Des divans profonds comme des tombeaux,
> Et d'étranges fleurs sur des étagères,
> Écloses pour nous sous des cieux plus beaux.
>
> Usant à l'envi leurs chaleurs dernières,
> Nos deux cœurs seront deux vastes flambeaux,
> Qui réfléchiront leurs doubles lumières
> Dans nos deux esprits, ces miroirs jumeaux.
>
> Un soir fait de rose et de bleu mystique,
> Nous échangerons un éclair unique,
> Comme un long sanglot, tout chargé d'adieux;
>
> Et plus tard un Ange, entr'ouvant les portes,
> Viendra ranimer, fidèle et joyeux,
> Les miroirs ternis et les flammes mortes.

This poem has recently been discussed by two English critics.
Professor Mansell Jones describes it as 'one of his most perfect
trifles—if a thing so perfect can be called a trifle'.[1] Mr. J. G.
Weightman, on the other hand, is 'reasonably sure' that it 'is one
of the great poems on which Baudelaire's reputation rests'.[2] The
first of these judgments seems to me to make too little of the poem
and the second to err on the side of generosity. It is unquestionably a poem of extraordinary beauty, but I do not think that
it possesses the range or the weight—it is significantly written in
decasyllabic lines—of the great masterpieces like *La Chevelure*,
Le Cygne, and *Le Voyage*.

It will be seen at once that the poem strikes a note which is
completely new in the *Fleurs du mal*. The tension has vanished
and is replaced by an immense feeling of exaltation. Death is not
the end, but the crown of life and its fulfilment; not something to
be feared, but something that is passionately desired. The death
of the lovers is, indeed, a ceremonial death, almost a religious
rite. They are not dying of old age, but in the prime of life when

[1] *Baudelaire*, p. 52.
[2] In *The Twentieth Century*, Vol. CLIII, No. 912, February 1953, p. 136.

they are full of vigour, and the 'dernières chaleurs' is qualified
by 'deux vastes flambeaux'. We have met the comparison between
beds and tombs in other poems, but the feeling it conveyed was
very different. The 'torches', 'mirrors', and even the 'Angel' are
all part of the furniture of the *Fleurs du mal*, but the only other
poem in the book to which it can be profitably compared is
Harmonie du soir which is far less impressive. For this is a poem
in Baudelaire's Symbolist manner. The ritual element, the
'étranges fleurs', the hearts merging into one another, and the
'soir fait de rose et de bleu mystique' will reappear in the work
of the movement of 1886, but no one will equal the beauty of
Baudelaire's poem. It reaches a climax in the tenth and eleventh
lines:

> Nous échangerons un éclair unique,
> Comme un long sanglot, tout chargé d'adieux,

where the high sharp notes of 'éclair unique' dissolve into the
slow, rich sounds of 'long sanglot' which dies away in 'tout
chargé d'adieux'. The note of exaltation goes with it and the
second tercet seems to be written in a mood of grave, restrained
confidence.

The interpretation of the poem only presents one real difficulty.
That is the figure of the Angel. Mr. Weightman suggests that
'the figure is female . . . and that she is a combination of "la
servante au grand cœur" and Baudelaire's mother. The richness
of the sonnet comes, therefore, from a fusion of adult love, with
its intellectual and mystical overtone, and the cosiness and
security of childhood, marked by filial, and possibly sensual,
love.'[1] This is an ingenious and convincing explanation of the
richness of the sonnet, but I find it less easy to follow him when
he goes on to suggest that the entry of the Angel is like that of a
devoted servant who comes in to dust the room and make up the
fire. This leads him to the conclusion that Baudelaire's conception of immortality in this poem is an endless repetition of the
love-death. The difficulty about this explanation is that it does
not pay sufficient attention to the *finality* of the ceremonial death,

[1] *Art. cit.*, p. 140.

to the '*dernières* chaleurs' or to the 'long sanglot, tout chargé d'adieux', and that it is based on too literal an interpretation of the word 'ranimer'. Baudelaire had a good knowledge of the gloomier doctrines of the Church, but he seems to have been decidedly weak in his conception of immortality and heaven. In the first three poems of this chapter he sees death as a literal fulfilment of desires experienced on earth. I have no doubt that he planned an eternity of love for his two lovers, but it still seems to me that their death is meant to be unique in every sense, a final leave-taking of this life and the entry into another. Mr. Weightman is certainly right in describing the Angel as 'supernatural', but he turns him or her into a somewhat pallid, rationalist angel reviving the burnt-out embers of love with a wave of a magic duster. I think myself that the Angel is meant to be the Angel of the resurrection and that the second tercet describes the resurrection of the dead. The 'doors' are indeed the doors of the room where the lovers died, but the beginning of the poem suggests that the place of death is at the same time a 'tomb'. It appears therefore that the Angel is opening the doors or 'gates' of the tomb and calling the lovers to a life that is different from their earthly state. I shall try to show that this view gains some support from the next poem.

The same note of rapture and the same conception of death are apparent in *La Mort des pauvres*:

> C'est la Mort qui console, hélas! et qui fait vivre;
> C'est le but de la vie, et c'est le seul espoir . . .
>
> C'est la clarté vibrante à notre horizon noir;
> C'est l'auberge fameuse inscrite sur le livre,
> Où l'on pourra manger, et dormir, et s'asseoir . . .

The third and fourth lines are of particular interest. In Baudelaire the horizon is nearly always 'black', a symbol of the circle which imprisons the poet. Here death is seen as a light beckoning from beyond the dark horizon and offering the one chance of breaking the circle. The 'auberge' in line 4 is apparently the inn from the parable of the Good Samaritan. We have already met it in *L'Irréparable* and *L'Horloge*, but once again there are dif-

ferences. In the first of these poems it is the symbol of the extinction of all hope:

> L'Espérance qui brille aux carreaux de l'Auberge
> Est soufflée, est morte à jamais.

In the second it is equated with 'Repentance' which is described
as 'la dernière auberge'.

The Angel reappears in the first tercet:

> C'est un Ange qui tient dans ses doigts magnétiques
> Le sommeil et le don des rêves extatiques,
> Et qui refait le lit des gens pauvres et nus;
>
> C'est la gloire des Dieux, c'est le grenier mystique,
> C'est la bourse du pauvre et sa patrie antique,
> C'est le portique ouvert sur les Cieux inconnus!

Death is the subject of each of the sentences in the last six
lines, but they are descriptions of the different wishes and dreams
which will be fulfilled through death. There is, to be sure, something of the servant about the Angel who is shown this time not
as making up the fire, but as making the beds of the poor. It is
not, however, the Angel of death. It is once again more like the
Angel of the resurrection who comes to call the dead and minister
to their needs. What is clear in this poem is that death is an entry
into a new life. 'Le portique' is the gate to this new life and is
specifically described as 'ouvert sur les Cieux inconnus'.

To 'the poor' death brings a promise of food, drink, and rest;
to the artist the prospect of realizing his dreams and producing
the perfect work which had always eluded him. Baudelaire says of
the artist:

> Nous userons notre âme en de subtils complots . . .
> Avant de contempler la grande Créature . . .

The 'grande Créature' appears to stand for the elusive 'Beauty'
which fills them with an 'infernal désir'. There are some, he goes
on, 'qui jamais n'ont connu leur Idole', and it is to them that
death will bring fulfilment:

> C'est que la Mort, planant comme un soleil nouveau,
> Fera s'épanouir les fleurs de leur cerveau!

There is a pronounced change of tone and feeling in the next three poems. In *La Fin de la journée* death is still seen as something desirable, but instead of a new vision it is something vaguely comforting which is identified with night:

> La nuit voluptueuse monte,
> Apaisant tout . . .

It is finally reduced to 'rafraîchissantes ténèbres'.

Le Rêve d'un curieux is an achievement of a different kind from any of the preceding poems. It is a poem of psychological subtlety and sardonic humour. The poet dreams that he is about to die, but death is no longer something positive to be desired for its own sake or for the benefits that it will bring. It is a wager, a novelty awaited with excitement certainly, but with mixed feelings:

> —J'allais mourir. C'était dans mon âme amoureuse,
> *Désir* mêle d'*horreur*, un mal particulier;
>
> *Angoisse* et vif *espoir*, sans humeur factieuse.
> Plus allait se vidant le fatal sablier,
> Plus ma torture était *âpre* et *délicieuse*;
> Tout mon cœur s'arrachait au monde familier.

He goes on to compare his mood to the excitement of the child at its first play:

> J'étais comme l'enfant avide du spectacle,
> Haïssant le rideau comme on hait un obstacle . . .
> Enfin la vérité froide se révéla.

The terse, prosaic third line carries expectation to its height. The close is a brilliant *tour de force*—a mixture of terror and disillusionment:

> J'étais mort sans surprise, et la terrible aurore
> M'enveloppait.—Eh quoi! n'est-ce donc que cela?
> La toile était levée et j'attendais encore.

Although *Le Voyage*, which has already been discussed in some detail, is included in this chapter, it is in reality an epilogue which corresponds to *Au Lecteur*. The poet's mood has changed again. Death is neither the crown of life nor a wager to titillate the weary man. It is the end to which the poet is inexorably driven by *ennui* and the failure of his hopes. He has completed his tour; he has tested every kind of experience so that logically there is only one thing left to try. He hopes that death will bring the novelty that life has denied; but it is only an expression of hope and not a statement of belief of any kind:

> Plonger au fond du gouffre, Enfer ou Ciel, qu'importe?
> Au fond de l'Inconnu pour trouver du *nouveau*!

Retrospect

'Morally and physically, I have always been conscious of the gulf, not only the gulf of sleep, but the gulf of action, dreams, memory, desire, regret, remorse, the beautiful, numbers, etc.'

Journaux intimes

It is tempting at this point to look back at the poet's itinerary and to draw some general conclusions. I have described *Le Voyage* as an allegory of man's life from the cradle to the grave, but I think we have to admit that the real journey begins sooner and ends later. At the start of Baudelaire's journey, and much further back than the cradle, lies 'the lost paradise' which is the great symbol of unity. At the close is not death, but the vision of dissolution which follows death and which is graphically evoked in the last words of *Une Charogne*.

The *Fleurs du mal* is therefore a record not merely of a circular tour of the modern world, but of the progressive loss of spiritual unity. The world described by the poet is continually growing smaller and the sense of stifling oppression greater. He had seen at the outset that his problem was the resolution of the conflict between man and his environment, between the inner and the outer life, and the recovery of unity. He had tried to achieve it through art and love, but all his attempts had failed. He found himself driven further and further into himself, into the desolating inner solitude. His revolt was short-lived and destructive, and we leave him waiting in a mood of resignation

BAUDELAIRE

Portrait from H. Fantin-Latour's Hommage à Delacroix
exhibited at the Salon of 1864 (*Louvre*)

for death which is the prelude to dissolution, but which alone offers a way out of a world where he is at once a 'prisoner' and an 'exile'.

The drama is twofold. It lies in the impact of a hostile environment on his consciousness which continually cheats his dream of reaching a unity outside him, and in the sudden eruption of destructive impulses from the depths of the unconscious which destroys internal unity. For this reason the 'tour' is an exploration of the inner and the outer worlds. He speaks in one poem of the 'voûte d'airain' and in the fourth *Spleen* he writes:

> Quand le ciel bas et lourd pèse comme un couvercle
> Sur l'esprit gémissant en proie aux longs ennuis,
> Et que de l'horizon embrassant tout le cercle
> Il nous verse un jour noir plus triste que les nuits,

bringing home to us the sense of constriction and oppression which weighs on the poet imprisoned—the familiar image is there—in a 'circle'.

In *De profundis clamavi* he describes a world in which the sun has lost its warmth and which is plunged into night:

> Un soleil sans chaleur plane au-dessus six mois,
> Et les six autres mois la nuit couvre la terre;
> C'est un pays plus nu que la terre polaire;
> —Ni bêtes, ni ruisseaux, ni verdure, ni bois!

Images of the external prison have their counterpart in those of the internal prison of the heart and the mind:

> —Mon âme est un tombeau que, mauvais cénobite,
> Depuis l'éternité je parcours et j'habite . . .

In *Obsession* he writes:

> dans nos cœurs maudits,
> Chambres d'éternel deuil où vibrent de vieux râles,
> Répondent les échos de vos *De profundis*.

When he surveys the outer world he finds that his material has gone rigid and hard, that it is peopled with robots—the 'spectres' of the 'Tableaux Parisiens' and the mechanical courtesans of the

P

love cycles—for human faculties have not escaped the general petrifaction. In the line

> Je suis belle, ô mortels! comme un rêve de pierre,

there is a contrast between the fluid 'dream' and the rigid 'stone'. For there are two processes at work in Baudelaire's poetry. The domination of metal and stone, the sense of the human becoming part of the soulless machine, gives his world its nightmare quality. This quality is heightened by the reverse process, by the disconcerting way in which cracks and fissures suddenly appear and the surface disintegrates to reveal the 'gulf' which threatens to swallow him up. 'Gouffre', 'abîme', and 'néant' are key-words in Baudelaire's poetry. The 'gulfs' and 'abysses' which lie beneath the surface of the stone and metal world are matched, as I have suggested, by the gulfs and abysses of the mind. In *Le Gouffre*, a poem first published in 1862, the gulf becomes a moving gulf:

> Pascal avait son gouffre, avec lui se mouvant.
> —Hélas! tout est abîme,—action, désir, rêve . . .

For the woman in *Femmes damnées* the abyss is her heart:

> Je sens s'élargir dans mon être
> Un abîme béant; cet abîme est mon cœur!

In these passages the gulfs and abysses are symbols of negation and frustration, the nightmare sensation of futility and despair which paralyses 'action, désir, rêve'. But Baudelaire sometimes uses the words in a different sense. When he writes in *Le Léthé*:

> Pour engloutir mes sanglots apaisés
> Rien ne me vaut l'abîme de ta couche,

the 'abyss' is a refuge and the poet is driven on by a desire to blot out the horror of the present by plunging into the purely instinctual life, into an orgasm of such violence that consciousness itself is temporarily obliterated.

The desire to resolve tension, to break out of prison, which is apparent in the general construction of the *Fleurs du mal*, is also reflected in the imagery of the individual poems. I have shown that *ennui* and *spleen* correspond to the positives, *extase* and *volupté*; but we also find that images expressing constriction and frustration like 'prison', 'tomb', and 'abyss' are matched by their opposites which at least provide a temporary release, or more precisely, a tantalizing hope of release. 'Ships' and the 'sea' are the commonest, but in addition there are the images of 'oases', 'gourds', and 'drinking':

> N'es-tu pas l'oasis où je rêve, et la gourde
> Où je hume à longs traits le vin du souvenir?

> Quand vers toi mes désirs partent en caravane,
> Tes yeux sont la citerne où boivent mes ennuis.

It is characteristic of Baudelaire that many of his key-words are used in both a positive and a negative sense. One of the most striking examples of the reversal of meaning is a line from *Le Voyage* where the 'oasis' becomes

> Une oasis d'horreur dans un désert d'ennui,

while in *L'Ennemi* water, instead of irrigating and fertilizing the poet's garden, is the agent of destruction:

> . . . il faut employer la pelle et les râteaux
> Pour rassembler à neuf les terres inondées,
> Où l'eau creuse des trous grands comme des tombeaux.

This habit of perpetually pitting words and images against one another is a further reflection of the insoluble conflict at the heart of the *Fleurs du mal*. For every emotion and every sensation is balanced by its opposite or by the hope or fear of its opposite, and is undermined by it the moment it comes into being. The poignancy of much of his finest work lies in his immense appreciation of life coupled with the simultaneous feeling that what he wants is just out of reach or just behind him. In

> Le Printemps adorable a perdu son odeur!

we are conscious of a muffled note of doom which is faintly heard in the repeated d's, and it is fatal. The passionate desire for new life behind the 'Printemps adorable' can never be realized, and the poet is left contemplating the dry scentless spring which has lost its magic and its tremulous beauty.

Baudelaire is with Racine the greatest master of the single line in French poetry, but if we examine his most famous and beautiful lines we find that they express an almost unbearable sense of loss, absence, distance. When he writes

> L'air est plein du frisson des choses qui s'enfuient,

the very essence of life seems to slip away in the sighing f's and s's. In other places the whole tragedy of life is packed into a simple word like 'loin', 'absent', 'lointain', or 'perdu':

> Comme vous êtes loin, paradis parfumé!
>
> Tout un monde lointain, absent, presque défunt.
>
> Les cocotiers absents de la superbe Afrique.
>
> Les bijoux perdus de l'antique Palmyre.

In all these lines we find the same balance between positive and negative: the despairing 'loin' and the richly suggestive 'paradis parfumé'; the 'absents' and exotic associations of 'superbe Afrique'; the 'perdus' and the 'antique Palmyre' which stands for a mysterious but vanished civilization.

Discussion of the structure of the *Fleurs du mal* leads naturally to an examination of individual poems and images, but in order to discover the ultimate meaning it is necessary to make the return journey and analyse the main themes. Three of the most important are religion, art, and love.

A poet's religion should not be an excuse for sectarian battles as it almost invariably is with Baudelaire; and Catholics and rationalists share a heavy responsibility for confusing the issue. The literary critic is not primarily concerned with Baudelaire's beliefs as a man or in deciding whether, as Mr. T. S. Eliot suggests, he needs our prayers. He is concerned with the function of religion in his work, and the proper place to begin is the poems themselves. The *Fleurs du mal* is filled with images and words drawn from the Christian religion. The devil stalks through its pages. We are continually reading of angels, evil, sin, repentance, vices, and ecstasy. Yet we have to admit with the Abbé Jean Massin that Baudelaire's Christianity is 'a very odd form of Christianity'.[1] Although he often uses theological terms in an orthodox sense, he gives them just as often a personal nuance. The devil is sometimes the Christian devil and sometimes the devil of the Romantics. His angels are sometimes guardian angels, avenging angels, or angels of evil; but the word is also used to describe a mistress or the divine element in man. There is one significant omission. The term 'grace' is frequently used to denote the elegance and beauty of woman, but it is never used in the poetry as distinct from the prose in its theological sense.[2] On the other hand, 'ecstasy' is used as a rough equivalent; but, as I have shown, it means the temporary rapture of *La Chevelure*, never the ecstasy of the religious mystics.

We must turn next to the poet's pronouncements on religion in his letters and diaries which provide a commentary on the poetry. In a letter to his mother dated 6 May 1861 he wrote:

'I desire with all my heart—and with a sincerity which no one but myself will ever understand—to believe that an external invisible being is interested in my fate; but what do you have to do in order to believe it?'[3]

In another letter written to Flaubert on 26 June of the previous year, he had said:

'After probing very deeply into the memory of my dreams, I perceived that I was obsessed by the impossibility of explaining certain actions and sudden thoughts of man without the hypothesis of the intervention of an evil power which is external to him. That is a great admission, but the whole of the nineteenth century may rise in arms without making me blush for it.'[4]

There are numerous references to original sin in the letters and

---

[1] *Baudelaire entre Dieu et Satan*, Paris, 1946, p. 9.

[2] *Une Charogne* contains an example of the ironic use of theological terms and the word 'grâces' in its profane sense:

> Oui! telle vous serez, ô la reine des grâces,
> Après les derniers sacrements . . .

[3] *Corr. gén.*, 3, p. 280.   [4] *Corr. gén.*, 3, pp. 124–5.

the criticism, but the classic examples are the famous entries in the diaries:

'Theory of true civilization.—It does not lie in steam or gas or table-turning, but in the diminution of the marks of original sin.'[1]

'There are in every man at every hour of the day two simultaneous postulations, one towards God, the other towards Satan. The invocation to God, or spirituality, is a desire to mount in the scale; that of Satan or animality, is a joy in going downwards.'[2]

There are two things which strike us about these passages. The first is the evident sincerity of the words, 'I desire with all my heart . . .' For there is little doubt that Baudelaire felt that he was, unwillingly, part of a general movement away from traditional beliefs. The second is that the emphasis on man's fallen state is not balanced by any belief in his redemption.[3]

I must glance back for a moment to the sentence from the letter to Alfred de Vigny quoted in an earlier chapter. 'All the new poems are designed to fit into the singular framework that I had chosen.' A poet living like Dante in a stable universe had no need to worry about a 'framework'. It was provided for him in the form of a body of commonly accepted beliefs which gave his experience its unity and its pattern. Baudelaire lived in an age in which there was no longer a body of commonly accepted beliefs. He was therefore obliged to create a new 'framework' in which religion, so far from imposing its pattern, appears in a fragmentary mutilated form. It follows that though religion is present in his poetry it only exists *à l'état de mythe*. It is a convenient poetic fiction—a 'hypothesis'—which provides an explanation of the dark forces that pervade his work. It is not a faith in which as a *poet* or a *man* he believes, but it is a symbol of the order or 'Ideal' towards which he was striving, and as such it is of great importance.

'De la vaporisation et de la centralisation du *Moi*. Tout est

---

[1] *Journaux intimes*, p. 80.   [2] *Ibid.*, p. 62.

[3] When we compare the letters to Flaubert and his mother, we can hardly avoid noticing that belief in an evil force seems to have presented none of the difficulties of belief in God.

là', said Baudelaire.[1] I have suggested that his negative aim in the *Fleurs du mal* was to resolve tension and his positive aim the recovery of unity—the unity as opposed to the multiplicity of experience, the 'centralisation' as opposed to the 'vaporisation' of the '*Moi*'. This could only be accomplished in an order which was in the widest sense religious. For in the religious order man has his appointed place; there can be no conflict between him and his milieu and no internal division of the self. The attempt to achieve this unity through poetic experience accounts at one level for his preoccupation with what must be called the transcendental element in experience and at the technical level for his preoccupation with form as a means of organizing experience. In some of the poems of positive vision, the momentary sense of unity comes either through the identification of the poet with a work of art or through union with another person. In *L'Invitation au voyage* it seems to be largely Dutch art:

> Là, tout n'est qu'ordre et beauté,
> Luxe, calme et volupté.

Mr. Eliot is certainly right in insisting that 'ordre' was intentionally placed first.[2] It is a symbol of unity in the sense of everything having its appointed place. 'Beauté' is an equivocal word. It often has transcendental associations both in Baudelaire's poetry and in his prose, and it can be applied to the supernatural and the natural orders. 'Calme' is absence of tension, while 'luxe' and 'volupté' emphasize the material element in his personal vision of beatitude. It can be put in another way by saying that his 'Ideal' is based on a compromise between two orders, that instead of hierarchy there is an attempt to fuse elements which are heterogeneous and to invest them with a quasi-religious aura. This is what happens in the final verse of *Tout entière*:

> O métamorphose mystique
> De tous mes sens fondus en un!
> Son haleine fait la musique,
> Comme sa voix fait le parfum!

[1] *Journaux intimes*, p. 51.
[2] *Essays Ancient and Modern*, London, 1936, p. 71.

'Mystique' is a word that occurs frequently in the *Fleurs du mal* and its meaning varies. In its present context it gives a vague religious overtone to 'métamorphose' and is, at the same time, a disguised superlative. 'Métamorphose' is the operative word and it stands not for unity but for the constant twisting and turning of the poet in search of his goal, of the alchemist trying to find the right formula.

This brings me to the parallel between religion and love. Baudelaire aimed at a religious-aesthetic unity on one plane, but on the human plane he also aimed at emotional unity through personal relationships which was to be the symbol of or the path to a higher unity. The passages on prostitution in the diaries have an obvious bearing on the breakdown of personal relations in his work and the failure to achieve unity:

'Love is the taste for prostitution. There is not a single noble pleasure which cannot be reduced to prostitution. At a play or a ball, each one enjoys everybody.

'What is art? Prostitution.'[1]

'What is love? The need to go out of yourself. Man is an animal who worships. To worship is to sacrifice and prostitute yourself. All love is therefore prostitution. . . .'[2]

'Invincible taste for prostitution in the heart of man which is the source of his horror of solitude.—He wants to be two. The man of genius wants to be *one*, therefore alone. Glory consists in remaining *one* and prostituting yourself in a special way.'[3]

'Prostitution' is another of the words on which Baudelaire set his personal stamp, but its meaning varied. I have shown that the prostitute was a symbol of rebellion, but in its present context prostitution stands for degradation. The conjunctions, 'art-prostitution', 'amour-prostitution', are striking examples of the way in which opposites either balance or undermine one another. Love is debased and degraded from within and becomes a form of prostitution. The poet's predicament is plain. As a man, he feels the need to 'go out of himself' in order to achieve union with another; but this simply causes an internal division without real

[1] *Journaux intimes*, p. 7.   [2] *Ibid.*, p. 79.   [3] *Ibid.*, p. 94.

union with the other. The genius strives to create an internal unity at the price of remaining within himself, but in doing so he is exposed to the internal stresses and divisions which make unity impossible. The first term of the equation may vary, but the final term is always 'prostitution' which is the negation of any form of unity.

The contrast goes still deeper. The prostitute, who degrades love, is the symbol of those forces which were undermining man in modern civilization. For in the last resort it is not only the man of genius, but every man who wishes to remain 'one' and to preserve the inner citadel against the forces of destruction which were perpetually undermining the unity of the individual. Religion, art, and love represent the three highest ideals of man, but instead of becoming the means of unity and wholeness by imposing their form on man, it is man who drags them down to his level, robbing them of their efficacy and making them an excuse for the dispersal instead of the organization of his potentialities. God becomes 'l'être le plus prostitué'[1] and love 'cette sorte de décomposition'.

'Original sin', said Baudelaire in the diaries, 'is unity become duality.' The ultimate explanation of his predicament is metaphysical. The whole of his poetry, as I have tried to show, is dominated by the search for unity. Now since 'duality', which is the root of the dilemma, was caused by original sin and since there was no place in his world for grace and redemption, it follows that the attempt was condemned to failure and frustration from the start. The drama of the *Fleurs du mal* lies therefore in an intense desire for unity coupled with the knowledge that it is impossible. The poet remains, ironically, 'riche, mais impuissant', a being without a centre in a world without direction, haunted by the 'gulf' and tortured by his own divisions:

—Ah! ne jamais sortir des Nombres et des Êtres!

His successors tried to solve the problem by turning poetry into an autonomous activity and by denying the relevance of religious and metaphysical problems. Baudelaire himself occupies

[1] *Ibid.*, p. 79.

an intermediate position. He recognized that the origin of the dilemma was metaphysical or religious, but he tried to solve it by æsthetic means. He translated his opposites into subjective terms —'the horror of life and the ecstasy of life'—and attempted to reconcile them in the act of poëtic creation. The result is paradoxical. The greatest poetry written in the nineteenth century is not merely the record of an *échec*; it is the record of the final collapse and ruin of the individual trying in vain to 'remain one'. I have spoken of the prevalence in the *Fleurs du mal* of images of death and dissolution, but the images of *physical* destruction are completed by images of *psychological* destruction, or what the poet chose to call 'La vaporisation du *Moi*':

> Mon *esprit* est pareil à la tour qui succombe
> Sous les coups du bélier infatigable et lourd.
>
> Et le riche métal de notre *volonté*
> Est tout vaporisé par ce savant chimiste.
>
> Mon *cœur* est un palais flétri par la cohue.
>
> Vainement ma *raison* voulait prendre la barre;
> La tempête en jouant déroutait ses efforts,
> Et mon *âme* dansait, dansait, vieille gabarre
> Sans mâts, sur une mer monstrueuse et sans bords!

The lines are a masterly expression of the destructive forces which attack the individual. The admirable precision of the language brings home to us the general paralysis which creeps over man, infecting his 'heart', rotting the 'will', corroding the 'mind', rendering 'reason' impotent and finally reducing the whole man—this is the sense of 'âme'—to a state of helplessness, drifting on the stormy shoreless seas where he finally disintegrates like an old barge.

For Baudelaire's poetry is the picture of a general breakdown of traditional relationships: the relations between Man and God— a world without redemption; between Man and Man—the community dissolves into the anonymous crowd of 'exiles'; between Man and Woman—a fragmentary mutilated religion is matched by a fragmentary mutilated love; and between the different faculties of the Individual—the destruction of the self.

VI

STYLE

1. Versification

'Car il est évident que les rhétoriques et les prosodies ne sont pas des tyrannies inventeés arbitrairement, mais une collection de règles réclaméé par l'organisation même de l'être spirituel. Et jamais les prosodies et les rhétoriques n'ont empêché l'originalité de se produire distinctement. Le contraire, à savoir qu'elles ont aidé l'éclosion de l'originalité, serait infiniment plus vrai.'

Curiosités esthétiques

'VOUS CRÉEZ un frisson nouveau', said Hugo in a famous letter to Baudelaire. 'Il y avait autre chose dans *Les Fleurs du mal* qu'un "frisson nouveau",' retorted Remy de Gourmont; 'il y avait un retour au vers français traditionnel.'[1] In stressing the combination of classical diction and a modern sensibility, Gourmont drew attention to one of the secrets of Baudelaire's art, but his remarks were largely confined to a parallel between the dream in *Athalie* and *Les Métamorphoses du vampire*. Baudelaire was steeped in the poetry of the sixteenth and seventeenth centuries. We have seen that in *Au Lecteur* he went back to the writers of the pre-classic period and borrowed a number of their technical devices. It is not difficult to find lines in the *Fleurs du mal* which might have been written by Racine:

Andromaque, des bras d'un grand époux tombée.

Ses bras vaincus, jetés comme de vaines armes.

Veuve d'Hector, hélas! et femme d'Hélenus.

L'une, par sa patrie au malheur exercée,
L'autre, que son époux surchargea de douleurs.

[1] *Promenades littéraires*, 2 ième série, Paris, 1906, p. 85.

235

It would be no less easy to pick out examples of his use of the eighteenth-century antithesis, but his connection with traditional French versification goes much deeper than a few isolated lines and echoes. The alexandrine is the staple of his verse. There are whole poems like 'J'aime le souvenir', *Paysage*, and *Le Crépuscule du matin* which are written in alternate masculine and feminine rhymes in the best classic manner; and the poet made extensive use of the traditional *rimes plates*, *rimes croisées*, and *rimes embrassées*.[1] He himself speaks in one of the draft prefaces to the *Fleurs du mal* of the need of a prosody 'dont les racines plongent plus avant dans l'âme humaine que ne l'indique aucune théorie classique'. The problem is a twofold one. We have to discover why Baudelaire, who dwelt on the importance of suppleness and fluidity, did in fact make such extensive use of traditional versification; and we also have to discover in what way he adapted it to his particular purposes.

'J'aime le souvenir' is an early and not altogether successful poem, but like the lesser works of great writers it throws a good deal of light on what he was trying to do:

> J'aime le souvenir de ces époques nues,
> Dont Phœbus se plaisait à dorer les statues.
> Alors l'homme et la femme en leur agilité
> Jouissaient sans mensonge et sans anxiété,
> Et, le ciel amoureux leur caressant l'échine,
> Exerçaient la santé de leur noble machine.
> Cybèle alors, fertile en produits généreux,
> Ne trouvait point ses fils un poids trop onéreux,
> Mais, louve au cœur gonflé de tendresses communes,
> Abreuvait l'univers à ses tétines brunes.
> L'homme, élégant, robuste et fort, avait le droit
> D'être fier des beautés qui le nommaient leur roi;
> Fruits purs de tout outrage et vierges de gerçures,
> Dont la chair lisse et ferme appelait les morsures!
>
> Le Poëte aujourd'hui, quand il veut concevoir
> Ces natives grandeurs, aux lieux où se font voir

---

[1] In English: rhyming couplets, alternate rhymes, and the rhyme scheme ABBA.

La nudité de l'homme et celle de la femme,
Sent un froid ténébreux envelopper son âme
Devant ce noir tableau plein d'épouvantement.
O monstruosités pleurant leur vêtement!
O ridicules troncs! torses dignes des masques!
O pauvres corps tordus, maigres, ventrus ou flasques,
Que le dieu de l'Utile, implacable et serein,
Enfants, emmaillota dans ses langes d'airain!
Et vous, femmes, hélas! pâles comme des cierges,
Que ronge et que nourrit la débauche, et vous, vierges,
Du vice maternel traînant l'hérédité
Et toutes les hideurs de la fécondité!

Nous avons, il est vrai, nations corrompues,
Aux peuples anciens des beautés inconnues:
Des visages rongés par les chancres du cœur,
Et comme qui dirait des beautés de langueur;
Mais ces inventions de nos muses tardives
N'empêcheront jamais les races maladives
De rendre à la jeunesse un hommage profond,
—A la sainte jeunesse, à l'air simple, au doux front,
A l'œil limpide et clair ainsi qu'une eau courante,
Et qui va répandant sur tout, insouciante
Comme l'azur du ciel, les oiseaux et les fleurs,
Ses parfums, ses chansons et ses douces chaleurs!

The weaknesses of the poem are apparent. There is little
rhythmical subtlety. Two orders are described consecutively and
compared, while the third section of the poem contains some
reflexions on their differences. The first section is evidently a
description of the golden age. Feuillerat suggests that 'l'homme et
la femme' are Adam and Eve, but the absence of any religious
accent and the presence of classical mythology seem to me to
make this doubtful.[1] In spite of Baudelaire's dislike of the
eighteenth century, the first section is little more than a versified
exhibition of Rousseau's theory of the 'noble savage' decorated
by the classical jargon of the time. It seems untrue, however, to
suggest, as Mr. Middleton Murry has done in a capital essay, that
Baudelaire 'made no technical innovations'.[2] The application of

[1] *Studies*, p. 228.   [2] *Op. cit.*, p. 121.

the grand style to a contemporary subject is in itself an important innovation. Baudelaire does not use it, as Corneille had done, to express the regularity, the stability of an established order. He uses it to express the sudden realization that the old order—the order based on the community life ('tendresses communes') and a sense of the dignity of man—had vanished and been replaced by an alien order and the tyranny of the new industrialism which was gradually stifling man's natural aspirations.

There is always in Baudelaire's poetry a contrast between the hard metallic words and words suggesting softness, corruption, and collapse. They are juxtaposed in such a way that the hard words bring out the softness of the other words. Baudelaire uses the device with great effect in his mature poetry and even in the contrast between the first and second sections of this poem it is not without a certain effectiveness. The real merits of the piece, however, depend on the contrast between diction and subject. We are made to feel the 'dieu de l'Utile' enfolding his children, who were once 'élégant(s), robuste(s) et fort(s)' in the 'langes d'airain' from which they emerge 'tordus, maigres, ventrus ou flasques'. They have been transformed by an unnatural environment into misshapen, shrunken, flabby, paunchy robots, into the anonymous slaves of a hideous machine who are only interesting on account of their emotional ravages and their 'visages rongés par les chancres du cœur'.

'They seem', said Mr. Eliot of the poems, 'to have the external but not the internal form of classic art.'[1] That is undoubtedly true, but it does not seem to me to be a matter for reproach. The diction is deliberately used to evoke the old order which becomes a point of reference, a standard by which the present is tested and condemned. There are moments in *Phèdre* when we catch a glimpse of a metaphysical gulf, when we seem to be watching the beginning of a dissolution of order inside the regular frame; but by the time we reach Baudelaire dissolution is an accomplished fact. That is why Baudelaire's *frisson* does depend in a very large degree on the contrast between form and content, on the spectacle

---

[1] *Selected Essays*, pp. 371–2.

of the individual and his world falling to pieces *inside the classical mould*.[1]

In his notes on Baudelaire Laforgue speaks with felicity of the 'allure solennelle, le vers qui *enchasuble* en ses plis lamés . . . la pensée subtile comme un parfum' and of 'cette noblesse immuable qui annoblit les vulgarités intéressantes, captivantes'.[2] The grand manner was essential to the expression of Baudelaire's tragic vision, but the contrast between past and present, actuality and ideal, was only one of the reasons for its use. The inner experience of the individual is the core of his poetry and the traditional form has a normative influence, creating a bridge between the poet and his milieu. This accounts to some extent for the connection between abstract words and homely images drawn from everyday life which will be examined in greater detail later in this chapter. The alexandrine is also used, as Laforgue suggests, for still another purpose. It is used to magnify and enoble 'les vulgarités intéressantes, captivantes', and it invests his themes with a curious ambiguous dignity:

> Je t'adore à l'égal de la voûte nocturne,
> O vase de tristesse, ô grande taciturne,
> Et t'aime d'autant plus, belle, que tu me fuis,
> Et que tu me parais, ornement de mes nuits,
> Plus ironiquement accumuler les lieues
> Qui me séparent mes bras des immensités bleues.
>
> Je m'avance à l'attaque, et je grimpe aux assauts,
> Comme après un cadavre un chœur de vermisseaux,
> Et je chéris, ô bête implacable et cruelle!
> Jusqu'à cette froideur par où tu m'es plus belle!

This poem shows that the courtesans, who provided the inspiration for some of his greatest poetry, have undergone a transformation, have been drawn up into the poet's own sphere where they become symbols in a universal drama. The mistress is, indeed, 'created' by the large use of 'poetical' expressions like

---

[1] 'Parce que la forme est contraignante, l'idée jaillit plus intense' (letter to Armand Fraisse on the sonnet, 18 February 1860, *Corr. gén.*, 3, p. 39).

[2] *Entretiens Politiques et Littéraires, art. cit.*, p. 116. *Mélanges posthumes*, p. 117.

'la voûte nocturne', 'vase de tristesse', 'grande taciturne', and 'immensités bleues' as well as by the slow enveloping rhythms until she becomes a goddess poised in space above the world. The dignity, however, remains ambiguous. All Baudelaire's poetry, particularly his love poetry, is based on sharp contrasts. There is a violent change of tone in the last four lines with their vertiginous descent towards the flesh which is expressed by an obscene *upward* movement—'je grimpe'. The poet does not scruple to use a deliberately crude expression like 'grimpe aux assauts' to describe the woman being taken by force or the 'chœur de vermisseaux' to emphasize the mortality of the goddess, while the 'ornement de mes nuits' becomes a 'bête implacable et cruelle'. Yet the precarious dignity is somehow preserved and the rape or attempted rape is a rape in the grand manner.

Another poem closes with the striking apostrophe:

> O fangeuse grandeur! sublime ignominie!

where the destructive conjunction of adjectives and substantives shows a creature at once 'sublime' and 'ignominious' who possesses for the poet a quasi-religious significance.

Baudelaire also employs the reverse process—the process of deflation—in a way that reminds us a little oddly of the English poets of the Augustan Age. One of the best examples occurs in a poem that I have already examined in detail:

> Resplendit à jamais, comme un astre inutile,
> La froide majesté de la femme stérile.

The 'femme stérile' effectively punctures the pretensions of 'majesté' and reveals its hollowness.

We find the same process of enobling 'les vulgarités intéressantes, captivantes' at work in the descriptions of city life:

> Je ne vois qu'en esprit tout ce camp de baraques,
> Ces tas de chapiteaux ébauchés et de fûts,
> Les herbes, les gros blocs verdis par l'eau des flaques,
> Et, brillant aux carreaux, le bric-à-brac confus.

Laforgue remarked that the last line shows the touch of the

master, and we understand what Mr. Eliot meant when he spoke of 'the elevation of such imagery to the *first intensity*'.[1]

There are two other uses of the grand manner which deserve mention. The first is the sudden switch from the solemn to the ludicrous which was extremely popular with Baudelaire's successors and which was employed with considerable effect by Corbière in *Le Bossu Bitord*, *Le Poète contumace*, and *Femme*:

> Notre âme est un trois-mâts cherchant son Icarie;
> Une voix retentit sur le pont: 'Ouvre l'œil!'
> Une voix de la hune, ardente et folle, crie:
> 'Amour . . . gloire . . . bonheur!' Enfer! c'est un écueil!

The second is the mock-heroic style that we find in *Les Chats*:

> Amis de la science et de la volupté,
> Ils cherchent le silence et l'horreur des ténèbres;
> L'Erèbe les eût pris pour ses coursiers funèbres,
> S'ils pouvaient au servage incliner leur fierté.

I think that these examples are sufficient to show that Baudelaire's use of the grand manner and the intentionally ambivalent attitudes expressed are something new in poetry, and they explain in part the extraordinary fascination, the *envoûtement* of his verse.

Once the novelty of his approach is grasped, it becomes relatively easy to understand his comment on the need of a new prosody and to illustrate not merely the variety of his own diction, but the reasons for its variety. Gourmont's 'return to traditional French versification' is an imprecise phrase. We know that there are certain qualities which are native to all good writing whether it is verse or prose; but it is impossible to return to the style of a past age or to make a complete break with it. The development of literature consists largely in a series of small but significant changes in traditional forms. Baudelaire's aim was the preservation and extension of traditional French versification. It would not be altogether an exaggeration to describe his work as a continuation of Racine's. It was a continuation in the sense that the poet's instrument becomes much subtler and much more

---

[1] *Selected Essays*, p. 374.

flexible because it is being applied to a far greater range of feelings and to a far greater width of experience than was possible in the seventeenth century.

'Quant à ma ponctuation,' he wrote in a letter to Poulet-Malassis four months before the appearance of the *Fleurs du mal*, 'rappelez-vous qu'elle sert à noter non seulement le sens, mais LA DÉCLAMATION.'[1] The word 'déclamation' is a very important one for a study of Baudelaire's versification. He showed a marked preference for the dramatic form. It enabled him not merely to probe more deeply into emotional states, but to expose the tensions and conflicts of the *homo duplex* that he was. I have glanced at his use of it in the Cycle of Jeanne Duval, *Le Voyage*, and *Un Voyage à Cythère*, but I want to carry the examination a stage further.

In the poems dealing with large issues like *Le Voyage* he uses dialogue with two or more speakers. The first speaker puts forward a point of view which is usually elaborated by a second 'voice' and attacked by a speaker on the other side. The poem becomes a dramatic debate, and its intensity is generated by the vigour with which the conflicting points of view are attacked and defended. The stay-at-home in *Le Voyage*, who addresses the travellers ironically as 'Étonnants voyageurs!', is evidently expecting to hear some tall stories about the sights they have seen or to be told that the voyage has been a disappointment. In either case he is prepared to enjoy himself at their expense. His mockery provokes a fierce attack on the conventional idea of travel which clearly disconcerts him. He drops the tone of banter and when he says: 'Et puis; et puis encore?' he seems to be begging for reassurance. But this simply leads to the final indictment of the futility and vulgarity of civilization, and a second traveller winds up the debate with

—Tel est du globe entier l'éternel bulletin.

Un Voyage à Cythère is a debate on Cythera. The poet is in a

---

[1] *Corr. gén.*, 3, p. 25. The poems contain plenty of 'déclamation' in the literal sense. No one can fail to notice Baudelaire's fondness for exclamation marks and for fitting an 'hélas' into the middle of many of his lines.

carefree mood sailing the peaceful seas. He suddenly catches sight
of the 'île triste et noire' and asks what it is. Someone answers
that 'It is Cythera, a country which is famous in song, or so we
are told'. He adds, disparagingly: 'Look, it's a poor sort of place
after all.' It is the beginning of an attack on the Cythera of legend
which is defended with equal warmth by a third speaker. This
time the question is settled by the travellers' arrival at the island,
by the impact of actuality, which shows that it is not 'a poor sort
of place', but a terrifying sort of place. The same thing happens
that happened in *Le Voyage*. The victory of the disillusioned
parties to the debate produces a complete change of mood and the
poem closes with the poet's sombre monologue on the new
situation.

The theme of *Femmes damnées* (Delphine et Hippolyte) is a
moral debate. Delphine states the case for homosexual relationships. Hippolyte—it is the crux of the poem—is conscious of the
immense seductiveness of Delphine, but her pleasure is poisoned
by moral scruples. In her second speech Delphine tries to demolish
the scruples, but Hippolyte's last speech shows that the debate
has simply produced that destructive insight into feeling which is
one of the outstanding characteristics of the seventeenth-century
dramatists. The arguments on the ethics of homosexuality are
clinched by the final intervention of the poet.

In the love poems Baudelaire generally uses monologue and
the drama of the Cycle of Jeanne Duval lies, as I have shown, in
the contrasted tones of the different poems and this makes each
poem an episode in a drama which extends over a number of
years. He uses monologue because the woman is passive and he
addresses her alternately in tones of adoration, supplication, and
denunciation. The Cycle of Mme Sabatier is a partial exception.
Confession is a debate on the problem of the society woman,
Semper eadem on the nature of love. The second of these poems
illustrates a slightly different mode:

> 'D'où vous vient, disiez-vous, cette tristesse étrange,
> Montant comme la mer sur le roc noir et nu?'
> —Quand notre cœur a fait une fois sa vendange,
> Vivre est un mal . . .

It is a no less successful example of Baudelaire's adaptation of
the alexandrine to the tone of casual conversation. It is 'dramatic',
but it is the drama of the undertone, the muttered confidence
which is as different as it could well be from the 'déclamation' of
'Tu mettrais l'univers entier':

> Quand la nature, grande en ses desseins cachés,
> De toi se sert, ô femme, ô reine des péchés,
> —De toi, vil animal,—pour pétrir un génie . . .

In an early poem like *Châtiment de l'orgueil*, he seems to use a
number of different 'voices' in the manner of a broadcast 'feature'
simply in order to vary the tone and to maintain the interest of
what is in fact a short dramatic narrative.

The examples that I have discussed all have one thing in
common. They are in no sense versified arguments, and it is possibly misleading to speak of the characters' 'points of view' at all.
They are not dealing with abstract ideas. The positions that they
attack or defend are emotionally apprehended and the 'idea' or
'point of view' is transformed into a mood or an impression.
What we are really witnessing is a conflict of attitudes. Baudelaire's method of presenting the conflict is strictly poetic. The
urgency and intensity of the poetry, the alternate clashing and
blending of the tones which reflect the different attitudes—*Un
Voyage à Cythère* is the outstanding example—decide the outcome of the 'argument' and give the poems their particular
appeal. A debate on travel or Cythera becomes the means of
revealing some of the profoundest and most disturbing of human
problems.

I want finally to look at a poem in a somewhat different manner
because it illustrates nearly all the qualities that I have mentioned.
M. Vivier has spoken disparagingly of the 'transitions d'écolier'
of *Le Masque*, but in doing so he seems to me to take the poem
too seriously and to do less than justice to its virtuosity.[1] It is,
admittedly, a minor poem, but the sub-title—'Statue Allégorique
dans le Goût de la Renaissance'—suggests the way in which it
should be read. It is an ironic sketch in the style of the heroic

[1] *Op. cit.*, p. 25.

comedies of the seventeenth century. Two people are standing
in front of the statue discussing its beauties:

> Contemplons ce trésor de grâces florentines;
> Dans l'ondulation de ce corps musculeux
> L'Élégance et la Force abondent, sœurs divines.
> Cette femme, morceau vraiment miraculeux,
> Divinement robuste, adorablement mince,
> Est faite pour trôner sur des lits somptueux,
> Et charmer les loisirs d'un pontife ou d'un prince.

It is the enthusiastic tone of the 'art-lover'. We catch the very
accent of the speaking voice, almost see him stretching out his
hand and demonstrating the curves of the muscular, seductive
body. The poet's intention, however, is ironical, and in the
'morceau vraiment miraculeux', 'divinement robuste, adorable-
ment mince', we detect the note of pompous fatuity which Baudelaire himself must often have heard when visiting exhibitions for
his *Salons*. The second connoisseur, fired by his enthusiasm,
breaks in with:

> —Aussi, vois ce souris fin et voluptueux
> Où la Fatuité promène son extase.

He deliberately uses the archaic, poetical 'souris'; the allusion
to 'Fatuité' emphasizes the statue's physical charms at the
expense of its supposed mental qualities and may be a sly comment on the speaker. Yet as we listen to his voice, the statue
almost seems to come to life:

> Ce long regard sournois, langoureux et moqueur;
> Ce visage mignard, tout encadré de gaze,
> Dont chaque trait nous dit avec un air vainqueur:
> 'La Volupté m'appelle et l'Amour me couronne!'
> A cet être doué de tant de majesté
> Vois quel charme excitant la gentillesse donne!

He invites his companion to look at the statue from the other
side:

> Approchons, et tournons autour de sa beauté.

Then we hear the shocked cry as he discovers, dramatically, that the figure is two-headed:

> O blasphème de l'art! ô surprise fatale!
> La femme au corps divin, promettant le bonheur,
> Par le haut se termine en monstre bicéphale!

The first speaker cuts in again:

> —Mais non! ce n'est qu'un masque, un décor suborneur,
> Ce visage éclairé d'une exquise grimace,
> Et, regarde, voici, crispée atrocement,
> La véritable tête, et la sincère face
> Renversée à l'abri de la face qui ment.
> Pauvre grande beauté! le magnifique fleuve
> De tes pleurs aboutit dans mon cœur soucieux;
> Ton mensonge m'enivre, et mon âme s'abreuve
> Aux flots que la Douleur fait jaillir de tes yeux!

The excited exchange takes us further and further away from the tone of delighted and mildly salacious connoisseurship with which the poem opened; but the reader's interest is heightened as he wonders what the outcome will be. The triumphant

> —Mais non! ce n'est qu'un masque, un décor suborneur

gives way to a calmer tone as the speaker meditates on the meaning of the 'allegory' and seems to identify himself with the woman's sufferings:

> Pauvre grande beauté! le magnifique fleuve
> De tes pleurs aboutit dans mon cœur soucieux;
> Ton mensonge m'enivre, et mon âme s'abreuve
> Aux flots que la Douleur fait jaillir de tes yeux!

The word 'mensonge' shows that his reflections belong to a world of make-believe, a world of 'allegory'. They are rudely disturbed by a sudden question from the other:

> —Mais pourquoi pleure-t-elle? Elle, beauté parfaite
> Qui mettrait à ses pieds le genre humain vaincu,
> Quel mal mystérieux ronge son flanc d'athlète?

The violent retort finally shatters the world of illusion:

> —Elle pleure, insensé, parce qu'elle a vécu!

It is driven home by a change of tense:

> Et parce qu'elle vit!

The poem opened in a mood of complacent dilettantism, but by a series of shocks the spectators are brought back to *living* problems, to their own predicament. For the sculptor has caught and preserved a moment of suffering, reminding them that

> ce qu'elle déplore
> Surtout, ce qui la fait frémir jusqu'aux genoux,
> C'est que demain, hélas! il faudra vivre encore!
> Demain, après-demain et toujours!—comme nous!

Although Baudelaire's use of the grand manner is highly original, it remains true that he did not invent any technical devices in the narrow sense of the term. The reason is not difficult to discover. The task of the poet in his time was to explore the resources already at his disposal and to make proper use of the inventions of the Romantics whose technical competence was more impressive than the quality of their experience. This meant that Baudelaire had to rid poetry of its vagueness and the large oratorical flourishes, and to bring it much closer to our mental processes. It was not until the next generation—the generation of Rimbaud and Laforgue—that alterations in sensibility made radical innovations in French prosody a necessity. When we examine the structure of Baudelaire's verse, we find that though he made skilful use of the cæsura, *enjambement*, the three-foot line, and alliteration, he seldom indulged in the more daring tricks of the Romantics. His approach, indeed, appears in many ways to be conservative; but he was not conservative out of respect for the rules for their own sake. If he made comparatively little use of the mobile cæsura, it was largely because a high degree of regularity was necessary for his particular purposes. This does not mean that the cæsura is always given the same value and falls monotonously at the hemistich. In one of his letters to an editor he stresses the importance that he attached to punctuation, and said that he would prefer a whole poem to be omitted rather than a

single comma because his commas always had a *raison d'être*.[1]
What he did was to introduce very considerable variations into
the value given to the cæsura, either to prevent it from inter-
fering with the sense already marked by the punctuation or to
reinforce the sense. In some lines it is so attenuated that it becomes
practically imperceptible; in others it is moderately accentuated,
and in others still it falls powerfully at the hemistich, giving
tremendous emphasis to certain words. In a number of lines in *Le
Voyage* it is carefully attenuated so that it will not disturb the
flow of the narrative:

> Les uns, joyeux de fuir une patrie infâme;
> D'autres, l'horreur de leurs berceaux, et quelques uns,
> Astrologues noyés . . .

In these lines Baudelaire is describing the 'ordinary' travellers
in contrast to the 'vrais voyageurs' whose adventures are the
main theme of the poem. He is therefore careful to ensure that no
special emphasis is given to any single word or words. Their
'joy' at escaping is balanced against their dislike of a 'patrie
infâme' or 'l'horreur de leurs berceaux'. The second line is a
good example of the way in which the poet achieves his aim. The
cæsura comes at the insignificant word 'leurs', and we shall find
that in other places it comes at a preposition or a conjunction.
The cæsura is more pronounced in the lines describing the 'vrais
voyageurs':

> Mais les vrais voyageurs sont ceux-là seuls qui partent
> Pour partir; cœurs légers, semblables aux ballons,
> De leur fatalité jamais ils ne s'écartent,
> Et, sans savoir pourquoi, disent toujours: Allons!

Here a certain stress is given to the words 'voyageurs',
'légers', 'fatalité', 'jamais', and 'pourquoi'. But the persons who
travel are much less important than the unexplained desire to
travel: that is why the *enjambement* heavily emphasized the verb
'partir'.

Another interesting example is provided by the line:

> Comme au long d'un cadavre un cadavre étendu.

---

[1] *Corr. gén.*, 4, p. 171 (letter to Gervaise Charpentier, 20 June 1863).

Baudelaire might have written:

> Comme un cadavre au long d'un cadavre étendu

with an attenuated cæsura at 'long'. He did not do so because he wanted to give the effect of two motionless bodies stretched side by side like corpses. The two 'cadavres' are therefore placed next to one another, and the cæsura coming between them gives precisely the same value and the same degree of lifelessness to both.

The heavily accentuated cæsura is used to give a strong emphasis to a particular word, but it is interesting to observe that even in a three-foot line—a line with a double cæsura—the word that the poet wishes to stress usually comes after the sixth syllable:

> Du ciel—se détachant en noir,—comme un cyprès.

The word 'noir' is heavily stressed and linked with 'cyprès' in order to bring out the intense preoccupation with death that pervades the whole poem. When Baudelaire wrote:

> Où saint Antoine—a vu surgir—comme des laves
> Les seins nus et pourprés—de ses tentations,

he used the double cæsura in the first line and the regular cæsura at the hemistich in the second line. This gives a powerful emphasis to 'surgir', which comes significantly at the seventh syllable, and links it with 'laves'. In the second line he gives equal emphasis to 'pourprés', which comes immediately before the cæsura, because the lurid glimpse of the breasts is far more important than 'tentations'.

Causerie is a disappointing poem, but it illustrates some of the effects that Baudelaire achieved by varying the force of the cæsura:

> Vous êtes un beau ciel d'automne, clair et rose!
> Mais la tristesse en moi monte comme la mer,
> Et laisse, en refluant, sur ma lèvre morose
> Le souvenir cuisant de son limon amer.

French writers differ about the place of the cæsura in the first

line. Flottes thinks that it comes after the ninth syllable in order
to isolate 'clair et rose', but I feel that Cassagne is right in reading it as a three-foot line stressing 'automne' and 'rose':

> Vous êtes—un beau ciel d'automne,—clair et rose![1]

The cæsura is barely perceptible in the second line because the
poet intends to convey the impression of the continuous movement of the sea creeping up, and the impression is heightened by
the cluster of m's. In the last two lines the cæsura is regular and
pronounced, suggesting the regular lines left on the shore as the
tide recedes. This in turn stresses the persistent bitterness left
behind by the 'tide of sadness' in contrast to the suavity of 'clair
et rose'. There is one other point which deserves notice. The
rising tide in line 2 makes us feel that the autumn landscape in
the first line has been obliterated, and this feeling is more marked
when our attention is fixed on the monotonous furrows of the
empty shore in lines 3 and 4.

In the same poem we read:

> Mon cœur est un palais flétri par la cohue;
> On s'y soûle, on s'y tue, on s'y prend aux cheveux!
> —Un parfum nage autour de votre gorge nue! . . .

The regular cæsura in the first two lines stresses the word
'flétri' and the violent actions of the mob. In the third there is a
very light cæsura at the preposition 'autour', so that the violence
suddenly subsides into the gentle 'swimming' movement of the
perfumes, creating a sense of release and relaxation. The intention is underlined by the dash at the beginning of the line which
is almost invariably a sign used by Baudelaire to indicate either
a change of 'voice' or, as here, a change of tone.

The aim of all these variations is to bring out the physical
basis of sensation, to make words perform the actions that they
describe. *Chant d'automne* is an immensely effective presentation
of an autumn scene:

> Bientôt nous plongerons dans les froides ténèbres;
> Adieu, vive clarté de nos étés trop courts!

[1] P. Flottes, *Charles Baudelaire: l'homme et le poète*, Paris, 1922, p. 212.
Cassagne, *Versification et métrique de Ch. Baudelaire*, Paris, 1906, p. 39.

J'entends déjà tomber avec des chocs funèbres
Le bois retentissant sur le pavé des cours . . .

J'écoute en frémissant chaque bûche qui tombe;
L'échafaud qu'on bâtit n'a pas d'écho plus sourd.
Mon esprit est pareil à la tour qui succombe
Sous les coups du bélier infatigable et lourd.

Il me semble, bercé par ce choc monotone,
Qu'on cloue en grande hâte un cercueil quelque part.
Pour qui?—C'était hier l'été; voici l'automne!
Ce bruit mystérieux sonne comme un départ.

It will be seen that the choice of words—'tombe', 'succombe', 'sourd', 'lourd', 'infatigable', 'monotone'—and the repetition of -*ou* sounds, which alternate with the sharp i's and the abrupt short o in 'choc', are brilliantly successful in conveying the dull thud of the wood falling on the paving-stones. The muffled vibration of 'retentissant' registers the impact of wood on stone, 'frémissant' its echo in the mind of the spectator. The effect is greatly increased by the regular fall of the cæsura at the hemistich in the first eight lines. It not only reflects the monotonous fall of the logs; it creates a sensation of numbness as the regular thud of wood on stone imposes its rhythm on the mind. Baudelaire was extremely skilful in creating patterns in which asymmetrical movements are set against a background of symmetry. It happens with the double cæsura in line 11. The hammering suggests coffins. The poet shakes off the feeling of mental numbness and asks in terror:

Pour qui?—C'était hier l'été; voici l'automne.

The pattern reforms with the regular fall of the cæsura in the last line, and the first section of the poem closes on a quiet note as the terror subsides and the sound of the logs fades away in

Ce bruit mystérieux sonne comme un départ.

The three-foot line is often said to be the invention of the Romantics. This is not correct—it is occasionally found in the seventeenth-century dramatists—but the Romantics undoubtedly exploited it very effectively and greatly extended its range and use. Baudelaire employs it to diminish the monotony of the alexandrine, to express sudden changes of mood or tone, and to vary the tempo of his verse. One of the best examples of the first use occurs in some lines from *Le Flacon* quoted in an earlier chapter:

> Mille pensers dormaient,—chrysalides funèbres,
> Frémissant doucement—dans les lourdes ténèbres,
> Qui dégagent leur aile—et prennent leur essor,
> Teintés d'azur,—glacés de rose,—lamés d'or.

In the first three lines the 'thoughts' are perceived collectively as a struggling mass, but as they sail into the air they separate like a cluster of coloured lights from a bursting rocket. We find ourselves contemplating them as individual objects possessing their own identity, and at the same time there is a pronounced slowing down of the tempo:

> Teintés d'azur,—glacés de rose,—lamés d'or.

In the second tercet of *La Destruction*:

> Il me conduit ainsi,—loin du regard de Dieu,
> Haletant—et brisé de fatigue,—au milieu
> Des plaines de l'Ennui,—profondes et désertes,

the broken rhythms of the second line express the terror and the exhaustion of the panting, breathless individual who in the next line seems to be swallowed up in the vast, empty, unending plains.

The effect is similar and still more successful in the second verse of *Obsession*:

> Je te hais, Océan!—tes bonds et tes tumultes,
> Mon esprit—les retrouve en lui;—ce rire amer
> De l'homme vaincu,—plein de sanglots—et d'insultes,
> Je l'entends dans le rire—énorme de la mer.

The versification stresses what I have called the *décousu* of the images. The speaker is identifying his stormy, uncontrolled emotions with the beating of the waves, and the second and third lines reflect the tossing of the waves as well as the body shaken by sobs and the choking 'insultes'. In the last line we simply hear the mighty roar of the sea which swallows up the man, the sobs, and the insults.

In the last two lines of *Le Flacon*:

> Cher poison—préparé par les anges!—Liqueur
> Qui me ronge,—ô la vie et la mort—de mon cœur!

the broken rhythms suggest the faltering thoughts and movements of a person on the point of death.

In *Le Beau navire* the three-foot lines reflect the swaying motion of a ship weighed down under its heavy sails:

> Quand tu vas—balayant l'air—de ta jupe large,
> Tu fais l'effet—d'un beau vaisseau—qui prend le large.

When he writes:

> Le jour décroît;—la nuit augmente;—*souviens-toi!*

the two abrupt statements followed by the injunction give the impression of life running relentlessly away and leaving the poet waiting helplessly for death.

Although the number of syllables in each line naturally does not alter, the length of the different feet varies considerably, reminding us of the primary function of what French prosodists call the *trimètre*. The 'count' of the last eight examples is 2, 6, 2 (*Chant d'automne*); 4, 5, 3 (*Le Flacon*); 3, 6, 3 (*La Destruction*); 3, 5, 4 / 5, 4, 3 (*Obsession*); 3, 7, 2 / 3, 6, 3 (*Le Flacon*); 3, 4, 5 / 4, 4, 4 (*Le Beau navire*); 4, 5, 3 (*L'Horloge*).

The rules of classical prosody did not allow *enjambement*. The practice of later generations of poets, however, shows that it belongs to the genius of the language, that it not only contributes to the sweep and the muscular qualities of the alexandrine, but that it can also have the reverse effect, enabling the poet to switch from the grand manner to the casual tone of conversation. The sweep is apparent in

> Mais les vrais voyageurs sont ceux-là seuls qui partent
> Pour partir; cœurs légers, semblables aux ballons . . .

where the travellers float away into space, and the sense of light-

ness and airiness is accentuated by the l's in the second line. The
effect is similar in two magnificent lines from *Le Gouffre*:

> Sur le fond de mes nuits, Dieu de son doigt savant
> Dessine un cauchemar multiforme et sans trêve.

The *enjambement*, following the alternation of d's and s's,
gives us the sensation of being propelled firmly but smoothly
into a nightmare world. The cæsura at the hemistich stresses
both 'cauchemar' and 'multiforme', so that we see the myriad
shapes of the nightmare fanning out against the sombre background of night, endlessly.

The sense of compulsion can be intensified by the use of a
double *enjambement* in conjunction with the three-foot line:

> Voilà le souvenir enivrant qui voltige
> Dans l'air troublé; les yeux se ferment; le Vertige
> Saisit l'âme vaincue . . .

The second *enjambement* and the transitive verb following two
intransitive verbs:

> le Vertige
> Saisit l'âme vaincue . . .

creates an impression of almost irresistible force, and the impression is naturally heightened by the peculiar sense of weakness
which Baudelaire's three-foot lines so often convey.

When he writes in *Les Aveugles*:

> Leurs yeux, d'où la divine étincelle est partie,
> Comme s'ils regardaient au loin, restent levés
> Au ciel; on ne les voit jamais vers les pavés
> Pencher rêveusement leur tête appesantie.

the double *enjambement* contributes to the compactness of the
syntax and at the same time creates a startling impression of the
unseeing eyes glued to the sky, which distinguishes the blind
from other pedestrians passing by with hanging heads.

I have only room to comment briefly on Baudelaire's use of
alliteration. It is usually regarded as a primitive device which
enabled early poets to give their verse a lilt or helped them to

memorize their lines. In Baudelaire it is an auxiliary device which is often extremely effective in intensifying physical impressions. In the lines

> Quand la *p*ierre, o*pp*rimant ta *p*oitrine *p*eureuse
> Et tes flancs qu'assou*p*lit un charmant nonchaloir,
> Em*p*êchera ton *c*oeur de battre et de vouloir,
> Et tes pieds de *cou*rir leur *cou*rse aventureuse . . .

we feel the stone pressing on the body and stifling the lithe, supple movements suggested by the labials and the soft -*ch* sounds in line 2 as well as putting a brake on the rapid movement of '*cou*rir' and '*cou*rse'. A similar sense of constriction is perceptible in

ces affreuses nuits

Qui *c*ompriment le *c*oeur *c*omme un papier qu'on froisse.

where the -*co*'s give the sensation of something clutching at the heart and closing round it.

Flottes points out that in the line

> . . . la gri*ff*e et la dent *f*éroce de la *f*emme

the f's have something 'crochu' about them and seem to dig into the soft flesh.[1]

In *Bénédiction* the poet strikes a note of embittered denunciation:

> Et je tordrai si bien cet arbre misérable,
> Qu'il ne *p*ourra *p*ousser ses boutons em*p*estés!

The play of the consonants, particularly the b's, p's, and s's, gives the impression that the speaker is spitting and spluttering with rage.

'Que diras-tu ce soir' shows the lengths to which Baudelaire was capable of pushing his undeniable virtuosity:

> Qui ce soit *dans* la nuit et *dans* la solitude,
> Que ce soit *dans* la rue et *dans* la multitude,
> Son fantôme *dans* l'air *danse* comme un flambeau.[2]

[1] *Op. cit.*, pp. 212–13.
[2] It was certainly a conscious virtuosity. In the MS. version sent to Mme Sabatier the last line reads:
> Son Fantôme en dansant marche comme un Flambeau.

Le Jet d'eau, a poem first published in a magazine in 1865, is a brilliant example of virtuosity of another kind:

> Tes beaux yeux sont las, pauvre amante!
> Reste longtemps, sans les rouvrir,
> Dans cette pose nonchalante
> Où t'a surprise le plaisir.
> Dans la cour le jet d'eau qui jase
> Et ne se tait ni nuit ni jour,
> Entretient doucement l'extase
> Où ce soir m'a plongé l'amour.
>
> > La gerbe épanouie
> > En mille fleurs,
> > Où Phœbé réjouie
> > Met ses couleurs,
> > Tombe comme une pluie
> > De larges pleurs.

The scene is the lovers' bedroom. The building stands in a courtyard and the sound of the fountain playing comes in through the open windows. The poet's aim is to describe the rise and fall of desire, the pleasure that it brings, and the melancholy that follows its satisfaction. He expresses these contrasted feelings through two contrasted movements—the heavy movements of the lovers and the light airy movement of the water—for which he uses two different verse-forms. The words 'amante', 'long-temps', 'nonchalante' suggest the weariness of the woman, but in the fifth line the sound of the water breaks in with the sharp i's and the nasals of 'entretient', mingling with the heavier 'douce-ment' and 'm'a plongé l'amour' with its voluptuous associations. In the refrain the sharp, clear -*ie*'s alternate with the thick 'fleurs', 'couleurs', and 'pleurs', reflecting the rise and fall of the water in a sort of pantomime of what has been happening in the bed-room. The effect was carefully calculated as we can see from the original version of the refrain which read:

> La gerbe d'eau qui berce
> Ses mille fleurs
> Que la lune traverse

> De ses lueurs
> Tombe comme une averse
> De larges pleurs.

The substitution of 'épanouie', 'réjouie', and 'pluie' for 'berce', 'traverse', and 'averse' produces the thin sharp sound which contrasts so strikingly with the heavier syllables.[1]

In the second verse the lovers recover and—*ils recommencent*:

> Ainsi ton âme qu'incendie
> L'éclair brûlant des voluptés
> S'élance, rapide et hardie,
> Vers les vastes cieux enchantés.
> Puis, elle s'épanche, mourante,
> En un flot de triste langueur,
> Qui par une invisible pente
> Descend jusqu'au fond de mon cœur.

The real theme of the poem is evidently making love to music. The gay, airy movement of the fountain communicates itself to the lovers and the first four lines are dominated by the sharp -*ie*'s and the é's, while in the word 's'élance' the image of rising desire merges into the visual image of the water spouting into the air, and the speaker seems to identify his subjective feelings with the fountain. The climax is reached in line 5, but the reaction sets in at once. For just as the words in -*eurs* in the refrain reflect the falling water, so in these four lines the words 'mourante', 'langueur', 'pente', and 'fond' mark the dying down of desire and the feeling of sadness—also apparent in the 'pleurs' of the refrain—which follows.

In the third and last verse we leave the poet meditating on what has happened:

> O toi, que la nuit rend si belle,
> Qu'il m'est doux, penché vers tes seins,
> D'écouter la plainte éternelle
> Qui sanglote dans les bassins!
> Lune, eau sonore, nuit bénie,
> Arbres qui frissonnez autour.
> Votre pure mélancolie
> Est le miroir de mon amour.

[1] See Cassagne, *op. cit.*, p. 64.

R

In these lines he sounds all the notes—sharp i's, nasals, liquid l's, ending with the muted 'autour', 'amour'—and the final impression is one of rich, mature satisfaction which seems to eddy outwards, gradually embracing the whole world in 'la plainte éternelle', the ecstatic 'nuit bénie', and the 'pure mélancolie' which becomes

. . . le miroir de mon amour.

2. Language

Any discussion of Baudelaire's versification leads to a consideration of the actual language of his poetry. 'Baudelaire's language is still classic,' as one authority said to me, 'but Rimbaud and Mallarmé set to work to demolish the French language.'[1] Mr. Eliot has expressed what may appear at first to be a divergent view. 'This invention of language,' he writes, 'at a moment when French poetry in particular was famishing for such invention, is enough to make of Baudelaire a great poet, a great landmark in poetry. Baudelaire is indeed the greatest exemplar in *modern* poetry in any language, for his verse and language is the nearest thing to a complete renovation that we have experienced.'[2] The divergence between these views is only apparent. Language can never stand still. A living language is always changing, developing, and sometimes decaying. It is in the great writer—particularly the great poet—that change and development first appear. We find in Baudelaire a combination of three elements: a classical French style, a remarkable originality, and unmistakable signs of decay. The classical element can be seen in his syntax and in his reliance on verb, substantive, and adjective; his originality in his power of suggestion and in fresh combinations of words; the element of decay in his macabre imagery and in the excessive use of poetic clichés, which reveals a tendency to slip back into conventional emotions and stock responses that is more pronounced than in any other French poet of comparable stature.

[1] M. Charles Bruneau, the present author of the great *Histoire de la langue française.*
[2] *Selected Essays*, p. 374.

Syntax

M. Henri Peyre has lately observed that in his syntax Baudelaire is 'un attardé plus qu'un novateur'.[1] Although he assures us
that 'attardé' is not necessarily a word of blame, I cannot help
feeling that in its context the word creates a misleading impression. Compared with Baudelaire's, Mallarmé's syntax may appear
highly original, but this is a superficial judgment. There is in
Mallarmé's later work an extraordinary brittleness which we
never find in Baudelaire's and which is not a sign of strength. Too
much has been made of the supposed influence of Sainte-Beuve's
Pensées d'août on Baudelaire—Baudelaire transformed what he
took from Sainte-Beuve as only a very great poet could have
done—but the nineteenth-century prosodists who discussed the
precise 'dose of prose' which is necessary in good verse were
working on the right lines. Poetry should possess the qualities
of good prose, and Baudelaire was to a greater extent than Proust
'un disciple de l'ancienne rhétorique'.[2] His sinewy, muscular
syntax contributes in a large measure to the solidity and tautness
of his verse.[3] The influence of Latin is apparent in his fondness for
introducing comparisons by the words 'comme' and 'ainsi que',
but it is the long flexible sentences beginning in one verse and
ending in another that bind some of his poems together:

> Tout à coup, un vieillard dont les guenilles jaunes
> Imitaient la couleur de ce ciel pluvieux,
> Et dont l'aspect aurait fait pleuvoir les aumônes,
> Sans la méchanceté qui luisait dans ses yeux,
>
> M'apparut.

It is generally agreed by grammarians that the separation of the
subject from its verb, and the verb from its object, by the inser-
tion of relative or other clauses is the commonest and most effec-

---

[1] *Connaissance de Baudelaire*, Paris, 1951, p. 118.

[2] Jean Mouton, *Le Style de Marcel Proust*, Paris, 1948, p. 151.

[3] 'Plus que tout autre écrivain de son époque, Baudelaire se rapproche
du grand siècle par la solidité de l'ossature qu'il donne à sa phrase' (Vivier,
op. cit., p. 159).

tive way of giving style its cohesion. It is by these means that Baudelaire succeeds in welding disparate elements into tightly constructed sentences which contribute to the density and drive of his verse. In the sentence from *Les Sept vieillards* the initial adverb raises the pitch of the verse by creating a sense of expectancy. The subject is separated from the main verb by a relative clause which describes the old man's physical appearance. It is qualified by a conditional clause which contrasts his pathetic appearance with the evil disposition that can be seen in his eyes. The fusion of the conflicting impressions is made possible by the choice of two verbs describing visual sensations—'imitaient' and 'luisait'—one governing a concrete and the other an abstract noun. In this way the physical appearance of the subject, the 'unfriendly' skies, and his unfriendly disposition are all linked together and emphasized by the bold use of 'pluvieux' and 'pleuvoir'. There is no need to stress the immense impact of 'M'apparut'—the past definite coming after the imperfect and conditional tenses and pushed into the next verse—which has behind it the whole force of the complex sentence. Baudelaire achieves an equally striking effect in the same poem by the use of short sentences:

> Aurais-je, sans mourir, contemplé le huitième,
> Sosie inexorable, ironique et fatal,
> Dégoûtant Phénix, fils et père de lui-même?
> —Mais je tournai le dos au cortège infernal.

The decisiveness of the last brief sentence points to a sudden change of mood, throwing into relief the indecision of the feelings and the fear expressed in the straggling first sentence with its qualifications and its final note of interrogation.

The poems of the Cycle of Spleen are particularly good examples of the way in which syntax is used to weld disparate elements into what Mr. Eliot calls 'a whole of tangled feelings':

> Il est amer et doux, pendant les nuits d'hiver,
> D'écouter, près du feu qui palpite et qui fume,
> Les souvenirs lointains lentement s'élever . . .

The auxiliary verb is separated from its infinitive and the

infinitive from its object by two adverbial clauses. In this way the poet's emotions are so closely related to his surroundings that he becomes part of them.

In the second *Spleen* the separation of subject and verb enables the poet to weave the collection of objects that he is describing into his verse, preserving the impression of wholeness and compactness which is essential to the effect that he is trying to give:

> Un gros meuble à tiroirs encombré de bilans,
> De vers, de billets doux, de procès, de romances,
> Avec de lourds cheveux roulés dans des quittances,
> Cache moins de secrets que mon triste cerveau.

Baudelaire made very skilful use of the archaic inversion to tighten the texture of his sentences and to throw a particular word or object into relief. In the third *Spleen* we read:

> Le savant qui lui fait de l'or n'a jamais pu
> De son être extirper l'élément corrompu . . .

The relative clause separates the subject from its verb and the inversion the auxiliary verb from its infinitive. This throws into relief 'l'élément corrompu', and the verb 'extirper' gains considerably in force by coming immediately in front of its object. There is another example in 'Tu mettrais l'univers entier':

> Comment n'as-tu pas honte et comment n'as-tu pas
> Devant tous les miroirs vu pâlir tes appas?

The separation of the second auxiliary verb from its participle emphasizes 'miroirs', but the participle coming at the hemistich and immediately before the infinitive intensifies the shock of 'pâlir tes appas'.

The close of *A une Malabaraise* has been greatly admired:

> L'œil pensif, et suivant, dans nos sales brouillards,
> Des cocotiers absents les fantômes épars!

The Malabar woman, lost in the Paris fog, is thinking dreamily of her native land. Her eye wanders over the blurred outlines of people and things, moving from the material to the immaterial. Her mind rests for a moment on the clear outline of 'cocotiers absents' which suddenly dissolve into 'fantômes épars' and merge into the dim figures seen in the fog. The impression is brilliantly conveyed, but the aim could only have been achieved by the inversion. If the poet had followed the normal grammatical rule and written, 'Les fantômes épars des cocotiers absents', his effect would have been ruined.

The care with which Baudelaire built up his sentences can be seen in the first verse of one of his less serious poems, *Les Chats*:

> Les amoureux fervents et les savants austères
> Aiment également, dans leur mûre saison,
> Les chats puissants et doux, orgueil de la maison,
> Qui comme eux sont frileux et comme eux sédentaires.

The aim of the sentence is to isolate qualities which are common to two different types of men and to cats. The conjunction in the first line does no more than place the two types of men side by side. The verb reveals a taste which they share and the adverb, besides reinforcing the verb, seems to place them on the same level. The clause separating the verb from its object introduces a qualification. The lovers and scholars are both fond of cats, but only at a particular period of their lives. The cats are invested with two opposing qualities—'puissants et doux'—which belong alike to 'fervent' lovers and 'austere' scholars. The inserted clause builds up cats, raising them to the level of lovers and scholars. The relative clause, which concludes the comparison, provides a certain relief. The elderly lovers and elderly scholars like cats feel the cold and are engaged, ironically, in 'sedentary' occupations.

The construction of the fourth *Spleen* is particularly interesting. It consists of only two sentences and the first occupies sixteen of its twenty lines. The first three verses are adverbial clauses describing the physical conditions which cause *spleen*:

> Quand le ciel bas et lourd . . .
>
> Quand la terre est changée . . .
>
> Quand la pluie étalant . . .

The poet's aim is to express the disruption of feeling produced by these conditions:

> Des cloches tout à coup sautent avec furie
> Et lancent vers le ciel un affreux hurlement,
> Ainsi que des esprits errants et sans patrie
> Qui se mettent à geindre opiniâtrement.

There is a sudden explosion of violent, senseless, discordant sounds in the depressing landscape. The familiar 'ainsi que' links them to the 'esprits errants et sans patrie' who have also lost their direction. Their relegation to the subordinate clause seems intended to stress the dominance of material surroundings over human beings whose 'obstinate moaning' contrasts with the 'affreux hurlement'. In the short second sentence the poet turns on himself and identifies his plight with the 'esprits errants et sans patrie'.

Writers who have praised the clear, firm, logical structure of Baudelaire's poems have certainly been right to do so, but it must be remembered that it is only achieved when there is a correspondence between the internal and the external logic. When his inspiration flags the framework is inclined to stick out awkwardly and nakedly, but in his best work we are aware of an internal logic in the sequence of the images and in the way in which they reinforce or are deliberately contrasted with one another. Baudelaire's normal method is to start with a strking image and then to develop its latent implications in the images that follow. His occasional failures and faults of construction are usually due either to building his poems on two or more key-images, as he does in *Le Flacon*, or to multiplying images when the implications of the opening image are exhausted as he does in the later verses of *Le Beau navire*. The virtues of his method can be seen in the sonnet, 'Une nuit que j'étais près d'une affreuse Juive':

> Une nuit que j'étais près d'une affreuse Juive,
> Comme au long d'un cadavre un cadavre étendu,
> Je me pris à songer près de ce corps vendu
> A la triste beauté dont mon désir se prive.
>
> Je me représentai sa majesté native,
> Son regard de vigueur et de grâces armé,

Ses cheveux qui lui font un casque parfumé,
Et dont le souvenir pour l'amour me ravive.

Car j'eusse avec ferveur baisé ton noble corps,
Et depuis tes pieds frais jusqu'à tes noires tresses
Déroulé le trésor des profondes caresses,

Si, quelque soir, d'un pleur obtenu sans effort
Tu pouvais seulement, ô reine des cruelles!
Obscurcir la splendeur de tes froides prunelles.

The adverbial clause in the first two lines describes, in Baudelaire's accustomed manner, the situation in which the poet happened 'one night' to find himself. The main sentence states that he began to think of the woman whom he really loved because his reflexions on her are the theme of the poem. The 'corps vendu' reinforces the horror of 'un cadavre étendu' and is contrasted with 'la triste beauté' in line 4. The 'affreuse Juive' is relegated to a subordinate clause because the poem records an imaginary movement away from an actual situation towards another person and another situation which for the moment can only be enjoyed mentally. For this reason the second quatrain opens with another main sentence, and 'Je me représentai' carries the process begun in 'Je me pris à songer' a stage further. The 'cadavre' and the 'corps vendu' are behind him as he looks towards the 'majesté native' with her 'vigueur' and 'grâces' whose memory brings the temporary corpse back to life by rescuing him from prostitution and making him fit for love again. The last six lines consist of a single sentence. Baudelaire uses a double conditional. The first, 'J'eusse avec ferveur baisé . . .' looks back to the situation described in the first quatrain and forward to the second conditional in lines 13 and 14—'Si . . . tu pouvais seulement'. He would have kissed her from her feet to her hair *if* he had not been stretched beside the degrading harlot and *if* only he were able to move the woman he loved. The 'noble corps' is a backward glance at the 'corps vendu' which at the same time reinforces the 'majesté native', the 'vigueur', the 'grâces', and the 'casque parfumé' of the second quatrain. It also leads up to the word 'splendeur' in the last line. The same is true of 'trésor' which contains an allusion to 'corps vendu' and contrasts the money paid for 'hired love' with the 'treasures' of true love.

The poem is clearly a comparison between two kinds of love. One stands for death and degradation, the other for life and happiness. The key-images are all either life-symbols or death-symbols. When we look at the poem as a whole, we cannot fail to be impressed by the way in which all the images develop from the initial picture and by the closeness with which they are interlocked. They form literally a chain because each of them depends either on what is coming or on what has gone before, or on both.

The sting, as usual, comes in the tail. For life and happiness depend on whether the 'triste beauté' in her 'majesté native' is capable of the tear which will show that she is also a human being. The answer is that she is not and that nothing can dim the 'splendeur' of her 'froides prunelles'. The poem has described a complete circle. It began with a picture of death and degradation, but it ends with a hollow, inhuman splendour which no less certainly than the monstrous harlot spells death.

The merit of the poem lies to a large extent in the correspondence between its internal and external logic. The adverbial clause at the beginning does its preparatory work efficiently and builds up the background of squalor with a couple of brief touches. The conditional clauses in the tercets postpone the climax until the last line and increase its impact. The only awkward line is the eighth because the inversion is not functional, but is necessary for the rhyme.

I think that we can conclude that syntax not only contributes to the solidity of Baudelaire's verse, but that it is its very foundation. It is one of the essentials of his diction that it both creates atmosphere in the grand manner and on occasion deals with the sordid details of everyday life without losing the degree of elevation proper to poetry. And this could only be accomplished through the clarity as well as the firmness of the syntax which supports it.

Substantives

'En matière d'art, j'avoue que je ne hais pas l'outrance; la
modération ne m'a jamais semblé le signe d'une nature
artistique vigoureuse.'

L'Art romantique

Baudelaire's diction is closely connected with certain characteristics of his vocabulary. It explains to some extent his taste for
archaisms like 'appas', 'souris', 'pleur', 'pensers', and 'belle' in
the sense of 'belle femme'; his liking for generic terms, 'l'homme',
'la femme', 'l'humanité', 'la multitude'; his insistence on size
and depth or, most striking of all, the prevalence of abstract
nouns in his work. The use of generic terms and abstractions is
part of the classical inheritance. It comes naturally to the moralist
who is accustomed to making large pronouncements about the
human condition or to a writer like Baudelaire who was very
conscious of the general laws that regulate life and constantly
referred to them in his poetry. The generic terms are much in
evidence in a derivative poem like 'J'aime le souvenir':

> Alors l'homme et la femme en leur agilité
> Jouissaient sans mensonge et sans anxiété.

So are the abstractions:

> Le Poëte aujourd'hui, quand il veut concevoir
> Ces *natives grandeurs*, aux lieux où se font voir
> La *nudité* de l'homme et celle de la femme,
> Sent un froid ténébreux . . .

Le Vin des chiffonniers contains a much more arresting example
of his use of a generic term:

> Au cœur d'un vieux faubourg, labyrinthe fangeux
> Où *l'humanité* grouille en ferments orageux . . .

The particularity of the setting throws the word 'humanité'
into strong relief. Humanity is reduced to its lowest terms, is
seen as a seething mass of twisted subterranean instincts huddled
into the 'muddy labyrinth' of the decrepit 'faubourg'.

The moralist is apparent in lines like

> O toi, tous mes *plaisirs*! ô toi, tous mes *devoirs*!

where his relationship with the woman is seen to consist in a balance between 'pleasure' and 'duty', or

> Tes yeux . . .
> Usent insolemment d'un pouvoir emprunté,
> Sans connaître jamais *la loi de leur beauté*,

where the words that I have italicized reveal the moralist's conviction that every action is or should be governed by its proper 'law'.

These examples illustrate the legitimate use of abstractions, but there is no doubt that Baudelaire was sometimes tempted like the seventeenth-century poets to conceal failures of inspiration by the use of rhetoric and the multiplication of abstractions or generalized words like 'sphères étoilées', 'l'immensité profonde', 'les espaces limpides', while even 'abîmes' and 'gouffres' are not invariably a sign of psychological insight. When we come across the lines:

> Homme, nul n'a sondé le fond de tes abîmes
>
> . . . ce cœur profond comme un abîme

we feel that we are being offered a spurious impression of depth in the manner of the Romantics.

Another common device which Baudelaire borrowed from the classics and turned to good account was personification:

> L'Espérance qui brille aux carreaux de l'Auberge
> Est soufflée . . .

The image of 'shining' hope has become a commonplace, but in

> . . . la Vengeance bat un infernal rappel,
> Et de nos facultés se fait le capitaine,

the figure of Vengeance is invested with a compulsive force, and the brilliance with which Baudelaire adapted the device to his own use is fully apparent in

> La Prostitution s'allume dans les rues.

The use of abstract terms, personification, and the preoccupation with size have still deeper implications. We know that Baudelaire's poetry reflects a perpetual oscillation between opposite poles. This naturally encouraged the expression of emotion in its extreme forms and the continual search for the superlative which appears in his insistence on size and depth.[1] There is also a continual oscillation between the material and the immaterial, a tendency for the immaterial to become material and for the material to dissolve into the immaterial which has been exhaustively studied by Dr. Ratermanis.[2] The passage on prostitution in *Le Crépuscule du soir* to which I have referred is a perfect example of these tendencies:

> La Prostitution s'allume dans les rues;
> Comme une fourmilière elle ouvre ses issues;
> Partout elle se fraye un occulte chemin,
> Ainsi que l'ennemi qui tente un coup de main.

It is possible that the image in the first line was suggested by the lamps hung outside brothels. The abstract term and the personification give 'Prostitution' a sinister force, but personification is already the beginning of 'materialization'. The process is continued in 's'allume' which lessens the gap between it and the life of 'the streets'. It is carried further in the second line where the subterranean activities of 'Prostitution' are compared to ants tunnelling in the soil, and the word 'ouvre' has a curious erotic overtone. 'Occulte chemin' in the third line marks a slight movement in the direction of the immaterial, and the adjective underlines the sinister implications of the original image. There is a movement back to the material in the fourth line, but the generality of the unknown and unseen 'enemy' makes it more alarming and increases the force of the passage.

[1] 'For I have a confession to make, my dear fellow, which may perhaps cause you a smile. Assuming that their other merits are equal, in nature and in art I prefer *big* things to all others, big animals, big landscapes, big ships, big men, big women, big churches, and, transforming my tastes into principles like many other people, I believe that size is not a consideration which is without importance in the eyes of the muse' (*Curiosités esthétiques*, pp. 312–13).

[2] R. B. Ratermanis, *Étude sur le style de Baudelaire*, Baden, 1949, *passim*.

The process is similar in:

> Les mystères partout coulent comme des sèves
> Dans les canaux étroits du colosse puissant.

> Je sens fondre sur moi de lourdes épouvantes
> Et de noirs bataillons de fantômes épars.

> Derrière les ennuis et les vastes chagrins
> Qui chargent de leur poids l'existence brumeuse . . .

When we examine Baudelaire's imagery in more detail, we shall find that he was continually trying to translate obscure perceptions into concrete terms. What we are concerned with here is something different. We are concerned with a two-way movement between the material and the immaterial. The fears, mysteries, and depression are psychological entities, but their effects are physical. The 'mysteries' remain mysteries, but circulate like 'sap'. 'Fear' is intangible, but it is 'heavy' on us. We are haunted by the spectre of 'noirs bataillons', but find ourselves grasping at 'fantômes *épars*'.

All these passages are in a sense examples of personification. Now personification is derived from medieval allegory. Its aim was to give general ideas a concrete embodiment so that they would be readily intelligible to simple, direct minds. In Baudelaire it serves a different purpose. The generality of the concept increases its power and by 'materializing' it, Baudelaire invests it with a hostile life of its own, makes us feel that it is an immediate threat to *us*.

The movement from the material to the immaterial is not only less common; it is in the nature of things incapable of complete realization because the tension of Baudelaire's work depends largely on the fact that his goal is inaccessible, that the rapture signified by 'extase' must be perceptible to the senses and therefore to some extent concrete or materialized. When he writes in *Mœsta et errabunda*:

> Loin du noir océan de l'immonde cité,
> Vers un autre océan où la splendeur éclate,
> Bleu, clair, profond, ainsi que la virginité,

we are very conscious of his striving to escape from the 'noir océan' and 'l'immonde cité'; but the vision is so elusive that the poet, not content with three adjectives which are disguised superlatives, reinforces 'splendeur' with a second abstraction also implying a superlative—'virginité'.

The limits of immaterialization can be seen in

> Le Plaisir vaporeux fuira vers l'horizon,

where, as Dr. Ratermanis would put it, the substantive 'suffers a diminution of materiality'.

The process is more interesting in its negative form. When the poet compares himself in *Un Fantôme* to a painter

> qu'un Dieu moqueur
> Condamne à peindre, hélas! sur les ténèbres,

we do have the feeling that the world is suddenly melting away in front of the artist.

We come across a somewhat different use of abstractions in a line from *Rêve parisien*:

> J'ai vu l'horreur de mon taudis,

or in another from *Une Martyre*:

> Le singulier aspect de cette solitude.

For here there are no comparisons and no supporting images. The 'horror' and the 'solitude' are directly apprehended. The word 'singulier' always produces a shock of surprise in Baudelaire, and in the second line it adds considerably to the horror of the 'solitude' in which the headless trunk is reclining.

In the lines from *Les Bijoux* and *Le Beau navire*:

> . . . la candeur unie à la lubricité
> Donnait un charme neuf à ses métamorphoses.

> . . . ta beauté,
> Où l'enfance s'allie à la maturité,

the perception of contrasted attributes—'candour' and 'lubricity', 'childhood' and 'maturity'—is conveyed entirely by the impact of abstract substantives on one another. It can be argued that as they both belong to women, they are by implication 'materialized'; but it will be agreed that the use of two abstract words with the definite article creates a far more powerful effect than could have been achieved with adjectives.

In other places the effect is obtained by the combination of abstract and concrete. When he writes:

> Des grands sphinx allongés au fond des solitudes,
> Qui semblent s'endormir dans un rêve sans fin,

we have the impression of the sphinxes receding into the far distance. It is strengthened by the 'rêve sans fin' which makes them more remote and at the same time endows them with human or animal attributes. In

> —Désormais tu n'es plus, ô matière vivante!
> Qu'un granit entouré d'une vague épouvante,

we feel that the formidable strength of 'granit' is being attacked and undermined by the impalpable and intentionally vague 'épouvante'.

The combination of abstract and concrete—abstract substantives with concrete adjectives or concrete substantives with abstract adjectives—is not something that is confined to Baudelaire. It is found in other French poets of the same period, but like all great writers Baudelaire takes a common stylistic device and moulds it to his own purposes. What he does all through the *Fleurs du mal* is to create a sense of acute instability. He does so by the double process of making the intangible tangible and the tangible intangible. One moment we feel ourselves menaced by a horror that we can almost touch and see; the next we feel that the world about us is on the point of melting away. This contributes to the general sense of malaise. It is clearly connected with the poet's obsession with 'gouffres' and 'abîmes', but they represent the sudden violent crises which occur when the malaise reaches a certain pitch of intensity.

Verbs

The verb is the pivot of Baudelaire's poetry. The predominance of the verb is essentially a classical trait and I make no apology for insisting on it. What distinguishes Baudelaire from his successors more than any other single factor is the place occupied by the verb in his poetry. The most decisive of the revolutionary changes which took place in French prosody in the next generation—I am thinking particularly of the free verse of Laforgue —was the suppression of main verbs in the attempt to come closer to our mental processes. The classical use of verbs is not merely the sign of the craftsman; it reveals a determination to shape and direct experience, to relate the experience of the individual to a larger scheme or pattern, to maintain contact with something outside him. What Laforgue tried to do, and very largely succeeded in doing, was to subordinate poetry to the inner experience of the individual with the result that the pattern was imposed by what was going on inside him. His poetry was an immensely delicate instrument which was designed to reflect the changes taking place in a world conceived not as something stable, but as a state of flux.

The verb is not simply the pivot that gives Baudelaire's verse its life and vigour; it is, as Vivier observes, 'the psychological element par excellence'.[1] He was strangely deficient in visual imagination, but his psychological sense was extraordinarily acute. He shows himself supremely gifted in the expression of movement, atmosphere, the shift and change of mood. It is through movement that he reveals the psychology of the personages who appear in his poetry, the impact of other people and of material reality on himself, and the play of his own sensibility.

Baudelaire's use of verbs is not ostentatious or 'showy', and it is this no doubt that led M. Henri Peyre to speak disparagingly of 'le vague, la généralité, parfois le manque de couleur de ses verbes' and to compare him unfavourably in this respect with Hugo.[2] The lines from *Le Poison* and *A une Passante* in which he

[1] *Op. cit.*, p. 63.   [2] *Op. cit.*, pp. 117–18.

speaks of

> ta salive qui *mord*,

or

> La rue assourdissante autour de moi *hurlait*

are on the whole exceptional. He obtains some of his most striking effects by the use of verbs which are certainly 'general' and 'colourless' though not in M. Peyre's unfavourable sense. The prodigious psychological effect of the lines,

> Je frissonne de peur quand tu me dis: 'Mon ange!'
> Et cependant je sens ma bouche aller vers toi,

is achieved by the commonplace verbs, 'sentir' and 'aller', and by the double cæsura:

> Et cependant—je sens ma bouche—aller vers toi.

It will be observed that each foot is of the same length and this intensifies the sense of psychological compulsion, the feeling that one of the women is being drawn slowly and relentlessly towards the other.

In the description of Goya's pictures in *Les Phares*, where he speaks of

> De vieilles au miroir et d'enfants toutes nues,
> Pour tenter les démons ajustant bien leurs bas,

the simple, 'colourless' verb not only catches and fixes the sly, salacious gesture; it associates the 'children', who have already lost their innocence, with the elderly harlots and shows them aptly picking up the tricks for pleasing and sedulously practising them in front of the mirror.

Les Petites vieilles illustrates the way in which Baudelaire uses movement to reveal the psychology of other people:

> Ils rampent, flagellés par les bises iniques,
> Frémissant au fracas roulant des omnibus,
> Et serrant sur leur flanc, ainsi que des reliques,
> Un petit sac brodé de fleurs ou de rébus;

S

> Ils trottent, tout pareils à des marionnettes;
> Se traînent, comme font les animaux blessés,
> Ou dansent, sans vouloir danser, pauvres sonnettes
> Où se pend un Démon sans pitié! Tout cassés
>
> Qu'ils sont . . .

Baudelaire employs the present or the past definite to describe particular actions, and the present participle to build up an impression of continual movement which serves as a background for the particular actions. In these lines verbs describing cringing frightened movements and jerky helpless movements—'rampent' and 'trottent', 'traînent' and 'dansent'—alternate with one another. They are reinforced by the perpetual shuddering fear of 'frémissant' and the desperate clutching of the handbags in 'serrant'. The fear and bewilderment are related to the roar of the traffic in the background—the 'fracas roulant des omnibus'. Nor must we overlook the way in which the combination of the three-foot line and *enjambement* intensifies what Cassagne calls 'la boiterie sautillante' of the poem:[1]

> Ou dansent,—sans vouloir danser,—pauvres sonnettes
> Où se pend—un Démon sans pitié!—Tout cassés
>
> Qu'ils sont . . .

In *Les Petites vieilles* the spectator's impression is created by a detached contemplation of the scene and is, in a sense, incidental to it. In *Le Beau navire* the movement seems to be directed to rousing a particular feeling in the onlooker:

> Quand tu vas balayant l'air de ta jupe large,
> Tu fais l'effet d'un beau vaisseau qui prend le large,
>   Chargé de toile, et va roulant
> Suivant un rhythme doux, et paresseux, et lent . . .
>
> Ta gorge qui s'avance et qui pousse la moire,
> Ta gorge triomphante est une belle armoire . . .

The present participle in the first line creates the background of continual movement, but it also serves another purpose. In Baudelaire's poetry life usually moves at two different tempos—

[1] *Op. cit.*, p. 48.

slow motion and the speed of normal life. The present participle creates the languid, dreamy movement—the slow motion—which is the background of the poem and is stressed by the adjectives in the fourth line:

> Suivant un rhythme doux, et paresseux, et lent.

Against this background the woman's breast is suddenly projected, provocatively, towards the poet making the silk dress swell and bulge. It is reinforced again by the adjective 'triomphante' which already conveys the idea of domination and surrender.

In the lines,

> Avec ses vêtements ondoyants et nacrés,
> Même quand elle marche on croirait qu'elle danse,

ordinary speed changes to the slow lilt of a dance. The two adjectives in the first line do the work of present participles and we are aware of them in the background throughout the poem.

Harmonie du soir is probably the best illustration of Baudelaire's conception of a world in a perpetual state of movement:

> Voici venir les temps où *vibrant* sur sa tige
> Chaque fleur *s'évapore* ainsi qu'un encensoir;
> Les sons et les parfums *tournent* dans l'air du soir;
> Valse mélancolique et langoureux vertige!

'Vibrant' describes the preliminary trembling of the flowers which in 's'évapore' droop and die. The word 'tournent' transforms the sounds and scents into something almost palpable and this creates the impression of a slow, swooning dance.

The blending of moving scents and sounds is also the theme of the last verse of *Parfum exotique*:

> Pendant que le parfum des verts tamariniers,
> Qui *circule* dans l'air et m'enfle la narine,
> Se mêle dans mon âme au chant des mariniers.

The word 'circule' like the word 'tournent' in *Harmonie du soir* should be noticed for reasons which will be apparent presently.

The second verse of *Sed non satiata* shows how he uses verbs to combine internal and external movement:

> Je préfère au constance, à l'opium, au nuits,
> L'élixir de ta bouche, où l'amour *se pavane*;
> Quand vers toi mes désirs *partent* en caravane,
> Tes yeux sont la citerne où *boivent* mes ennuis.

'Se pavane' has the effect of isolating love and making it a tangible entity instead of a subjective attraction between two people, while 'partent' and 'boivent' invest 'désirs' and 'ennuis' with a strange individuality which is separate from the person who experiences them. This exteriorization of emotion is one of Baudelaire's highly personal characteristics and we find it again in *Les Bijoux* where he speaks of

> . . . mon amour profond et doux comme la mer,
> Qui vers elle montait comme vers sa falaise,

as well as in *A une Madone*, where he writes:

> Onduleux, mon Désir qui monte et qui descend.

What happens in all these poems is not merely the exteriorization or projection of emotion, but the projection of an inner world of feeling which is in *a perpetual state of ferment*.

In *Lesbos* he uses a combination of massed verbs and massed adjectives to achieve what M. Vivier would call a 'mythological' effect:[1]

> Lesbos, où les baisers sont comme les cascades
> Qui se jettent sans peur dans les gouffres sans fonds
> Et courent, sanglotant et gloussant par saccades,
> Orageux et secrets, fourmillants et profonds;
> Lesbos, où les baisers sont comme les cascades!

In these lines the 'baisers', like the 'désirs' and the 'ennuis' of the other poems I have quoted, are invested with an individual identity which is detached from the lovers who have in fact vanished from the scene; and just as the desires 'partent en caravane', the kisses are 'comme les cascades'. 'Se jettent' and 'courent' describe their desperate, headlong movement which is prolonged and intensified by the contrasted 'sanglotant' and

---

[1] 'Le verbe est peut-être le seul élément de la phrase baudelairienne qui donne parfois aux choses une sorte de *vie mythologique* (*op. cit.*, p. 63).

'gloussant'. 'Orageux et secrets' suggests a breathless, furtive eagerness; 'fourmillants' underlines the swarming, swirling movement, and 'profonds' reinforces 'gouffres sans fonds', conveying the impression of recklessness and disaster.

This discussion leads to certain other conclusions about Baudelaire's use of verbs. He not only presents a world in a perpetual state of movement. His movement is a two-way movement. The inward movement is the impact of his surroundings on the poet; the outward movement, which is in part provoked by it, is the attempt of the poet to exteriorize his emotions and to impose himself on his surroundings. This has the effect of constantly modifying the relation between the poet and the world. In the Parisian poems like *Les Petites vieilles* the scene described is interiorized, becoming part of the poet's own mental landscape, and he may well have been referring to this when he used the word 'allégorie'. The corresponding tendency is the assimilation of the poet and the world he is describing. The most prominent example is *Harmonie du soir*, where he is caught up by the whirling sounds and scents and becomes part of the garden.

The other striking thing about Baudelaire's movement is its absence of direction. This is apparent in a number of the examples that I have given. The old women wander through the streets of Paris as hopelessly lost as the travellers who imitate 'la toupie et la boule'; the kisses disappear into 'bottomless gulfs'; while in the activity of the women in *Le Beau navire* and 'Avec ses vêtements ondoyants et nacrés', and of the scents and sounds which 'turn' and 'circulate' in *Harmonie du soir* and *Parfum exotique*, we see reproduced once more the familiar circular movement which dominates Baudelaire's work.

Adjectives

A good deal of what I have said of Baudelaire's verbs and substantives applies to his use of adjectives. His lack of visual imagination accounts for the banality of many of his descriptions of material reality and the recurrence of conventional phrases like 'nectar vermeil', 'fruits vermeils', 'un rayon rose et gai', 'l'aube blanche et vermeille', 'voilé de vapeurs roses', 'ton corps blanc et rose'. The unfortunate influence of the less reputable Romantics and what I have called the decay of language are apparent in the maddening repetition of words like 'fatal', 'infernal', 'ténébreux', 'nocturne', and 'funèbre'. The same influence explains the prevalence of 'terrible', 'horrible', 'affreux', and 'effrayant', but in this case a distinction must be made. There are occasions when these words correspond to a genuine sensation of horror and are not mere counters; they are also like the abstract nouns to some extent the result of Baudelaire's natural tendency to express the extremes of feeling which frequently blurred genuine perceptions.

There is fortunately a credit side to the account which is decidedly impressive. It was not for nothing that Baudelaire remarked: 'La voix de l'adjectif me pénétra jusqu'aux mœlles.' For the adjective, too, is the psychological element. It has three main uses. It reinforces the verb; it records psychological impressions and judgments of value; and it is one of the principal factors in Baudelaire's sardonic humour.

We have seen something of the connection between verbs and adjectives, but I want to look again at the opening of *Au Lecteur* and *Les Sept vieillards*:

> La sottise, l'erreur, le péché, la lésine,
> Occupent nos esprits et travaillent nos corps,
> Et nous alimentons nos aimables remords,
> Comme les mendiants nourrissent leur vermine.
>
> Nos péchés sont têtus, nos repentirs sont lâches . . .

Professor Hackett has pointed out that in addition to their current meaning, 'occupent' and 'travaillent' must be interpreted in their classical sense of 'to take and hold a military position' and 'torment'.[1] This applies to the adjectives. 'Aimables remords' is a good example of Baudelaire's use of 'contrary' words to create a shock of surprise. 'Aimables' means indulgence towards sin, but in its present context it also implies absence of military discipline. The ironic intention is underlined by the figure of the dirty, verminous, undisciplined beggar. 'Têtus' emphasizes the aggres-

[1] *Op. cit.*, p. 189.

sive force of 'occupent'; the sins have 'invaded' humanity and
cannot be 'dislodged'. 'Lâches' refers back to 'aimables', but
besides meaning slack, it means 'cowardly' and continues the military associations of 'occupent' so that we have the image of a
cowardly 'repentance' retreating before invading 'sin'.

> Fourmillante cité, cité pleine de rêves,
> Où le spectre en plein jour raccroche le passant!

'Fourmillante' is an adjective which does the work of a present
participle. It describes the collective movement of the swarming,
anonymous crowd, creating the background of continual movement. 'Rêves' prepares us for the apparition which stands out
silhouetted against the crowd. We do not know what it is—it is
perhaps as well that it is a generalized figure—but it seems to be
supernatural and frightening. It pounces on one member of the
milling crowd. The short, sharp, decisive movement of 'rac-
croche' is thrown into startling relief by the indefinite movement
of the crowd. 'Raccrocher' normally means no more than to
'accost', but here it must be given its etymological sense of
croche or *crochu*, 'hooked'. We feel the hooked fingers clutch the
pedestrian's arm.

The first part of *Le Cygne* closes with an ironic comparison
which depends on two adjectives suggesting nervous movement
linked by a verb:

> Sur son *cou convulsif* tendant sa *tête avide*,
> Comme s'il adressait des reproches à Dieu!

It is an example of the use of the psychological adjective and,
as I pointed out earlier, the 'convulsive' movements of the swan
are a reflection of the *malaise* of the modern exile.

There is one marked difference between Baudelaire's verbs and
his adjectives. Unlike the verbs the adjectives—even commonplace adjectives—constantly call attention to themselves and
constantly create an impression of surprise:

> La reine de mon cœur au regard nonpareil,
> Qui riait avec eux de ma sombre détresse
> Et leur versait parfois quelque *sale caresse*.

Their effectiveness often depends on the contrast between the substantive and its adjective or on the use of an adjective in a sense which is slightly different from current usage, or is an extension of it. This is a sign of the creative use of language, of the way in which language grows and develops in the work of a major poet, and it calls for continual adjustment on the part of the reader.

One of Baudelaire's commonest devices is the application of words normally used to describe human feelings or human actions to inanimate objects and vice versa:

> La ruche qui se joue au bord des clavicules,
> Comme un ruisseau lascif qui se frotte au rocher,
> Défend pudiquement des lazzis ridicules
> Les funèbres appas qu'elle tient à cacher.

The 'ruisseau lascif' is a startling example of Baudelaire's verbal inventiveness. The adjective invests the stream with a queer indecent life, and the impression is strengthened by the verb 'frotter' which is coloured by 'lascif' and introduces the obscene movement that completes the image.

The effect is similar in

> la bûche enfumée
> Accompagne en fausset *la pendule enrhumée*

and

> Ne sont que des miroirs obscurcis et *plaintifs*!

In both cases the adjective associates inanimate objects with the human world. The clock is endowed with a sinister presence whose 'voice' mocks the feeble voice of the poet—the 'fantôme frileux'—mentioned a line or two earlier. The dulled mirror, which reflects the pathetic image of the poet, becomes in his imagination a reproachful voice calling attention to his failures. When he speaks in *Une Martyre* of 'meubles voluptueux', he succeeds in conveying the luxurious atmosphere of the sex-crime which is so potent that it seems an attribute of the furnishings. He achieves the same sharpness of impression in 'oreiller caressant'.

The opposite effect is seen in *Un Voyage à Cythère*:

et du *ventre effondré*
Les intestins pesants lui coulaient sur les cuisses,

where he applies an adjective which is normally used of material
things, particularly buildings, to a part of the body in such a way
that the whole body suddenly becomes part of the world of inanimate objects. The process is virtually the same when he calls
Jeanne Duval 'Machine aveugle et sourde', but the effect is less
spectacular because the comparison between a human being and
a machine was already in common use.

Un Voyage à Cythère contains another interesting example:

J'ai senti tous les becs et toutes les mâchoires
Des *corbeaux lancinants* et des panthères noires
Qui jadis aimaient tant à triturer ma chair.

It illustrates the way in which Baudelaire extends and transforms
a common idiom. 'Une douleur lancinante' describes a subjective
impression, a 'throbbing pain', which is only perceptible to the
person who suffers it. The sensation of pain is preserved, but the
movement is exteriorized in the relentless, mechanical pecking of
the crows and reinforced by the singular felicity of the verb
'triturer'.

Baudelaire had a particular fondness for 'contrary' words, for
the clash between the positive substantive and the negative or
destructive epithet, or the negative substantive and the positive
adjective which produces the same effect. In the lines from *Femmes
damnées* (Delphine et Hippolyte),

Elle cherchait dans l'œil de sa pâle victime
Le *cantique muet* que chante le plaisir,

there is a contrast between 'cantique' and 'muet', and the song
instead of being heard is perceived by the eye.

We have seen that in 'un pendu déjà mûr', the adjective 'mûr',
which usually has strong positive associations, is transformed
into an ironical negative. In *Une Charogne* he speaks of 'ce *ventre
putride*'; but though the effect is the same, in this instance the
negative adjective destroys the positive associations of the substantive which in the sense of 'womb' is a symbol of life and
fertility.

I want to glance briefly at the more specific use of adjectives
for the purpose of psychological notation. In the illustrations
which follow we shall find the same reliance on contrasts between
substantive and adjective, on the presentation of conflicting ideas
and on combinations of words which modify their normal sense;
but the impression is sometimes more complex because there is
a balance between conflicting ideas instead of the straight conversion of positives into negatives or negatives into positives.
'Myrtes infects' is an example of straight conversion and transforms love into something malignant; but when the poet addresses
his mistress as 'aimable pestilence' there is a blending of opposites.
Love is seen to be a contagious disease, but there is pleasure as
well as pain in the contagion. There is the same blending of
opposites in 'la douleur savoureuse'. When he writes,

De terribles plaisirs et d'affreuses douceurs,

the 'terrible plaisirs' is close to the common idiom, but in
'd'affreuses douceurs' the rasping adjective and the smooth substantive make the flesh creep.

'Molle enchanteresse' holds the balance between the impulses
to yield and to dominate, 'horreur sympathique' between violent
repulsion and strong attraction, and in both cases there is a pronounced moral overtone. 'Soleil monotone' demands a psychological adjustment on the part of the reader who is made to admit
that brilliant sunlight may be accompanied by a subjective sense
of monotony. This also applies to 'maigreur élégante' which recalls Gautier's 'Carmen est maigre'. For 'maigreur' has a slightly
deprecatory meaning which is emphasized by 'élégante'.[1] In
'Volupté, fantôme élastique' the adjective is used with great
ingenuity not simply to describe the changing shapes of the
wraith, but to 'materialize' it and suggest its extraordinary
variety. When he speaks of 'cheveux élastiques et lourds', the
adjective not only brings out the passiveness of the Baudelairean
woman, but the appeal to the sense of touch transforms her into
the passive *object* of an erotic game. 'Fantôme frileux' is an inver-

[1] Gautier's line creates the opposite effect. 'Maigre' ironically destroys
the exotic associations of Carmen. Compare: 'La maigreur est plus nue,
plus indécente que la graisse' (*Journaux intimes*, p. 13).

sion of the usual conception of 'fantôme'. For normally it is the 'fantôme' which is supposed to give us the sensation of fear accompanied by cold, but the poet has chosen to present himself as the shivering ghost.

In 'féconde paresse' the conjunction of positive and negative gives the impression of a positive feeling of expectancy, a sense that some form of creative activity is about to take place. In 'loisir embaumé' he creates an impression of luxury by the application of an adjective with a material connotation to an abstract noun. These examples also illustrate Baudelaire's power of condensation which is largely responsible for their impact on the reader. 'Loisir embaumé' describes a state of leisure and relaxation which is characterized by the presence of perfumes. They are at once artificial perfumes which evoke the *mundus mulierbris*, and the natural scent of flowers. In 'une île paresseuse' and 'rivages heureux' he certainly applies words normally used to denote human attributes to inanimate matter, but both phrases are a poetic shorthand for 'an island where I shall be able to sit back and enjoy a lazy luxury' and 'surroundings in which my *spleen* and sense of guilt will vanish and I shall feel happy'. Other examples are 'fièvres hurlantes', 'époques nues', 'boiteuses journées', 'neigeuses années', 'nuit voluptueuse' and 'nuits morbides'.

I must turn next to the use of adjectives for the purpose of making moral valuations. The intention is moral in 'magistrats curieux' which suggests in its context that the interest of magistrates in violent crime is not always purely professional. There is the same moral overtone in 'froides prunelles', 'rêve ruineux', 'poison perfide', 'astre inutile', and 'femme stérile'. Expressions like 'noirs ennuis' and 'noir chagrin' belong to common usage, but the varied use that Baudelaire makes of the word 'black', which often has a moral connotation, deserves study. Nor should we overlook his fondness for epithets describing moral and physical degradation like 'vil', 'servile', and 'décrépit'.

I have said something of the difference between the words 'extase' and 'volupté'. I want to look now at the different adjectives or, to use Dr. Ratermanis's term, *déterminants* that Baudelaire applies to the second of these words. The basic meaning of 'volupté' is physical pleasure, but the precise nature of the pleasure is determined by context and adjective. Its commonest meaning is sexual pleasure, particularly when it is used without an adjective at all. Baudelaire employs it in the singular in *Le Reniement de Saint Pierre* and *Le Voyage* to describe the masochistic sexual pleasure that he attributes to martyrs. In *A Celle qui est trop gaie* he goes still further. 'L'heure des voluptés' simply means the time of sexual intercourse. In *Mœsta et errabunda* 'la volupté pure' means the innocent love of childhood which is satisfied with a chaste kiss in the 'bosquets'; but the 'volupté noire' of *A une Madone*, the 'stérile volupté' of *Lesbos*, and the 'morne volupté' of *Femmes damnées* means the pleasure tainted with guilt and remorse which is associated with sexual perversion, and in all three cases the adjective seems to imply moral condemnation. It would be a mistake, however, to think that the word invariably possesses a sexual connotation. When Baudelaire speaks in *Bénédiction* of 'saintes voluptés', the expression is much stronger than the word 'extase' and apparently stands for the beatific vision that the poet will enjoy among 'the ranks of the blessed' in heaven. The 'mâle volupté' of *Élévation* describes the virile pleasure that the poet experiences during periods of inspiration. The 'voluptés calmes' of *La Vie antérieure* are the conditions of *physical* comfort in which he lived while 'naked slaves' were dealing with his *spiritual* problem, with 'Le secret douloureux qui me faisait languir'. Finally, in *Le Voyage*, the 'vastes voluptés, changeantes, inconnues' stand for the indefinable goal—it is clearly a spiritual or psychological goal—which drives the travellers on to continue their quest.

The discussion has so far been limited to single adjectives, but something must be said of Baudelaire's use of massed adjectives. I have written in another place of the difference between the use of massed adjectives in the classic periods and in the nineteenth century.[1] In the classic writers the adjectives preserve their individual identity, and are employed to express a number of dif-

[1] *The Novel in France*, London, 1950, pp. 223–6.

ferent and sometimes conflicting attributes which belong to the
same person or thing. In certain nineteenth-century writers—
Balzac is probably the best example—they lose their individual
identity and are used primarily for emphasis. In *Le Flacon*
Baudelaire applies no less than eight adjectives to the bottle:

> vieux flacon désolé,
> Décrépit, poudreux, sale, abject, visqueux, fêlé.

I think that we must admit that the aim here is largely emphasis
and that the distinction between 'décrépit', 'poudreux', 'sale',
and 'visqueux' is slight. It must be remembered, however, that
the bottle and its perfume are a symbol of the poet's work and of
his love. There is a moral nuance in 'désolé', 'abject', and possibly 'fêlé'. This example is somewhat exceptional and in general
Baudelaire employs the classic method. In the same poem he
speaks of

> . . . un vieil amour ranci, charmant et sépulcral.

Each of the adjectives is used to describe a distinctive trait of
his love, but they all contribute to the complex impression.
'Ranci'—a word usually applied to stale fats—is the destructive
adjective which is suggested by the comparison between love and
perfume, and its prosaic associations clearly add to its effectiveness. 'Charmant'—a word that might in the present context apply
to a 'keepsake' and does to some extent turn the poet's volume
into one—is the incongruous adjective which attenuates the effect
of 'ranci' and qualifies 'sépulcral' by making us feel that this
'death' is not to be taken entirely seriously. 'Sépulcral' is a
reference to the images drawn from tombs and coffins, but it also
gives precision to 'ranci'. The stale perfume which symbolizes the
'vieil amour' is also the smell of the corpse decaying in its coffin.

In the line from *Les Petites vieilles* ,

> Des êtres singuliers, décrépits et charmants,

'singuliers' stands for the general impression of oddity given by
the old women, 'décrépits' for their battered condition, while the
ironic 'charmants' expresses, in conjunction with the other two
adjectives, the poet's ambivalent attitude towards them. They are

pathetic and he is faintly sorry for them; but they are also rather repulsive and he transforms them into figures in a bitter little comedy.[1]

When he describes one of the old men as

> Sosie inexorable, ironique et fatal,

'inexorable' stands for the apparently unending procession; 'ironique' is used partly for its unexpectedness and partly to suggest that the poet is being mocked by the nightmare procession; while 'fatal', instead of being a cliché as it usually is in Baudelaire, reinforces 'inexorable' and refers to his own half-humorous, half-frightened question:

> Aurais-je, sans mourir, contemplé le huitième . . .?

When he describes beauty as 'monstre énorme, effrayant, ingénu', the final adjective stands for a quality which is seldom associated with a being who is 'énorme' and 'effrayant', and in this way saves the line from banality.

La Chevelure provides an example of a different kind in

> Tout un monde lointain, absent, presque défunt.

The actual difference in meaning of the three adjectives is relatively small, but the effect of the line depends precisely on the very slightness of the difference. For the three adjectives are carefully graduated and arranged in descending order. Their sound is nearly as important in the present context as their logical meaning. The sharp shrill nasals of 'lointain', which underline the poet's nostalgia, thicken in 'absent' and are almost completely muffled in 'défunt'.

It remains to add that the tension of Baudelaire's poetry is continually reflected in his use of the contrasted psychological epithet, particularly in the contrast between words suggesting *spleen* and words suggesting escape from *spleen*. 'Amer et doux', 'affreux et captivant', and 'âpre et délicieuse' are among the

---

[1] Baudelaire's use of the deliberately incongruous adjective was probably learnt from the eighteenth-century prose-writers. Compare Voltaire's comment on Candide:
'Il s'en retournait, se soutenant à peine, prêché, *fessé*, absous et béni . . .'

most effective examples, but the list is a long one and includes some of Baudelaire's most commonplace as well as some of his most personal epithets.

3. Imagery

I have examined some of Baudelaire's most famous images in other parts of this study and I need only recall them briefly here. They are the sea, ships, sails, masts, the movements of women and skirts, perfumes, *excitants*, metals, jewels, gulfs, abysses, prisons, tombs, water, oases, bells, and clocks. They reflect not merely his main interests, but the basic pattern of his experience. For his practice of using nearly all his principal images in both a positive and a negative sense or of pairing them off with their opposites, intensifies the contrasts and tensions which underlie his work. All that remains for me to do is to draw some general conclusions about his images and to examine two further types of imagery which have had a very considerable influence on his successors in France and in other countries.

'The whole of the visible universe', said Baudelaire in the *Salon de 1859*, 'is only a storehouse of images and signs to which imagination will give a place and a relative value. It is a sort of pasture that imagination must digest and transform.'[1] Not many poets have given such a concise description of the formation of the image in their work. For Baudelaire carries out his own prescription to the letter. One of the most important words in the sentence is the word 'visible'. In spite of the prevalence in his poetry of abstract words and the defectiveness of his visual imagination, he had a very firm grasp of the world of external perception. The starting-point of many of his poems is a material object or a homely, humdrum scene:

Rappelez-vous *l'objet* que nous vîmes, mon âme . . .

Il est de forts parfums pour qui toute *matière*
Est poreuse.

Pour l'enfant, amoureux de cartes et d'estampes,
L'univers est égal . . .

[1] *Curiosités esthétiques*, p. 283.

His imagination is concrete. He allows it to play on the visible world; he absorbs sights and sounds which are 'digested' and 'transformed' into the symbols of his poetry. This is the foundation of his technical innovations—the emotional equivalences and the recurring image. He could only have expressed the highly complex feelings that we find in his poetry by using concrete objects as signs for abstract or intangible emotions. The actual process is clarified by the famous passage from the diaries quoted in the opening chapter:

'Dans certains états de l'âme presque surnaturels, la profondeur de la vie se révèle dans le spectacle, si ordinaire qu'il soit, qu'on a sous les yeux. Il en devient le symbole.'

The words that I want to emphasize are 'si ordinaire qu'il soit'. It is in the moment of vision or of poetic inspiration that the imagination does its creative work. This work is the transfiguration of the actual. Objects which are valueless and meaningless in themselves are given a 'place' in the pattern of the poet's experience and a value which is 'relative' to the poem he is writing. The obvious example is the catalogue of objects at the beginning of the second *Spleen*. The objects are completely worthless and meaningless in themselves, but as I have pointed out, each of them becomes a strand in the emotion that the poet is expressing.[1] A still more impressive example is the image of the swan. For in *Le Cygne* the commonplace spectacle of an escaped swan scratching among the gravel becomes the symbol of the exiled modern man. When we compare Baudelaire's swan and Mallarmé's the differences are startling. The creative process at work in the two poems was probably not dissimilar and Mallarmé's swan is a symbol in much the same sense as Baudelaire's, but this is nothing to the differences. Baudelaire's swan is a living bird which belongs to everyday experience. It scratches in vain for water and is bewildered by the noise of the traffic and the scavengers' carts. Mallarmé's swan is a tenuous wraith living in a remote and rarefied region, a waste of ice and frost where it has contrived, in a way that defies imagination, to get itself trapped in a frozen lake.

[1] See pp. 161–2 above.

Although, as Miss Margaret Gilman observes in a remarkable article, Baudelaire usually moves 'from the outer to the inner reality . . . from the ordinary vision to the poetic vision', he does not invariably do so.[1] The movement, as always in Baudelaire, is a two-way movement. His images repeat to some extent the process that I described in the discussion of his substantives and verbs. The image is a passage from the tangible to the intangible, but it is also the instrument by which the intangible becomes tangible as it does in

> les vagues terreurs de ces affreuses nuits
> Qui compriment le cœur comme un papier qu'on froisse.

In these lines he not only gives point to the 'vagues terreurs' by the homely image of the crumpling paper; he succeeds in transmuting impalpable fears into physical sensation.

There is a similar but less striking instance in *L'Horloge*:

> Les vibrantes Douleurs dans ton cœur plein d'effroi
> Se planteront bientôt comme dans une cible,

where the subjective feeling of a throbbing pain crystallizes in the concrete image of vibrating arrows which have embedded themselves in a target.

It is apparent that in Baudelaire's work the concrete image is the bridge between everyday life and poetic experience. It ensures that whatever he has to say will be related to the experience of the common reader and will be intelligible to him. Miss Gilman is surely right in speaking of the disintegration in the poets who followed him of 'the Baudelairean synthesis of concrete experience, poetic vision, and creative activity' and of the tendency of 'the poetic experience' to become 'an end in itself, a way of knowledge'; but this is not confined to the 'Voyants'.[2] Mallarmé, who ranks as an 'Artist', sometimes gives the illusion of possessing a firm hold on the material world, but the comparison between his swan and Baudelaire's seems to me to demonstrate

[1] 'From Imagination to Immediacy in French Poetry' in *The Romanic Review*, Vol. XXXIX, No. 1, February 1948, p. 33.

[2] *Art. cit.*, pp. 35, 42.

T

conclusively that he inhabited a purely poetic world and that there is no bridge from this world to the everyday world.

We may conclude that the very concreteness of Baudelaire's imagination is one of the reasons why his poetry is the record of an *échec*. He works at a number of different levels, but he was himself firmly anchored in the natural plane and a poem of vision like *La Chevelure* derives its force not from any ascending movement—the Cycle of Mme Sabatier shows that Baudelaire's upward movements were not altogether impressive—but from the multiplication of images suggesting *material* ripeness and well-being.

In his essay on 'The Metaphysical Poets', Mr. Eliot has suggested that there is a similarity between the conceits of the English Metaphysical Poets and some of the images used by the French Symbolists, while more recently Mr. Cleanth Brooks has remarked that the metaphysical element is 'something basic in all poetry' and that there is a sense in which 'all poetry is symbolist poetry'.[1] No one supposes that the French poets were influenced by or had even read the English Metaphysicals, but the process at work in some of the most characteristic images of both groups is curiously alike. There is first what Aristotle, defining the essence of metaphor, called 'the intuitive perception of similarity in dissimilars', and secondly the use of unexpected comparisons in order to compel a fresh effort of attention on the part of the reader by a rearrangement of the objects of experience. The taste of the Metaphysicals for images drawn from mathematics to describe love, which we find in Donne's *Valediction: Forbidding Mourning* or Marvell's *Definition of Love*, has its counterpart in Baudelaire's use of metals, perfumes, or religious metaphors. In these instances a relationship is perceived between two spheres of experience which at first appear to have nothing in common. There are occasions, too, when we find the same sort of ingenuity in the work of both groups. In *A Valediction: of Weeping* Donne wrote:

---

[1] *Selected Essays*, pp. 275–6. *Modern Poetry and the Tradition*, London, 1948, pp. 48, 67.

LET me powre forth
My teares before thy face, whils't I stay here,
For thy face coines them, and thy stampe they beare,
And by this Mintage they are something worth.

In *La Mort des amants* Baudelaire imagines that the lovers'
minds have become twin mirrors which reflect their burning
hearts:

Nos deux cœurs seront deux vastes flambeaux,
Qui réfléchiront leurs doubles lumières
Dans nos deux esprits, ces miroirs jumeaux.

What is common to both these examples is the image of the
mirror and the idea that the reflection in a mirror, whether the
'mirror' is the tears or the minds of the lovers, of the external
signs of emotion enhances the value of the emotion and prolongs
its effect. Donne's tears are justified because they reflect the image
of his mistress which means that she is the cause of the tears. The
final *élan* of Baudelaire's lovers gains in value and intensity
because it is reflected in their minds, producing a complete union
of 'heart' and 'mind'.

Aristotle's intuitive perception corresponds to the distinction
made by Fiser in an illuminating book between 'the classic or
static symbol' and 'the "literary" or dynamic symbol'. The
'static' symbol means the formal comparison which is usually no
more than an elaboration or illustration of the poet's feeling. The
'dynamic' symbol is essentially creative. It consists of 'new
combinations' and the 'play of analogies' which not only reveal
'la durée profonde de la vie', but make possible a direct 'participation' in it.[1] It is through this form of image or symbol that the
scope of poetry is extended and our sensibility enlarged. Fiser
gives as an example of the 'symbole dynamique pur' four lines
from a poem of Verlaine's:

[1] *Le Symbole littéraire*, Paris, n.d. [1941], *passim.*
'Cette symbolisation de la vie profonde est faite par le jeu des images,
par la combinaison nouvelle des mots qui perdant leur signification conven-
tionnelle, parviennent à nous donner l'illusion de la mélodie, image fidèle de
la vie intérieure' (p. 41).

> Je suis un berceau
> Qu'une main balance
> Au creux d'un caveau.
> Silence, silence.

He points out that 'by the rhythm and by the new sense of the words the poet has shown the direction of the movement of the spirit in which we are free to participate more and more deeply'.[1]

What is interesting in these lines is the direct identification of the two disparate things:

> Je suis un berceau . . .

We frequently find direct identification in the work of the Metaphysicals and the Symbolists, but the conceit and the 'dynamic' symbol are also introduced by the conjunctions 'as' or 'like' in English and 'comme' or 'ainsi que' in French. Donne uses direct identification in

> The *spider love*, which transubstantiates all . . .

and a conjunction in

> If they [the souls] be two, they are two so
> As stiffe twin compasses are two . . .

Baudelaire also uses both forms, but he has a marked preference for the conjunction. In the second *Spleen* we find

> Je suis un cimetière abhorré de la lune,

and in *L'Horloge*:

> Le Plaisir vaporeux fuira vers l'horizon
> Ainsi qu'une sylphide au fond de la coulisse.

He did not carry his experiments with language and imagery nearly as far as his successors, but there are a number of images in his work which must be classified as conceits or 'dynamic' symbols. The expanded image in *L'Albatros* seems to me to be a good example of the 'static' symbol, but in spite of a certain

[1] *Ibid.*, *loc cit.*

obscurity the identification of poetry-perfume-love in *Le Flacon*
must be regarded as a 'dynamic' symbol. The imagery of *A une
Madone* is less daring and also contains fewer lapses than Corbière's in *Litanie du sommeil*, but it does recall in a striking way
the seventeenth-century conceit:

> Ta Robe, ce sera mon Désir, frémissant . . .
>
> Je te ferai de mon Respect de beaux Souliers
> De satin . . .
>
> Tu verras mes Pensers, rangés comme les Cierges . . .

There is a more striking example still in *Harmonie du soir*:

> Ton souvenir en moi luit comme un ostensoir!

The image of the white Host held in a monstrance, suggesting
the memory of the woman held in the mind and illuminating it,
depends as surely as Donne's 'spider love' on a knowledge of the
doctrine of transubstantiation. The 'substance' of his love has
been 'transubstantiated' and its memory is more potent than his
actual relations with the woman.

When he writes of Jeanne Duval:

> Ta mémoire, pareille aux fables incertaines,
> Fatigue le lecteur ainsi qu'un tympanon,

the immaterial 'mémoire' is endowed with attributes normally
belonging to material things. The very concreteness of 'tym-
panon', with its suggestion of an endless, monotonous clash, is
obviously much more effective than if he had merely said: 'The
reader is wearied by the memory or the thought of you.'

He mingles pathos and irony when, in the list of exiles and
outcasts in *Le Cygne*, he says:

> Je pense . . .
> Aux maigres orphelins séchant comme des fleurs,

assimilating the unhappy orphans to the fragile flowers drooping
after the rain.

Baudelaire like the Metaphysicals was particularly successful in
using the homely comparison to create an impression of surprise.
When he says to Jeanne Duval

> Pour exercer tes dents à ce jeu singulier,
> Il te faut chaque jour un cœur au râtelier,

the linking of 'jeu-cœur-râtelier' exposes her love as a hideous 'game' which is destroying the poet.

When he wants to express the demonic power of Beauty, he writes:

> Le Destin charmé suit tes jupons comme un chien,

with the result that, compared with Beauty, 'Destiny' is reduced to the status of a domestic pet.

In other poems we find:

> elle noyait
> Sa nudité voluptueusement
> Dans les baisers du satin et du linge,

where the attribution of human faculties to inanimate things in the unexpected conjunction of 'baisers-satin-linge' conveys an acutely voluptuous sensation.

The process is reversed in:

> Tes yeux, illuminés ainsi que des boutiques
> Et des ifs flamboyants dans les fêtes publiques,
> Usent insolemment d'un pouvoir emprunté,
> Sans connaître jamais la loi de leur beauté.

In these lines he is accusing the woman of using her charms mindlessly—'pouvoir emprunté' apparently means cosmetics—like the display of lights at a public festival which are designed to attract everybody without discrimination.

There is a more spectacular example at the end of the first part of *Le Voyage* where he speaks of

> Ceux-là dont les désirs ont la forme des nues,
> Et qui rêvent, ainsi qu'un conscrit le canon,
> De vastes voluptés, changeantes, inconnues.

The 'clouds' may have suggested cannon smoke. The poet appears to be saying that their insatiable pursuit of an unknown goal has reduced the travellers to the condition of a conscript who is compelled to face the cannon and who does so with a mixture of terror and fascination. The effect is to show the travellers, who a moment ago were described as 'cœurs légers, semblables aux ballons', in a fresh light and to introduce a new and unexpected emotion.

The most impressive example of all is the terrific image at the close of *Femmes damnées* (Delphine et Hippolyte):

> L'âpre stérilité de votre jouissance
> Altère votre soif et roidit votre peau,
> Et le vent furibond de la concupiscence
> Fait claquer votre chair ainsi qu'un vieux drapeau.

Some of the most effective of the conceits of the Metaphysicals depend not merely on the unexpected comparison, but on the daring use of hyperbole. So it is here. The climax can only be fully appreciated when it is remembered that eighty lines of the poem are devoted to a detailed description of the soft, voluptuous atmosphere of the perverse loves which are its subject. Then, suddenly, the smooth skin withers, shrinks, and bursts apart under the fiery blast, and we hear only the flapping of the tattered banner winding and unwinding round its pole which ironically recalls the spectacle of bodies twisting and turning in their lust. 'Stérilité' is the pivot of the whole poem. Baudelaire certainly means us to regard sexual perversity as the symbol of an unnatural civilization, but there is no moralizing. His attitude is completely fused in the image. The tattered flag is a sign of defeat and destruction.

The poetic conceit was the invention of the Age of Baroque, and there is often a baroque extravagance in the images of Donne and Crashaw and still more in those of their successors. It is matched in the French poets by a streak of preciosity which produces strange and beautiful effects, as it does in the close of *Recueillement*:

> Vois se pencher les défuntes Années,
> Sur les balcons du ciel, en robes surannées;
> Surgir du fond des eaux le Regret souriant;
>
> Le Soleil moribond s'endormir sous une arche,
> Et, comme un long linceul traînant à l'Orient,
> Entends, ma chère, entends la douce Nuit qui marche.

The personification of the 'défuntes Années' reclining on 'the balconies of heaven *en robes surannées*' and 'le Regret souriant', emerging somewhat surprisingly from the depths of the waters, might well have aroused the envious admiration of a seventeenth-century poet. The last three lines with their liquid l's and the soft, sighing -*ch*, -*che*, and -*ce* sounds are, musically, among the loveliest that Baudelaire wrote.

· Baudelaire also seems to have been one of the first French poets to use the baroque image which is deliberately intended to strike a discordant note and to shock us out of our conventional habits of seeing and feeling:

> Et, comme le soleil dans son enfer polaire,
> Mon cœur ne sera plus qu'un bloc rouge et glacé.
>
> .   .   .   .   .
>
> comme un œil sanglant qui palpite et qui bouge,
> La lampe sur le jour fait une tache rouge.

In their context these lines from *Chant d'automne* and *Le Crépuscule du matin* are highly effective examples of Baudelaire's shock tactics. They stand out like splashes of crude, violent colour against the sober background. But there are inevitably occasions when the image is not successful and we find something like the exaggerated conceits of a Cowley or a Benlowes:

> —Son cœur! son cœur racorni, *fumé comme un jambon.*

I have emphasized the use of contrast—sometimes violent contrast—in Baudelaire, and it is nowhere more apparent than in his sardonic humour. He is virtually the inventor of what has since become known as 'the ironic juxtaposition' which has been extensively employed by contemporary poets and particularly by Mr. Eliot. In *Les Petites vieilles* he asks:

> —Avez-vous observé que maints cercueils de vieilles
> Sont presque aussi petits que celui d'un enfant?

where the intention is obviously to insist on the smallness and triviality of the old women who have shrunk to childish proportions.

In *Le Vin des chiffonniers* the irony is turned against the poet who is compared to a rag-picker:

> On voit un chiffonnier qui vient, hochant la tête,
> Buttant, et se cognant aux murs comme un poëte.

Une Charogne does not seem to me to deserve all the praise that it has been given, but technically it is one of the most influential of Baudelaire's poems. He was obsessed to a greater degree than almost any other poet since the Elizabethan dramatists by images of physical decomposition, and in this poem his imagination dwells on them with a macabre relish. The poem is the classic source of the destructive image and the destructive use of language without which Rimbaud's early work could scarcely have been written. He begins with a contrast between the gracious setting and the hideous corpse:

> Rappelez-vous l'objet que nous vîmes, mon âme,
> Ce beau matin d'été si doux:
> Au détour d'un sentier une charogne infâme
> Sur un lit semé de cailloux. . .

The word 'infâme' is the ironical retort to 'âme' and destroys the impression created by 'doux'. 'Cailloux' qualifies 'lit' and leads to the shocking image in the next verse:

> Les jambes en l'air, comme une femme lubrique,
> Brûlante et suant les poisons,
> Ouvrant d'une façon nonchalante et cynique
> Son ventre plein d'exhalaisons.

The word 'lubrique' introduces the sexual element and fixes the obscenity of the spectacle. 'Nonchalante' and 'cynique' invest the stiffening corpse, grotesquely, with the shameless, impudent swagger of the prostitute. 'Ouvrant' underlines the obscenity by suggesting the posture of the prostitute lying on a bed ready to receive the male. The images that follow are all images of inverted fecundity. Instead of bringing forth life, the belly is the source of proliferating decay:

> Le soleil rayonnait sur cette pourriture,
> Comme afin de la cuire à point,

> Et de rendre au centuple à la grande Nature
>   Tout ce qu'ensemble elle avait joint;
>
> Et le ciel regardait la carcasse superbe
>   Comme une fleur s'épanouir . . .
>
> Les mouches bourdonnaient sur ce ventre putride,
>   D'où sortaient de noirs bataillons
> De larves, qui coulaient comme un épais liquide
>   Le long de ces vivants haillons. . . .
>
> On eût dit que le corps, enflé d'un souffle vague,
>   Vivait en se multipliant.
>
> Et ce monde rendait une étrange musique,
>   Comme l'eau courante et le vent.

The positive words, 'centuple', 'superbe', 'fleur', 'vivants', 'se multipliant', and 'musique' acquire a negative force which heightens the sense of destruction. 'Superbe' must be given its double sense of 'superb' and 'proud'. The corpse is a 'superb' specimen and at the same time recalls the swagger of the living prostitute.

The climax is reached in the last three verses when the speaker suddenly turns on the mistress and identifies her with the corpse:

> —Et pourtant vous serez semblable à cette ordure,
>   A cette horrible infection,
> Étoile de mes yeux, soleil de ma nature,
>   Vous, mon ange et ma passion!

The destructive effect is achieved by the clash between conventionally poetic images like 'Étoile de mes yeux', 'soleil de ma nature', and the 'ordure', the 'horrible infection'.

The poem closes with a final contrast between the immortal soul and the corrupt body made not in any religious sense, but in order to exploit the macabre possibilities of the theme:

> Alors, ô ma beauté! dites à la vermine
>   Qui vous mangera de baisers,
> Que j'ai gardé la forme et l'essence divine
>   De mes amours décomposés!

Once again positive and negative—'mangera de baisers'—
contribute to the destructive effect. The final effect, indeed, is one
of complete destruction. The 'forme' and the 'essence divine'
are both borrowings from theology, but their normal sense is
modified. They are not used to describe an essence which is
objectively indestructible. They are used to describe the memory
of the woman which will remain in the poet's mind after her death
and which will, he seems to imply, be her only form of immortality. The traditional sense of the words is undermined, but they
are nevertheless used ironically to heighten the savage 'amours
décomposés'.

Although Baudelaire's style is founded on contrast the final
impression is not one of discord, but of a unified vision of a
divided world. If I had to name the quality which most strikes
me in his work and which seems to comprehend all the others, I
should feel inclined to choose the balance between the poetic and
the prosaic. Laforgue was the first to point out that he creates
remarkable effects by the introduction of the prosaic comparison
or the commonplace word into the highly poetic passage, and we
remember the famous line in *Le Balcon*:

> La nuit s'épaississait ainsi qu'une cloison.

The effect is still more striking when he adopts the reverse
process and inserts the poetic line or the poetic word in the middle
of a prosaic passage or a description of squalor:

> C'est une femme belle et de riche encolure,
> Qui laisse dans son vin traîner sa chevelure.

> Piétinant dans la boue, et cherchant, l'œil hagard,
> Les cocotiers absents de la superbe Afrique
> Derrière la muraille immense du brouillard.

In the first example the word 'chevelure' sheds a poetic radiance
over the squalid scene. In the second the vision of an exotic
continent suddenly lights up the city of mud, then is just as suddenly extinguished by the fog. This corresponds to Baudelaire's
vision of the contemporary world. The sober unemphatic tone

and the neutral colours are the staple of his verse. They reflect the desolation of a world which is continually illuminated by a fleeting splendour. It is in such moments that we become aware that 'the horror of life' and 'the ecstasy of life' are simultaneous and inseparable.

I hope that this discussion of Baudelaire's style will have shown in what sense he stands for tradition and experiment. His versification and syntax, his use of verbs, and the sobriety of his language equipped him with a powerful flexible instrument. It enhanced his innovations and his departures from tradition, but at the same time it provided an admirable system of control which saved him from the extravagances and incoherence of later writers. His power of incantation was less than that of some of his successors; his images and epithets were less daring than theirs; but his work was essentially a work of liberation without which their different achievements would have been impossible. The main ground on which they can and must be criticized is the eagerness with which they jettisoned so many of the things that he had thought worth preserving.

CONCLUSION

I BEGAN this study by suggesting that the best way of approaching Baudelaire was to interrogate one of the closest of his disciples in the hope of discovering what his example meant to a fellow-practitioner. I chose Laforgue as one of the most intelligent and gifted of them, and his notes on his master did indeed provide a useful point of departure. Now that I have reached the end of my essay, I propose to repeat the procedure and interrogate not merely the disciples, but those who have devoted many years to the study and elucidation of Baudelaire's work and who must be regarded as the poet's friends.

The question that we now have to ask is this: What is to be the final judgment on Baudelaire? This time the answers are a little disconcerting.

'Ni grand cœur, ni grand esprit,' said Laforgue, 'mais quels nerfs plaintifs, quelles narines ouvertes à tout, quelle voix magique.'[1] 'Le premier voyant,' said Rimbaud, 'roi des poëtes, un vrai Dieu. Encore a-t-il vécu dans un milieu trop artiste; et la forme si vantée en lui est mesquine.'[2]

These may appear to be youthfully sweeping judgments, but the doubts expressed by Laforgue and Rimbaud have been shared by later writers who have felt that there was perhaps something lacking in Baudelaire. 'Il butte sans cesse à l'obstacle de son indigence imaginative,' remarks Vivier.[3] 'Il y a dans Hugo un excès du langage sur sa matière,' said Fondane; 'il y a dans Baudelaire un excès de matière sur le langage.'[4] The cry has been repeated

[1] *Entretiens Politiques et Littéraires, art cit.*, p. 102. *Mélanges posthumes,* p. 119.

[2] *Œuvres complètes*, ed. R. de Renéville and J. Mouquet, Paris, 1946, p. 257 (letter to P. Demeny of 15 May 1871).

[3] *Op. cit.*, p. 300.

[4] *Baudelaire et l'expérience du gouffre*, Paris, 1947, p. 352.

301

by foreign critics of Baudelaire. Bendetto speaks of 'la naturelle pauvreté de son imagination verbale, la ténuité de son souffle créateur'.[1] 'I should place him', writes Mr. Eliot, 'with men who are important first because they are human prototypes of new experience, and only second because they are poets.'[2] Finally, Professor Mansell Jones describes his achievement 'as that of a major, not a great, poet'.[3]

It will be seen that we are faced with two sharply differing points of view. Laforgue is filled with admiration for Baudelaire's mastery of the means of communication, but he is much less impressed by what is in fact communicated. The other six writers adopt precisely the opposite point of view. They are greatly impressed by what Baudelaire was trying to say, but they feel that the means of expression were not always adequate to the matter which accounts for phrases like 'indigence imaginative' and 'naturelle pauvreté de son imagination verbale'.

These views present certain obvious difficulties. It is difficult to see how Baudelaire could have been the superb artist for which Laforgue takes him if he was neither a 'grand esprit' nor a 'grand cœur'. I cannot help suspecting that Laforgue was, unconsciously, asking for something that Baudelaire never intended to offer, and that he failed to do justice to the toughness and resilience of his verse. We cannot expect a poet living in troubled times to possess the serene, unclouded vision of a Dante. What Baudelaire tried to express, and succeeded admirably in expressing, was the spiritual and emotional frustration of the contemporary man. His picture of him in love or in the grip of *spleen* differed so much from anything which had been seen or said before that it is not altogether surprising that he should appear to be a man with a 'magic voice', but without a 'grand cœur' or a 'grand esprit'.

The second view seems to me to be equally difficult to accept. I cannot believe in the significance of an experience which is only communicated, in so far as it is communicated, in spite of a grave deficiency in the means of communication. I do not see

---

[1] *Art. cit.*, p. 26.

[2] *The Criterion*, Vol. IX, No. 35, January, 1930, p. 358.

[3] *Baudelaire*, p. 50.

how a great poet can be more important 'as a human prototype of new experience' than as a poet. Nor do I see how a writer can be a 'major' poet without being a 'great' one, though it must be said in fairness to Professor Mansell Jones that his sensitive appreciation of the artist belies his somewhat puritanical conclusion.

We must, I think, take it as axiomatic that great poetry can only be written when two conditions are fulfilled. The poet must possess a new vision *and* the power of communicating it to his readers. At the same time, we cannot entirely dismiss the views of the seven critics whom I have quoted. There *are* moments when we feel doubts about the depth of Baudelaire's heart or the breadth of his mind, and there are comparatively few of his poems which do not contain weak lines. We judge a great poet by his best work, but I think that we must in honesty admit that the proportion of bad poems in the *Fleurs du mal* is much greater than most of us care to recognize, that Baudelaire's immense reputation rests mainly on a handful of masterpieces and a distinctly larger number of very fine poems. The criticisms that I have been discussing, however, overlook one very important factor. It is the pervasive charm of the 'voix magique' or what Valéry called the 'charme continu' of his poetry. The poems contain all sorts of *défaillances*, bad lines, and miserable clichés lifted from the lesser Romantics, but even the minor poems possess an inimitable accent of their own which is unique in nineteenth-century poetry. Open the *Fleurs du mal* at random and begin to read, and you find that you go on reading, oblivious of the *défaillances*, the clichés, and even the downright bad lines because you simply cannot stop listening to the 'voix magique'. This places Baudelaire in a class by himself among French poets of the last century, and indeed the only other French poet I can think of who possesses the same *envoûtement* is Racine. Hugo is supremely accomplished, but he remains the great craftsman, the superb virtuoso whose voice becomes first wearisome, then deafening, and finally intolerable. Rimbaud was a unique genius, but to read Rimbaud calls for an immense effort and the demands that he makes on us are so great that we can as a rule only take him in small doses. He was Baudelaire's sole rival and it is possible that he was potentially the greatest French poet of the century, but his actual achievement seems to me to fall short of Baudelaire's handful of masterpieces.

'He had enjoyed a *sense of his own age*,' writes Mr. Quennell, 'had recognized its pattern while the pattern was yet incomplete, and . . . had anticipated many problems, both on the æsthetic and the moral plane, in which the fate of modern poetry is still concerned.'[1] He also belonged to his age and while we must deplore the fact that some of its least admirable attitudes found their way into his poetry, this was to a large extent inseparable from his achievement. His own attitude is not consistent in the manner of the classic writer's, nor could we expect it to be. His purpose—it is this that distinguishes him from his predecessors—was not to examine experience from a fixed unchanging standpoint or to demonstrate the excellence of one particular attitude. It was to explore all the different possible attitudes which were open to contemporary civilized man.

It has been said of him that he gave expression to something that was diffused in the air about him. The measure of his success is, paradoxically, the completeness, the finality of his picture. No problem, no aspect of modern urban civilization eluded him. The great city is there with its bustle and its industrialism, its palaces and its slums, its stuffy middle-class apartments filled with ugly but expensive furniture and artificial flowers, the ragged poor and their hovels, the brothels and the gambling dens.

His mingling of classical diction with the conversational style, archaic words with modern colloquialisms, enabled him to reveal human nature to itself in a new way. For the man whose feelings are analysed is no rootless intellectual. He is the cultured European who is fully aware of his great heritage and the dangers to which it is exposed. The continuity of his work with the work of the past is absolute. Every line, every word has behind it layers and layers of civilized human experience. This gives his poetry its richness, its maturity, and its strange resonance. He is unrivalled in his exploration of the stresses of contemporary life, in detecting the least tremor of vibrating nerves. The love cycles not only

[1] *Baudelaire and the Symbolists*, London, 1929, p. 64.

transformed traditional conceptions of 'passion' and anticipated many of the discoveries made a generation or two later in the laboratories of the psychiatrists; they contain more genuine wisdom than most of the treatises and text-books which have proved such a formidable addition to our reading list. The experiences that he records are not something that happened to an isolated individual; they are something that happened to human nature at a particular stage of its development and affect us all. That is why his single volume of verse has modified the sensibility of generations of sensitive readers.

Although Baudelaire was the great laureate of a collapsing civilization and though the word 'vaincu' echoes through the Cycle of Spleen, it cannot be repeated too often that his attitude *as a poet* was not defeatist and that all his work bears the impress of a powerful personality. No other writer saw through the popular slogans of the day and the religion of progress more completely than he; but though the *Fleurs du mal* is an indictment of a corrupt society, Baudelaire was not a reformer; he had no 'policy' and nothing of the crusading spirit. His insistence on original sin shows that he did not try like later reformers to evade responsibility by attributing man's ills to economic factors or believe that they could be cured by some facile political reshuffle. He realized that the problems were spiritual, but his work was to present problems rather than to find solutions. Later in the century Lautréamont proclaimed that 'La poésie doit avoir pour but la vérité pratique', and Rimbaud's reforming zeal drove him out of poetry altogether. Their views would have been entirely alien to Baudelaire's nature. His poetry always halts at the point where it seems about to merge into theology and his 'tour' ends on a mark of interrogation. It was because he was so completely an artist, so disdainful of the theory that poetry should inculcate a moral, that he remains after all the greatest European poet of the century.

U

APPENDIX

COMPARATIVE TABLE OF THE CONTENTS OF THE FIRST AND SECOND EDITIONS OF THE FLEURS DU MAL [1]

ITALICS denote unpublished poems included in the first edition of the *Fleurs du mal*; a dagger poems which were added to the second edition. A dash in the second column indicates that the title of the poem is the same as that shown opposite in the first column.

1st Edition 1857	2nd Edition 1861
101 poems: 5 chapters	127 poems: 6 chapters

Au Lecteur	—

I. SPLEEN ET IDÉAL	I. SPLEEN ET IDÉAL
(77 poems of which 3 were condemned and 8 transferred to 'Tableaux Parisiens' in the second edition.)	(85 poems of which 66 came from the same chapter of the first edition and 19 were new.)

(The Cycle of Art)	(The Cycle of Art)
1. *Bénédiction*	I. —
2. *Le Soleil* (2nd ed., LXXXVII)	II. L'Albatros†
3. *Élévation*	III. —
4. *Correspondances*	IV. —
5. '*J'aime le souvenir de ces époques nues*'	V. —
6. *Les Phares*	VI. —

[1] These tables are reproduced from the critical edition by kind permission of M. José Corti. The editors give those of the first three editions, but I have omitted the third edition because it is discredited and only has a curiosity value. The sub-divisions of 'Spleen et Idéal' were added by me.

7. *La Muse malade*	VII.	—
8. *La Muse vénale*	VIII.	—
9. Le Mauvais moine	IX.	—
10. L'Ennemi	X.	—
11. Le Guignon	XI.	—
12. La Vie antérieure	XII.	—
13. *Bohémiens en voyage*	XIII.	—
14. L'Homme et la mer	XIV.	—
15. Don Juan aux enfers	XV.	—
16. Châtiment de l'orgueil	XVI.	—
17. La Beauté	XVII.	—
18. L'Idéal	XVIII.	—
19. La Géante	XIX.	—
(Cycle of Jeanne Duval)		
20. *Les Bijoux* (condemned poem)	XX. Le Masque†	
	XXI. Hymne à la beauté†	
	(Cycle of Jeanne Duval)	
21. *Parfum exotique*	XXII.	—
	XXIII. La Chevelure†	
22. '*Je t'adore à l'égal de la voûte nocturne*'	XXIV.	—
23. '*Tu mettrais l'univers entier dans ta ruelle*'	XXV.	—
24. *Sed non satiata*	XXVI.	—
25. 'Avec ses vêtements on- doyants et nacrés'	XXVII.	—
26. *Le Serpent qui danse*	XXVIII.	—
27. *Une Charogne*	XXIX.	—
28. De Profundis clamavi	XXX.	—
29. Le Vampire	XXXI.	—
30. *Le Léthé* (condemned poem)		
31. '*Une nuit que j'étais près d'une affreuse Juive*'	XXXII.	—
32. Remords posthume	XXXIII.	—
33. *Le Chat* ('*Viens, mon beau chat*')	XXXIV.	—
	XXXV. Duellum†	

34. *Le Balcon*   XXXVI. —
                                       XXXVII. Le Possédé†
                                       XXXVIII. Un Fantôme†

35. 'Je te donne ces vers afin   XXXIX. —
    que si mon nom'

                                     (Cycle of Mme Sabatier)
                                        XL. Semper eadem†

(Cycle of Mme Sabatier)
36. Tout entière   XLI. —
37. 'Que diras-tu ce soir,   XLII. —
    pauvre âme solitaire'
38. Le Flambeau vivant   XLIII. —
39. *A Celle qui est trop gaie*
    (condemned poem)
40. Réversibilité   XLIV. —
41. Confession   XLV. —
42. L'Aube spirituelle   XLVI. —
43. Harmonie du soir   XLVII. —
44. Le Flacon   XLVIII. —
  (Cycle of Marie Daubrun)   (Cycle of Marie Daubrun)
45. Le Poison   XLIX. —
46. *Ciel brouillé*   L. —
47. *Le Chat* ('Dans ma cer-   LI. —
    velle')
48. *Le Beau navire*   LII. —
49. L'Invitation au voyage   LIII. —
50. L'Irréparable   LIV. —
51. *Causerie*   LV. —
                                      LVI. Chant d'automne†
                                      LVII. A une Madone†
                                      (Secondary Heroines)
                                      LVIII. Chanson d'après-
                                              midi†
                                      LIX. Sisina†

  (Secondary Heroines)
52. L'Héautontimorouménos
    (2nd ed., LXXXIII)

53. Franciscae meae laudes   LX.   —
54. A une Dame créole   LXI.   —
55. Mœsta et errabunda   LXII.   —
                                    LXIII. Le Revenant
                                          (1st ed., 72)
                                    LXIV. Sonnet d'automne†
                                    LXV. Tristesses de la lune
                                          (1st ed., 75)
(Cycle of Spleen)   (Cycle of Spleen)
56. Les Chats   LXVI.   —
57. Les Hiboux   LXVII.   —
                                    LXVIII. La Pipe
                                          (1st ed., 77)
                                    LXIX. La Musique
                                          (1st ed., 76)
                                    LXX. Sépulture
                                          (1st ed., 74)
                                    LXXI. Une Gravure fan-
                                          tastique†
                                    LXXII. Le Mort joyeux
                                          (1st ed., 73)
                                    LXXIII. Le Tonneau de la
                                          haine
                                          (1st ed., 71)
58. La Cloche fêlée   LXXIV.   —
59. Spleen ('Pluviôse irrité')   LXXV.   —
60. *Spleen ('J'ai plus de*   LXXVI.   —
    souvenirs')
61. *Spleen ('Je suis comme le*   LXXVII.   —
    roi')
62. *Spleen ('Quand le ciel bas*   LXXVIII.   —
    et lourd')

                                    LXXIX. Obsession†
                                    LXXX. Le Goût du néant†
63. *Brumes et pluies*
    (2nd ed., CI)

                                    LXXXI. Alchimie   de   la

vous étiez jalouse'
(1st ed., 69)
CI. Brumes et pluies
(1st ed., 63)
CII. Rêve parisien†

68. Le Crépuscule du matin   CIII.   —

69. '*La servante au grand
cœur dont vous étiez jalouse*'
(2nd ed., C)   (LE VIN follows as Chap. III)

70. '*Je n'ai pas oublié, voisine
de la ville*'
(2nd ed., XCIX)

71. Le Tonneau de la haine
(2nd ed., LXXIII)

72. *Le Revenant*
(2nd ed., LXIII)

73. Le Mort joyeux
(2nd ed., LXXII)

74. *Sépulture*
(2nd ed., LXX)

75. *Tristesses de la lune*
(2nd ed., LXV)

76. *La Musique*
(2nd ed., LXIX)

77. *La Pipe*
(2nd ed., LXVIII)

II. FLEURS DU MAL   IV. FLEURS DU MAL
(12 poems)   (9 poems)

78. La Destruction   CIX.   —

79. *Une Martyre*   CX.   —

80. Lesbos (condemned
poem)

81. *Femmes damnées (Del-
phine et Hippolyte)*
(condemned poem)

82. *Femmes damnées ('Comme*   CXI.   —
un bétail pensif')

III. RÉVOLTE   V. RÉVOLTE
(3 poems)   (3 poems)

(LA MORT follows as Chap. VI)

IV. LE VIN   III. LE VIN
(5 poems)   (5 poems)

(FLEURS DU MAL follows as Chap. IV)

V. LA MORT   VI. LA MORT
(3 poems)   (6 poems)

SELECT BIBLIOGRAPHY

It would be impossible to provide anything like a complete bibliography here. I have therefore confined myself to a selection of those books and articles which I have read and found useful on some aspect of the poet's life and work.

I strongly recommend M. Henri Peyre's *Connaissance de Baudelaire* (Corti, 1951) which is an admirable survey of the present state of Baudelaire studies and contains a bibliography of over three hundred books and articles.

In the case of essays which have been published more than once, I have given only the latest and most accessible source unless the original place of publication appeared of particular interest.

Except where the contrary is stated, books in English and French are published in London and Paris respectively.

A. EDITIONS

Œuvres complètes, ed. J. Crépet. Conard-Lambert, 19 vols., 1922–53.

Œuvres, ed. Y. G. Le Dantec (Bibliothèque de la Pléiade). Gallimard, 2 vols., 1931–2. New edition in one volume under the title of *Œuvres complètes*, 1951.

Les Fleurs du mal, Édition critique établie par Jacques Crépet et Georges Blin. Corti, 1942.
(Indispensable.)

Journaux intimes, Fusées, Mon Cœur mis à nu, Carnet, Édition critique établie par Jacques Crépet et Georges Blin. Corti, 1949.

Douze poëmes de Charles Baudelaire, Publiés en fac-similé sur les manuscrits originaux de l'auteur avec le texte en regard des mêmes pièces, d'après les éditions des *Fleurs du mal*. G. Crès, 1917, ii + 40 pp.

B. COMMENTARIES

Asselineau, Charles, *Charles Baudelaire, sa vie et son œuvre*. A. Lemerre, 1869. Reprinted in *Baudelaire et Asselineau*, Textes recueillis et commentés par Jacques Crépet et Claude Pichois. Librairie Nizet, 1953.

315

(Asselineau's life was essentially a work of piety which has been used by most biographers, but which now only has a period interest.)

BARBEY D'AUREVILLY, *Poésie et poètes*. A. Lemerre, 1906, pp. 97–123.

BARRÈS, MAURICE, *La Folie de Charles Baudelaire*. Les Écrivains Réunis, 1926, 105 pp.

Baudelaire, Le Tombeau de, précédé d'une étude sur le texte des *Fleurs du mal* par le Prince Alex. Ourousof. (Bibliothèque Artistique et Littéraire), Éditions de la Société Anonyme 'La Plume', 1896, 125 pp.

BENEDETTO, L. F., 'L'Architecture des *Fleurs du mal*' in *Zeitschrift für Französische Sprache und Literatur*, Vol. 39, pp. 18–70.

BENNETT, JOSEPH D., *Baudelaire, a Criticism*. Princeton: Princeton University Press, London: Oxford University Press, 1944, 2nd ed. 1946, 165 pp.

BILLY, ANDRÉ, *La Présidente et ses amis*. Flammarion, 1945, 260 pp.
(The most accurate and up-to-date study of Baudelaire and Mme Sabatier.)

BLANCHOT, MAURICE, 'L'Échec de Baudelaire' in *La Part du feu*. Gallimard, 1949, pp. 137–56.

BLIN, GEORGES, *Baudelaire*. Gallimard, 1939, 217 pp.
(Interesting study of Baudelaire's thought.)

Le Sadisme de Baudelaire. Corti, 1948, 190 pp.
(Chapter on the *Petits poèmes en prose* and destructive criticism of J. P. Sartre's *Baudelaire, q.v.*)

BOURGET, PAUL, 'Baudelaire' in *Essais de psychologie contemporaine*, I, Édition définitive, Plon, 1926, pp. 2–33.
(Written in 1881–3. Interesting though Bourget's Baudelaire is no longer 'our Baudelaire'.)

CASSAGNE, ALBERT, *Versification et métrique de Ch. Baudelaire*. Hachette, 1906, iii + 126 pp.
(Still the only detailed study of Baudelaire's versification.)

COLÉNO, ALICE, *Les Portes d'ivoire*, Métaphysique et poésie, Nerval, Baudelaire, Rimbaud, Mallarmé. Plon, 1948, 245 pp.
(A valuable study of the visionary element in Baudelaire.)

CRÉPET, EUGÈNE, *Baudelaire*, Étude biographique revue et complétée par Jacques Crépet. Messein, 1907, 466 pp.
(Still the indispensable source book.)

DECAUNES, LUC, *Charles Baudelaire* (Poètes d'aujourd'hui No. 31). Seghers, 1952, 220 pp.

(A stimulating essay of 97 pages followed by a selection from Baudelaire's poetry and prose.)

DU BOS, CHARLES, 'Méditation sur la vie de Baudelaire' in *Approximations*, 1ère série. Plon, 1922, pp. 179–242.

'Introduction à *Mon cœur mis à nu*' in *Approximations*, 5ième série, Corrêa, 1932, pp. 19–105.

ELIOT, T. S., 'Baudelaire in our Time' in *Essays Ancient and Modern*, Faber & Faber, 1936, pp. 63–75.

(Criticism of Arthur Symons's interpretation of Baudelaire.)

'Baudelaire' in *Selected Essays*, Faber & Faber, 1932, pp. 367–78.

FAIRLIE, ALISON, 'Some Remarks on Baudelaire's *Poème du Haschisch*' in *The French Mind*, Oxford: Clarendon Press, 1952, pp. 291–317.

(An excellent study with some interesting views on the architecture of the *Fleurs du mal*.)

FERRAN, ANDRÉ, *L'Esthétique de Baudelaire*. Hachette, 1933, xii + 734 pp.

(The most comprehensive account available of Baudelaire's aesthetic theories.)

FEUILLERAT, ALBERT, 'L'Architecture des *Fleurs du mal*' in *Studies by Members of the French Department of Yale University* (Yale Romanic Studies No. XVIII). New Haven: Yale University Press, London: Oxford University Press, 1941, pp. 221–330.

Baudelaire et la Belle aux cheveux d'or. New Haven: Yale University Press, Paris: Corti, 1941, 97 pp.

Baudelaire et sa mère. Montreal: Les Éditions Variétés, 1944, 226 pp.

FISER, EMÉRIC, *Le Symbole littéraire*, Essai sur la Signification du Symbole chez Wagner, Baudelaire, Mallarmé, Proust. Corti, n.d. [1941], 226 pp.

(A valuable essay which is unfortunately difficult to obtain.)

FLOTTES, PIERRE, *Charles Baudelaire: l'homme et le poète*. Perrin, 1922, xii + 235 pp.

(Good chapter on the poet.)

FONDANE, BENJAMIN, *Baudelaire et l'expérience du gouffre*. Seghers, 1947, 383 pp.

(Stimulating. The author died in a concentration camp without being able to revise his work.)

GIDE, ANDRÉ, 'Baudelaire et M. Faguet' in *Nouveaux prétextes*. 9 ième éd., Mercure de France, 1921, pp. 134–55.

'Préface aux *Fleurs du mal*' in *Incidences*. Gallimard, 1924, pp. 159–163.

GILMAN, MARGARET, 'From Imagination to Immediacy in French Poetry' in *The Romanic Review*, Vol. XXXIX, No. 1, February 1948, pp. 30–49.

GOURMONT, REMY DE, 'Baudelaire et le songe d'Athalie' in *Promenades littéraires*, 2 ième série. Mercure de France, 1906, pp. 85–94.

HACKETT, C. A., *Anthology of Modern French Poetry* from Baudelaire to the present day. Oxford: Blackwell, xxxix + 305 pp.
(Valuable introductory essay on Baudelaire and his place in French poetry.)

HOOG, ARMAND, 'Le Poète vaincu ou Baudelaire' in *Littérature en Silésie*. Grasset, 1944, pp. 225–79.
(A good essay.)

JONES, P. MANSELL, *The Background to Modern French Poetry*. Cambridge: University Press, 1951, xii + 196 pp.
(An excellent study of the sources of Baudelaire's æsthetic theories.)
Baudelaire (Studies in Modern European Literature and Thought). Cambridge: Bowes & Bowes, 1952, 64 pp.
(Attractive essay.)

LAFORGUE, JULES, 'Notes Inédites de Laforgue sur Baudelaire' in *Entretiens Politiques et Littéraires*, Vol. II, No. 13, April 1891, pp. 98–120.
'Notes sur Baudelaire' in *Mélanges posthumes*. Mercure de France, 1903, pp. 111–19.
(Laforgue's notes should if possible be read in the review in which they were first published. The version given in *Mélanges posthumes* deserves all the harsh things that scholars have said about it. It is inaccurate and only about half the length of Laforgue's text, but it does contain the essentials of his criticism of Baudelaire.)

LEMONNIER, LÉON, *Enquêtes sur Baudelaire*. Crès, 1929, 133 pp.

MASSIN, ABBÉ JEAN, *Baudelaire entre Dieu et Satan*. Julliard, 1946, 341 pp.
(The best study of Baudelaire's religion.)

MOUQUET, JULES, and BANDY, W. T., *Baudelaire en 1848*. Émile-Paul, 1946, 340 pp.
(An account of Baudelaire's political activities in 1848 with a selection from the political articles attributed to him.)

NADAR, FÉLIX, *Charles Baudelaire: Le Poète vierge*. Blaizot, 1911, iii + 143 pp.

MURRY, JOHN MIDDLETON, 'Baudelaire' in *Countries of the Mind*, first series. Collins, 1922. New ed. Oxford University Press, 1931, pp. 115–36.
> (An excellent essay on Baudelaire's imagery.)

POMMIER, JEAN, *La Mystique de Baudelaire*. Les Belles Lettres, 1932, 202 pp.
> (The classic study of this aspect of Baudelaire's work.)

Dans les chemins de Baudelaire. Corti, 1945, 384 pp.
> (A collection of occasional essays and reviews.)

PORCHÉ, FRANÇOIS, *La Vie douloureuse de Charles Baudelaire* (Le Roman des Grandes Existences, No. 6). Plon, 1926, 302 pp.

Baudelaire: Histoire d'une âme. Flammarion, 1945, 452 pp.
> (One of the best critical biographies. A completely revised and greatly expanded version of *La Vie douloureuse de Charles Baudelaire*.)

Baudelaire et la Présidente (Collection: Les Amitiés Amoureuses). Geneva: Éditions du Milieu du Monde, 1941, 250 pp.
> (A charming monograph and like everything that Porché wrote on Baudelaire it should be read, but it is less full and less accurate than André Billy's study, *vide supra*.)

PRÉVOST, JEAN, *Baudelaire*, Essai sur l'inspiration et la création poétiques. Mercure de France, 1953, 382 pp.
> (An important book. It suffers to some extent from the fact that the author was less interested in poetry than investigating the nature of poetic inspiration. The preface makes it clear that Baudelaire was simply chosen as the most suitable of the various poets whom he considered for the experiment he wished to carry out. The chapter called 'Le Souffle chez Baudelaire' is of particular interest.)

PROUST, MARCEL, 'À propos de Baudelaire' in *Chroniques*. Gallimard, 1927, pp. 212–38.

QUENNELL, PETER, *Baudelaire and the Symbolists*. Chatto & Windus, 1929, 222 pp.

RATERMANIS, J. B., *Étude sur le style de Baudelaire* d'après *Les Fleurs du mal* et *Les Petits poèmes en prose:* Contribution à l'étude de la langue poétique du dix-neuvième siècle. Baden: Éditions Art et Science, 1949, 502 pp.
> (An important and illuminating study of Baudelaire's language, but it is too long, contains too many illustrations of most of the technical devices discussed, and would have

been more valuable if the author had confined himself more closely to points of style which are peculiar to Baudelaire. Its place of publication seems, unfortunately, to have prevented the book from becoming generally known. It was virtually unknown to the French authorities to whom I mentioned it recently, and the Bibliothèque de la Sorbonne appears to be the only one of the three principal Paris libraries which possesses a copy.)

RAYMOND, MARCEL, *De Baudelaire au surréalisme*, Essai sur le mouvement poétique contemporain. Corrêa, 1933. New ed., Corti, 1940, 369 pp.

RAYNAUD, ERNEST, *Charles Baudelaire*. Garnier, 1922, 411 pp.

REYNOLD, GONZAGUE DE, *Charles Baudelaire*. Geneva: Éditions Georg et Cie., Paris: G. Crès, 1920, 417 pp.
  (A good critical biography with an excellent chapter on Baudelaire's technique.)

RIVIÈRE, JACQUES, 'Baudelaire' in *Études*. Gallimard, 1911, pp. 13–31.

ROYÈRE, JEAN, 'L'Érotologie de Baudelaire' in *Le Mercure de France*, Vol. CXL, No. 528, 15 June 1920, pp. 618–37.
  (Curious and interesting.)

RUFF, M. A., *Sur l'architecture des 'Fleurs du mal'*. A. Colin, 1931, 30 pp.
  (Reprinted from *Revue d'Histoire Littéraire de la France*, January–March, July–September 1930.)

SARTRE, J. P., *Baudelaire* (Les Essais XXIV). Gallimard, 1947, xiii + 224 pp. Eng. tr. by M. Turnell. Horizon, 1949.
  (Existentialist interpretation of Baudelaire.)

SCHNEIDER, PIERRE, 'Baudelaire, poète de la fragmentation' in *Critique*, Vol. VII, Nos. 51–2, August–September 1951, pp. 675–85.
  (A remarkable essay.)

SMITH, JAMES, 'Baudelaire' in *Scrutiny*, Vol. VII, No. 2, September 1938, pp. 145–66.

STARKIE, ENID, *Baudelaire*. Gollancz, 1933, 518 pp.
  (The fullest life available.)

SUARÈS, ANDRÉ, 'Le Profond Baudelaire' in *Valeurs*. Grasset, 1936, pp. 152–7.
  Trois grands vivants: Cervantès, Baudelaire, Tolstoï. Grasset, 1937, 317 pp.
  (Baudelaire pp. 269–304.)

THIBAUDET, ALBERT, 'Baudelaire' in *Intérieurs*. Plon, 1924, pp. 1–61.

VALÉRY, PAUL, 'Situation de Baudelaire' in *Variété II*. Gallimard, 1930, pp. 141–73.

> (Reprint of a lecture delivered in 1924 at Mme Lesage's, taken down in shorthand and privately printed in the collection, 'Lesage et ses Amis', the same year. Subsequently published as an introduction to *Les Fleurs du mal* (Collection: Vers et Prose). Payot, 1926.)

VIVIER, ROBERT, *L'Originalité de Baudelaire*. Brussels: Académie Royale, Paris: La Renaissance du Livre, 1926, new ed., Académie Royale, 1953, 296 pp.

> (Still the best study of Baudelaire's style.)

INDEX OF POEMS

GENERAL INDEX

Ancelle, N. D., 42
Aquinas, St. Thomas, 18
Aristotle, 290
Arnold, M., 15
Asselineau, C., 48, 57, 92, 93, 100, 217
Aupick, General (*stepfather of the poet*), 41, 44–5, 46, 49
Aupick, Mme (*mother of the poet*), 41–54, 60, 61, 62, 74, 89, 229, 230
Autard de Bragard, M. and Mme, 46

Babou, H., 49
Balzac, H. de, 45, 205, 285
Bandy, W. T., 48
Barbey d'Aurevilly, J., 64, 92
Banville, T. de, 59, 75, 76, 77, 137
Baudelaire, C. A. (*half-brother of the poet*), 43, 44
Baudelaire, C. P.:
Belgium, visit to, 53–4; birth, 44; childhood, 44–5; *conseil judiciaire*, 42, 47, 51, 60; critic, work as, 47, 49; dandyism, 38–9, 48–9; death 54; drugs, habit of taking, 47, attitude towards, 94–5; East, voyage to, 45–6; education, 44–5; family, relations with, 41–2; financial difficulties, 42, 53; *Fleurs du mal*, prosecution for, 50, publication of, 49, revision of, 51, title of, 49, 200–1; French Academy, candidature for, 50; friendships, 45, 47–8; health, 43–4, 53, 54; mistresses, relations with, M. Daubrun, 71–6, J. Duval, 58–62, Mme

Sabatier, 62–71; E. A. Poe, influence of, 49; political activities, 48–9; sexual experience, 54–8, 65–9, 73; sexual perversion, interest in, 204–5; *spleen*, suffers from, 51–3; suicide, attempted, 47
Baudelaire, J. F. (*father of the poet*), 43–4
Baudelaire, Mme J. F., 43
Beauvoir, R. de, 47
Béguin, A., 32
Benedetto, L. F., 92–3, 136–7, 302
Benlowes, A., 296
Bennett, J. D., 181, 207, 213
Bernard, C., 44
Bernini, L., 148
Billy, A., 63, 64, 65, 68
Blin, G., 27, 28, 57, 97, 101, 120, 173, 186, 194
Boissard, F., 66
Bouilhet, L., 64
Bourget, P., 143
Bracquemond, 201
Broise, E. de, 50
Brooks, C., 290
Bruneau, C., 258

Carjat, E., 52
Cassagne, A., 250, 257, 274
Castelnau, Commandant, 70
Castelnau, J. A. C., *see* Wallace, Lady
Chaucer, 17, 88, 89
Chénier, A., 22, 80
Champfleury, 48
Choiseul-Praslin, Duc de, 43